Of Bunsen Burners, Bones, and Belles Lettres

NTC's Library of Classic Essays

Of Bunsen Burners, Bones, and Belles Lettres

Classic Essays across the Curriculum

James D. Lester
Austin Peay State University

NTC Publishing Group
Lincolnwood, Illinois USA

Executive Editor: John T. Nolan
Sponsoring Editor: Marisa L. L'Heureux
Cover and interior design: Ophelia M. Chambliss
Cover art: Celia Johnson/Gerald & Cullen Rapp, Inc.
Production Manager: Rosemary Dolinski

Acknowledgments for literary selections begin on page 223, which is to be considered an extension of the copyright page.

ISBN-0-8442-5882-2 (student text)
ISBN-0-8442-5883-0 (instructor's edition)

Published by NTC Publishing Group
© 1996 NTC Publishing Group, 4255 West Touhy Avenue
Lincolnwood (Chicago), Illinois 60646-1975 U.S.A.
Manufactured in the United States of America

Library of Congress Cataloging-in-Publication Data

Of bunsen burners, bones, and belles lettres : classic essays across
   the curriculum / [edited by] James D. Lester.
     p.   cm.
   ISBN 0-8442-5882-2 (pbk.)
     1. College readers.   2. Interdisciplinary approach in education.
3. Essays.   I. Lester, James D., 1935–   .
PE1122.O34   1995
082—dc20   95-11060
                                                         CIP

5 6 7 8 9 VP 0 9 8 7 6 5 4 3 2 1

Contents

vi Contents

A Day in Samoa, Margaret Mead   81
The Yellow Bus, Lillian Ross   86

❧

Classic Essays in the Physical Sciences   105

The Method of Scientific Investigation,
   Thomas Henry Huxley   107
Touch and Sight: The Earth and the Heavens,
   Bertrand Russell   112
What Is the Theory of Relativity? Albert Einstein   119
"But a Watch in the Night," A Scientific Fable,
   James C. Rettie   125
The Moving Tides, Rachel Carson   132
The Bird and the Machine, Loren Eiseley   147
The Long Habit, Lewis Thomas   157
Pain Is Not the Ultimate Enemy, Norman Cousins   163

❧

Classic Essays in Business and Economics   171

Division of Labour, Adam Smith   173
Alienated Labor, Karl Marx   181
The Gospel of Wealth, Andrew Carnegie   191
The Peter Principle, Laurence J. Peter and Raymond Hull   198
Why Women are Paid Less than Men, Lester C. Thurow   205
The Efficient Society, Jeremy Rifkin   209

Acknowledgments   223

Index of Authors and Titles   227

Preface

NTC's Library of Classic Essays

This is a four-volume collection of some of the finest essays ever written, providing a broad yet in-depth overview of the development and scope of the genre. In essence, an essay is a short prose composition, usually exploring one subject and often presenting the personal view of the author. An essay may take a variety of forms (from narration to description to autobiography) and may reflect any number of moods (from critical to reflective to whimsical).

Although we recognize a few early works by Plato, Aristotle, and others as essays, it was really Michel de Montaigne, a French philosopher and writer, who substantially defined the form when he published two volumes of his own essays under the title *Essais* in 1580. Montaigne considered himself to be representative of humankind in general; thus, his essays, though they are to be read as general treatises on the human condition, are largely reflective of Montaigne's own attitudes and experiences.

The essay proved to be a most adaptable form. In the eighteenth century, both journalists and philosophers in England and pamphleteers and patriots in the American colonies quickly discovered the power of a well-crafted and provocative essay. By the middle of the nineteenth century, the essay was the form of choice for such brilliant writers as the American Ralph Waldo Emerson and the British George Eliot. In the twentieth century, the essay has become the most widely read genre—from personal essays in periodicals to scholarly essays in scientific journals to argumentative essays on the editorial pages of newspapers worldwide.

Of Bunsen Burners, Bones, and Belles Lettres: Classic Essays across the Curriculum

This volume contains twenty-eight classic essays that illustrate the richness of the essay genre in several academic disciplines. Organized by discipline, these essays explore an amazing diversity of topics. If, however, one of your favorites is not included here, it may well be in one of the other volumes: *Plato's Heirs: Classic Essays; Daughters of the Revolution: Classic Essays by Women;* or *Diverse Identities: Classic Multicultural Essays.*

This volume brings you essays that explore how writers think and write in different disciplines. It is our hope that this collection will allow you to examine who you are and better enable you to explore your place—and the place of others—in the universe.

CLASSIC
ESSAYS
IN THE

Humanities

Why I Am an Agnostic

CLARENCE DARROW

Clarence Darrow (1857–1938) was born in Kinsman, Ohio. He became one of America's most famous trial lawyers in the years before and after the turn of the century. An opponent of the death penalty, he defended more than one hundred murderers, but none was executed. He also became known as a lawyer for labor, and he defended Eugene V. Debs in a high-profile case that resulted from the 1894 labor strike. His most famous case, however, was the 1925 trial of John T. Scopes, whom he defended against the legal maneuverings of William Jennings Bryan. Darrow argued for Scopes's right to teach evolution in Tennessee schools. Darrow also wrote two novels, *Farmington* (1904) and *An Eye for an Eye* (1905). He also published *Crime: Its Cause and Its Treatment* (1922) and *The Story of My Life* (1932).

"Why I Am an Agnostic" provides a provocative point of view on ideas about the human spirit that usually concern readers in the humanities. Darrow confesses to being a doubter, just as individual members of a church are doubters about the religion of other denominations. To the public mind, he says, "an agnostic is one who doubts or disbelieves the main tenets of the Christian faith." Darrow then questions his own ability to identify God, to find any existence of the immortal soul, and to accept the Bible as anything more than a human document. He defends his skepticism by showing that many doubtful people using scientific methods have brought civilization to new levels, not with miracles but with rational wisdom. As he puts it, "skepticism and doubt lead to study and investigation, and investigation is the beginning of wisdom."

1   An agnostic is a doubter. The word is generally applied to those who doubt the verity of accepted religious creeds of faiths. Everyone is an agnostic as to the beliefs or creeds they do not accept. Catholics are agnostic to the Protestant creeds, and the Protestants are agnostic to the Catholic creed. Anyone who thinks is an agnostic about something, otherwise he must believe that he is possessed of all knowledge. And the proper place for such a person is in the madhouse or the home for the feeble-minded. In a popular way, in the western world, an agnostic is one who doubts or disbelieves the main tenets of the Christian faith.

2   I would say that belief in at least three tenets is necessary to the faith of a Christian: a belief in God, a belief in immortality, and a belief in a supernatural book. Various Christian sects require much more, but it is difficult to imagine that one could be a Christian, under any intelligent meaning of the word, with less. Yet there are some people who claim to be Christians who do not accept the literal interpretation of all the Bible, and who give more credence to some portions of the book than to others.

3   I am an agnostic as to the question of God. I think that it is impossible for the human mind to believe in an object or thing unless it can form a mental picture of such object or thing. Since man ceased to worship openly an anthropomorphic God and talked vaguely and not intelligently about some force in the universe, higher than man, that is responsible for the existence of man and the universe, he cannot be said to believe in God. One cannot believe in a force excepting as a force that pervades matter and is not an individual entity. To believe in a thing, an image of the thing must be stamped on the mind. If one is asked if he believes in such an animal as a camel, there immediately arises in his mind an image of the camel. This image has come from experience or knowledge of the animal gathered in some way or other. No such image comes, or can come, with the idea of a God who is described as a force.

4   Man has always speculated upon the origin of the universe, includ-

ing himself. I feel, with Herbert Spencer, that whether the universe had an origin—and if it had—what the origin is will never be known by man. The Christian says that the universe could not make itself; that there must have been some higher power to call it into being. Christians have been obsessed for many years by Paley's argument that if a person passing through a desert should find a watch and examine its spring, its hands, its case and its crystal, he would at once be satisfied that some intelligent being capable of design had made the watch. No doubt this is true. No civilized man would question that someone made the watch. The reason he would not doubt it is because he is familiar with watches and other appliances made by man. The savage was once unfamiliar with a watch and would have had no idea upon the subject. There are plenty of crystals and rocks of natural formation that are as intricate as a watch, but even to intelligent man they carry no implication that some intelligent power must have made them. They carry no such implication because no one has any knowledge or experience of someone having made these natural objects which everywhere abound.

5   To say that God made the universe gives us no explanation of the beginnings of things. If we are told that God made the universe, the question immediately arises: Who made God? Did he always exist, or was there some power back of that? Did he create matter out of nothing, or is his existence coextensive with matter? The problem is still there. What is the origin of it all? If, on the other hand, one says that the universe was not made by God, that it always existed, he has the same difficulty to confront. To say that the universe was here last year, or millions of years ago, does not explain its origin. This is still a mystery. As to the question of the origin of things, man can only wonder and doubt and guess.

6   As to the existence of the soul, all people may either believe or disbelieve. Everyone knows the origin of the human being. They know that it came from a single cell in the body of the mother, and that the cell was one out of ten thousand in the mother's body. Before gestation the cell must have been fertilized by a spermatozoön from the body of the father. This was one out of perhaps a billion spermatozoa that was the capacity of the father. When the cell is fertilized a chemical process begins. The cell divides and multiplies and increases into millions of cells, and finally a child is born. Cells die and are born during the life of the individual until they finally drop apart, and this is death.

7   If there is a soul, what is it, and where did it come from, and where does it go? Can anyone who is guided by his reason possibly imagine a soul independent of a body, or the place of its residence, or the character of it, or anything concerning it? If man is justified in any belief or disbelief on any subject, he is warranted in the disbelief in a soul. Not one scrap of evidence exists to prove any such impossible thing.

8   Many Christians base the belief of a soul and God upon the Bible. Strictly speaking, there is no such book. To make the Bible, sixty-six books are bound into one volume. These books are written by many people at different times, and no one knows the time or the identity of any author. Some of the books were written by several authors at various times. These books contain all sorts of contradictory concepts of life and morals and the origin of things. Between the first and the last nearly a thousand years intervened, a longer time than has passed since the discovery of America by Columbus.

9   When I was a boy the theologians used to assert that the proof of the divine inspiration of the Bible rested on miracles and prophecies. But a miracle means a violation of a natural law, and there can be no proof imagined that could be sufficient to show the violation of a natural law; even though proof seemed to show violation, it would only show that we were not acquainted with all natural laws. One believes in the truthfulness of a man because of his long experience with the man, and because the man has always told a consistent story. But no man has told so consistent a story as nature.

10   If one should say that the sun did not rise, to use the ordinary expression, on the day before, his hearer would not believe it, even though he had slept all day and knew that his informant was a man of the strictest veracity. He would not believe it because the story is inconsistent with the conduct of the sun in all the ages past.

11   Primitive and even civilized people have grown so accustomed to believing in miracles that they often attribute the simplest manifestations of nature to agencies of which they know nothing. They do this when the belief is utterly inconsistent with knowledge and logic. They believe in old miracles and new ones. Preachers pray for rain, knowing full well that no such prayer was ever answered. When a politician is sick, they pray for God to cure him, and the politician almost invariably dies. The modern clergyman who prays for rain and for the health of the politician is no more intelligent in this matter than the primitive man who saw a separate miracle in the

rising and setting of the sun, in the birth of an individual, in the growth of a plant, in the stroke of lightning, in the flood, in every manifestation of nature and life.

12 As to prophecies, intelligent writers gave them up long ago. In all prophecies facts are made to suit the prophecy, or the prophecy was made after the facts, or the events have no relation to the prophecy. Weird and strange and unreasonable interpretations are used to explain simple statements, that a prophecy may be claimed.

13 Can any rational person believe that the Bible is anything but a human document? We now know pretty well where the various books came from, and about when they were written. We know that they were written by human beings who had no knowledge of science, little knowledge of life, and were influenced by the barbarous morality of primitive times, and were grossly ignorant of most things that men know today. For instance, Genesis says that God made the earth, and he made the sun to light the day and the moon to light the night, and in one clause disposes of the stars by saying that "he made the stars also." This was plainly written by someone who had no conception of the stars. Man, by the aid of his telescope, has looked out into the heavens and found stars whose diameter is as great as the distance between the earth and the sun. We know that the universe is filled with stars and suns and planets and systems. Every new telescope looking further into the heavens only discovers more and more worlds and suns and systems in the endless reaches of space. The men who wrote Genesis believed, of course, that this tiny speck of mud that we call the earth was the center of the universe, the only world in space, and made for man, who was the only being worth considering. These men believed that the stars were only a little way above the earth, and were set in the firmament for man to look at, and for nothing else. Everyone today knows that this conception is not true.

14 The origin of the human race is not as blind a subject as it once was. Let alone God creating Adam out of hand, from the dust of the earth, does anyone believe that Eve was made from Adam's rib—that the snake walked and spoke in the Garden of Eden—that he tempted Eve to persuade Adam to eat an apple, and that it is on that account that the whole human race was doomed to hell—that for four thousand years there was no chance for any human to be saved, though none of them had anything whatever to do with the temptation; and that finally men were saved only through God's son

dying for them, and that unless human beings believed this silly, impossible and wicked story they were doomed to hell? Can anyone with intelligence really believe that a child born today should be doomed because the snake tempted Eve and Eve tempted Adam? To believe that is not God-worship; it is devil-worship.

15   Can anyone call this scheme of creation and damnation moral? It defies every principle of morality, as man conceives morality. Can anyone believe today that the whole world was destroyed by flood, save only Noah and his family and a male and female of each species of animal that entered the Ark? There are almost a million species of insects alone. How did Noah match these up and make sure of getting male and female to reproduce life in the world after the flood had spent its force? And why should all the lower animals have been destroyed? Were they included in the sinning of man? This is a story which could not beguile a fairly bright child of five years of age today.

16   Do intelligent people believe that the various languages spoken by man on earth came from the confusion of tongues at the Tower of Babel, some four thousand years ago? Human languages were dispersed all over the face of the earth long before that time. Evidences of civilizations are in existence now that were old long before the date that romancers fix for the building of the Tower, and even before the date claimed for the flood.

17   Do Christians believe that Joshua made the sun stand still, so that the day could be lengthened, that a battle might be finished? What kind of person wrote that story, and what did he know about astronomy? It is perfectly plain that the author thought that the earth was the center of the universe and stood still in the heavens, and that the sun either went around it or was pulled across its path each day, and that the stopping of the sun would lengthen the day. We know now that had the sun stopped when Joshua commanded it, and had it stood still until now, it would not have lengthened the day. We know that the day is determined by the rotation of the earth upon its axis, and not by the movement of the sun. Everyone knows that this story simply is not true, and not many even pretend to believe the childish fable.

18   What of the tale of Balaam's ass speaking to him, probably in Hebrew? Is it true, or is it a fable? Many asses have spoken, and doubtless some in Hebrew, but they have not been that breed of asses. Is salvation to depend on a belief in a monstrosity like this?

19 Above all the rest, would any human being today believe that a child was born without a father? Yet this story was not at all unreasonable in the ancient world; at least three or four miraculous births are recorded in the Bible, including John the Baptist and Samson. Immaculate conceptions were common in the Roman world at the time and at the place where Christianity really had its nativity. Women were taken to the temples to be inoculated of God so that their sons might be heroes, which meant, generally, wholesale butchers. Julius Caesar was a miraculous conception—indeed, they were common all over the world. How many miraculous-birth stories is a Christian now expected to believe?

20 In the days of the formation of the Christian religion, disease meant the possession of human beings by devils. Christ cured a sick man by casting out the devils, who ran into the swine, and the swine ran into the sea. Is there any question but what that was simply the attitude and belief of a primitive people? Does anyone believe that sickness means the possession of the body by devils, and that the devils must be cast out of the human being that he may be cured? Does anyone believe that a dead person can come to life? The miracles recorded in the Bible are not the only instances of dead men coming to life. All over the world one finds testimony of such miracles: miracles which no person is expected to believe, unless it is his kind of a miracle. Still at Lourdes today, and all over the present world, from New York to Los Angeles and up and down the lands, people believe in miraculous occurrences, and even in the return of the dead. Superstition is everywhere prevalent in the world. It has been so from the beginning, and most likely will be so unto the end.

21 The reasons for agnosticism are abundant and compelling. Fantastic and foolish and impossible consequences are freely claimed for the belief in religion. All the civilization of any period is put down as a result of religion. All the cruelty and error and ignorance of the period has no relation to religion. The truth is that the origin of what we call civilization is not due to religion but to skepticism. So long as men accepted miracles without question, so long as they believed in original sin and the road to salvation, so long as they believed in a hell where man would be kept for eternity on account of Eve, there was no reason whatever for civilization: life was short, and eternity was long, and the business of life was preparation for eternity.

22 When every event was a miracle, when there was no order or

system or law, there was no occasion for studying any subject, or being interested in anything excepting a religion which took care of the soul. As man doubted the primitive conceptions about religion, and no longer accepted the literal, miraculous teachings of ancient books, he set himself to understand nature. We no longer cure disease by casting out devils. Since that time, men have studied the human body, have built hospitals and treated illness in a scientific way. Science is responsible for the building of railroads and bridges, of steamships, of telegraph lines, of cities, towns, large buildings and small, plumbing and sanitation, of the food supply, and the countless thousands of useful things that we now deem necessary to life. Without skepticism and doubt, none of these things could have been given to the world.

23   The fear of God is not the beginning of wisdom. The fear of God is the death of wisdom. Skepticism and doubt lead to study and investigation, and investigation is the beginning of wisdom.

24   The modern world is the child of doubt and inquiry, as the ancient world was the child of fear and faith.

The Patron and the Crocus

VIRGINIA WOOLF

Virginia Woolf (1882–1941) was born in London, the daughter
of Sir Leslie Stephen, who was renowned for his biographies of
Alexander Pope, Samuel Johnson, and others. She received a good
education and, in 1912, married the writer Leonard Woolf. They
became one of the most celebrated literary couples in England.
They were central figures in the Bloomsbury Group of literary
figures and artists. The Woolfs also founded Hogarth Press, which
published not only their own works but the works of many notable
British writers.

Woolf wrote a number of innovative novels: *Mrs. Dalloway*
(1925), *To the Lighthouse* (1927), *Orlando* (1928), *The Waves*
(1931), and *Between the Acts* (1941). She also wrote many essays,
both critical and meditative, which were collected, in part, in *The
Common Reader* (1925), *The Second Common Reader* (1933), and
The Death of the Moth and Other Essays (1942), which was published
after her suicide in 1941.

"The Patron and the Crocus" is taken from *The Common Reader*.
Here she discusses the divided attention of any writer who must
focus carefully both on the subject, which is often a thing of beauty
like the crocus, and on the audience, which she calls the *patron*.
While the crocus might remain the same throughout the years, she
says, the audience shifts and changes. The writer's task is made more

difficult by the fact that the modern patron has many faces in a "bewildering variety."

1   Young men and women beginning to write are generally given the plausible but utterly impracticable advice to write what they have to write as shortly as possible, as clearly as possible, and without other thought in their minds except to say exactly what is in them. Nobody ever adds on these occasions the one thing needful: "And be sure you choose your patron wisely," though that is the gist of the whole matter. For a book is always written for somebody to read, and, since the patron is not merely the paymaster, but also in a very subtle and insidious way the instigator and inspirer of what is written, it is of the utmost importance that he should be a desirable man.

2   But who, then, is the desirable man—the patron who will cajole the best out of the writer's brain and bring to birth the most varied and vigorous progeny of which he is capable? Different ages have answered the question differently. The Elizabethans, to speak roughly, chose the aristocracy to write for and the playhouse public. The eighteenth-century patron was a combination of coffee-house wit and Grub Street bookseller. In the nineteenth century the great writers wrote for the half-crown magazines and the leisured classes. And looking back and applauding the splendid results of these different alliances, it all seems enviably simple, and plain as a pikestaff compared with our own predicament—for whom should we write? For the present supply of patrons is of unexampled and bewildering variety. There is the daily Press, the weekly Press, the monthly Press; the English public and the American public; the best-seller public and the worst-seller public; the high-brow public and the red-blood public; all now organised self-conscious entities capable through their various mouthpieces of making their needs known and their approval or displeasure felt. Thus the writer who has been moved by the sight of the first crocus in Kensington Gardens has, before he sets pen to paper, to choose from a crowd of competitors the particular patron who suits him best. It is futile to say, "Dismiss them all; think only of your crocus," because writing is a method of communication; and the crocus is an imperfect crocus until it has been shared. The first

man or the last may write for himself alone, but he is an exception and an unenviable one at that, and the gulls are welcome to his works if the gulls can read them.

3   Granted, then, that every writer has some public or other at the end of his pen, the high-minded will say that it should be a submissive public, accepting obediently whatever he likes to give it. Plausible as the theory sounds, great risks are attached to it. For in that case the writer remains conscious of his public, yet is superior to it—an uncomfortable and unfortunate combination, as the works of Samuel Butler, George Meredith, and Henry James may be taken to prove. Each despised the public; each desired a public; each failed to attain a public; and each wreaked his failure upon the public by a succession, gradually increasing in intensity, of angularities, obscurities, and affectations which no writer whose patron was his equal and friend would have thought it necessary to inflict. Their crocuses in consequence are tortured plants, beautiful and bright, but with something wrynecked about them, malformed, shrivelled on the one side, overblown on the other. A touch of the sun would have done them a world of good. Shall we then rush to the opposite extreme and accept (if in infancy alone) the flattering proposals which the editors of the *Times* and the *Daily News* may be supposed to make us—"Twenty pounds down for your crocus in precisely fifteen hundred words, which shall blossom upon every breakfast table from John o'Groats to the Land's End before nine o'clock tomorrow morning with the writer's name attached"?

4   But will one crocus be enough, and must it not be a very brilliant yellow to shine so far, to cost so much, and to have one's name attached to it? The Press is undoubtedly a great multiplier of crocuses. But if we look at some of these plants, we shall find that they are only very distantly related to the original little yellow or purple flower which pokes up through the grass in Kensington Gardens about this time of year. The newspaper crocus is amazing but still a very different plant. It fills precisely the space allotted to it. It radiates a golden glow. It is genial, affable, warmhearted. It is beautifully finished, too, for let nobody think that the art of "our dramatic critic" of the *Times* or of Mr. Lynd of the *Daily News* is an easy one. It is no despicable feat to start a million brains running at nine o'clock in the morning, to give two million eyes something bright and brisk and amusing to look at. But the night comes and these flowers fade. So little bits of glass lose their lustre if you take them out of the sea;

great prima donnas howl like hyenas if you shut them up in telephone boxes; and the most brilliant of articles when removed from its element is dust and sand and the husks of straw. Journalism embalmed in a book is unreadable.

5 The patron we want, then, is one who will help us to preserve our flowers from decay. But as his qualities change from age to age, and it needs considerable integrity and conviction not to be dazzled by the pretensions or bamboozled by the persuasions of the competing crowd, this business of patron-finding is one of the tests and trials of authorship. To know whom to write for is to know how to write. Some of the modern patron's qualities are, however, fairly plain. The writer will require at this moment, it is obvious, a patron with the book-reading habit rather than the play-going habit. Nowadays, too, he must be instructed in the literature of other times and races. But there are other qualities which our special weaknesses and tendencies demand in him. There is the question of indecency, for instance, which plagues us and puzzles us much more than it did the Elizabethans. The twentieth-century patron must be immune from shock. He must distinguish infallibly between the little clod of manure which sticks to the crocus of necessity, and that which is plastered to it out of bravado. He must be a judge, too, of those social influences which inevitably play so large a part in modern literature, and able to say which matures and fortifies, which inhibits and makes sterile. Further, there is emotion for him to pronounce on, and in no department can he do more useful work than in bracing a writer against sentimentality on the one hand and a craven fear of expressing his feeling on the other. It is worse, he will say, and perhaps more common, to be afraid of feeling than to feel too much. He will add, perhaps, something about language, and point out how many words Shakespeare used and how much grammar Shakespeare violated, while we, though we keep our fingers so demurely to the black notes on the piano, have not appreciably improved upon *Antony and Cleopatra*. And if you can forget your sex altogether, he will say, so much the better; a writer has none. But all this is by the way—elementary and disputable. The patron's prime quality is something different, only to be expressed perhaps by the use of that convenient word which cloaks so much—atmosphere. It is necessary that the patron should shed and envelop the crocus in an atmosphere which makes it appear a plant of the very highest importance, so that to misrepresent it is the one outrage not to be forgiven this side of

the grave. He must make us feel that a single crocus, if it be a real crocus, is enough for him; that he does not want to be lectured, elevated, instructed, or improved; that he is sorry that he bullied Carlyle into vociferation, Tennyson into idyllics, and Ruskin into insanity; that he is now ready to efface himself or assert himself as his writers require; that he is bound to them by a more than maternal tie; that they are twins indeed, one dying if the other dies, one flourishing if the other flourishes; that the fate of literature depends upon their happy alliance—all of which proves, as we began by saying, that the choice of a patron is of the highest importance. But how to choose rightly? How to write well? Those are the questions.

Comedy's Greatest Era

JAMES AGEE

James Agee (1909–1955) was born in Knoxville, Tennessee. He received a good education at St. Andrews Academy in Tennessee, Phillips Exeter Academy in New Hampshire, and Harvard University. Under the tutelage of I. A. Richards at Harvard, Agee honed his technique for communicating a story through a first-person narrator who served both as a main character and as a commentator on the aesthetic features of the story. Following his graduation from Harvard, Agee worked for *Fortune* magazine and found time to produce his first book, a set of poems entitled *Permit Me Voyage*. In 1936, *Fortune* editors sent Agee to Alabama to do a photo-essay (with photographer Walker Evans) about tenant farmers. The result, *Let Us Now Praise Famous Men* (1941), was the highlight of his career. It is an artistic portrait of a way of life, one that blends the art of photography with a prose poem. Agee also reviewed books and movies for *Time* and *Nation*. His reviews reflect his belief that film, as an artistic medium, could blend fiction and reality to produce masterful works of art. He demonstrated that prowess as coauthor with John Huston of the movie *The African Queen*.

"Comedy's Greatest Era," published in *Life* in 1949, remains Agee's most popular essay. It provides a parody of analytical criticism by ranking laughter in four grades—from the titter to the boffo. But Agee also examines the artistic essence of the silent comedians, rating them above the comedians who followed in the talking motion pictures. His comments on the artists, especially Charlie Chaplin, are so insightful that critics still today quote his words.

1   In the language of screen comedians four of the main grades of laugh are the titter, the yowl, the bellylaugh and the boffo. The titter is just a titter. The yowl is a runaway titter. Anyone who has ever had the pleasure knows all about a bellylaugh. The boffo is the laugh that kills. An ideally good gag, perfectly constructed and played, would bring the victim up this ladder of laughs by cruelly controlled degrees to the top rung, and would then proceed to wobble, shake, wave and brandish the ladder until he groaned for mercy. Then, after the shortest possible time out for recuperation, he would feel the first wicked tickling of the comedian's whip once more and start up a new ladder.

2   The reader can get a fair enough idea of the current state of screen comedy by asking himself how long it has been since he has had that treatment. The best of comedies these days hand out plenty of titters and once in a while it is possible to achieve a yowl without overstraining. Even those who have never seen anything better must occasionally have the feeling, as they watch the current run or, rather, trickle of screen comedy, that they are having to make a little cause for laughter go an awfully long way. And anyone who has watched screen comedy over the past ten or fifteen years is bound to realize that it has quietly but steadily deteriorated. As for those happy atavists who remember silent comedy in its heyday and the bellylaughs and boffos that went with it, they have something close to an absolute standard by which to measure the deterioration.

3   When a modern comedian gets hit on the head, for example, the most he is apt to do is look sleepy. When a silent comedian got hit on the head he seldom let it go so flatly. He realized a broad license, and a ruthless discipline within that license. It was his business to be as funny as possible physically, without the help or hindrance of words. So he gave us a figure of speech, or rather of vision, for loss of consciousness. In other words he gave us a poem, a kind of poem, moreover, that everybody understands. The least he might do was

to straighten up stiff as a plank and fall over backward with such skill that his whole length seemed to slap the floor at the same instant. Or he might make a cadenza of it—look vague, smile like an angel, roll up his eyes, lace his fingers, thrust his hands palms downward as far as they would go, hunch his shoulders, rise on tiptoe, prance ecstatically in narrowing circles until, with tallow knees, he sank down the vortex of his dizziness to the floor, and there signified nirvana by kicking his heels twice, like a swimming frog.

4   Startled by a cop, this same comedian might grab his hatbrim with both hands and yank it down over his ears, jump high in the air, come to earth in a split violent enough to telescope his spine, spring thence into a coattail-flattening sprint and dwindle at rocket speed to the size of a gnat along the grand, forlorn perspective of some lazy back boulevard.

5   Those are fine clichés from the language of silent comedy in its infancy. The man who could handle them properly combined several of the more difficult accomplishments of the acrobat, the dancer, the clown and the mime. Some very gifted comedians, unforgettably Ben Turpin, had an immense vocabulary of these clichés and were in part so lovable because they were deep conservative classicists and never tried to break away from them. The still more gifted men, of course, simplified and invented, finding out new and much deeper uses for the idiom. They learned to show emotion through it, and comic psychology, more eloquently than most language has ever managed to, and they discovered beauties of comic motion which are hopelessly beyond reach of words.

6   It is hard to find a theater these days where a comedy is playing; in the days of the silents it was equally hard to find a theater which was not showing one. The laughs today are pitifully few, far between, shallow, quiet and short. They almost never build, as they used to, into something combining the jabbering frequency of a machine gun with the delirious momentum of a roller coaster. Saddest of all, there are few comedians now below middle age and there are none who seem to learn much from picture to picture, or to try anything new.

7   To put it unkindly, the only thing wrong with screen comedy today is that it takes place on a screen which talks. Because it talks, the only comedians who ever mastered the screen cannot work, for they cannot combine their comic style with talk. Because there is a screen, talking comedians are trapped into a continual exhibition of

their inadequacy as screen comedians on a surface as big as the side of a barn.

8   At the moment, as for many years past, the chances to see silent comedy are rare. There is a smattering of it on television—too often treated as something quaintly archaic, to be laughed at, not with. Some two hundred comedies—long and short—can be rented for home projection. And a lucky minority had access to the comedies in the collection of New York's Museum of Modern Art, which is still incomplete but which is probably the best in the world. In the near future, however, something of this lost art will return to regular theaters. A thick straw in the wind is the big business now being done by a series of revivals of W. C. Fields's memorable movies, a kind of comedy more akin to the old silent variety than anything which is being made today. Mack Sennett now is preparing a sort of pot-pourri variety show called *Down Memory Lane* made up out of his old movies, featuring people like Fields and Bing Crosby when they were movie beginners, but including also interludes from silents. Harold Lloyd has re-released *Movie Crazy*, a talkie, and plans to revive four of his best silent comedies (*Grandma's Boy, Safety Last, Speedy* and *The Freshman*). Buster Keaton hopes to remake at feature length, with a minimum of dialogue, two of the funniest short comedies ever made, one about a porous homemade boat and one about a prefabricated house.

9   Awaiting these happy events we will discuss here what has gone wrong with screen comedy and what, if anything, can be done about it. But mainly we will try to suggest what it was like in its glory in the years from 1912 to1930, as practiced by the employees of Mack Sennett, the father of American screen comedy, and by the four most eminent masters: Charlie Chaplin, Harold Lloyd, the late Harry Langdon and Buster Keaton.

10   Mack Sennett made two kinds of comedy: parody laced with slapstick, and plain slapstick. The parodies were the unceremonious burial of a century of hamming, including the new hamming in serious movies, and nobody who has missed Ben Turpin in *A Small Town Idol*, or kidding Erich von Stroheim in *Three Foolish Weeks* or as *The Shriek of Araby*, can imagine how rough parody can get and still remain subtle and roaringly funny. The plain slapstick, at its best, was even better: a profusion of hearty young women in disconcerting bathing suits, frisking around with a gaggle of insanely incompetent policemen and of equally certifiable male civilians sporting museum-

piece mustaches. All these people zipped and caromed about the pristine world of the screen as jazzily as a convention of water bugs. Words can hardly suggest how energetically they collided and bounced apart, meeting in full gallop around the corner of a house; how hard and how often they fell on their backsides; or with what fantastically adroit clumsiness they got themselves fouled up in folding ladders, garden hoses, tethered animals and each other's headlong cross-purposes. The gestures were ferociously emphatic; not a line or motion of the body was wasted or inarticulate. The reader may remember how splendidly upright wandlike old Ben Turpin could stand for a Renunciation Scene, with his lampshade mustache twittering and his sparrowy chest stuck out and his head flung back like Paderewski assaulting a climax and the long babyish black hair trying to look lionlike, while his Adam's apple, an orange in a Christmas stocking, pumped with noble emotion. Or huge Mack Swain, who looked like a hairy mushroom, rolling his eyes in a manner patented by French Romantics and gasping in some dubious ecstasy. Or Louise Fazenda, the perennial farmer's daughter and the perfect low-comedy housemaid, primping her spit curl; and how her hair tightened a good-looking face into the incarnation of rampant gullibility. Or snouty James Finlayson, gleefully foreclosing a mortgage, with his look of eternally tasting a spoiled pickle. Or Chester Conklin, a myopic and inebriated little walrus stumbling around in outsize pants. Or Fatty Arbuckle, with his cold eye and his loose, serene smile, his silky manipulation of his bulk and his satanic marksmanship with pies (he was ambidextrous and could simultaneously blind two people in opposite directions).

11   The intimate tastes and secret hopes of these poor ineligible dunces were ruthlessly exposed whenever a hot stove, an electric fan or a bulldog took a dislike to their outer garments: agonizingly elaborate drawers, worked up on some lonely evening out of some Godforsaken lace curtain; or men's underpants with big round black spots on them. The Sennett sets—delirious wallpaper, megalomaniacally scrolled iron beds, Grand Rapids *in extremis*—outdid even the underwear. It was their business, after all, to kid the squalid braggadocio which infested the domestic interiors of the period, and that was almost beyond parody. These comedies told their stories to the unaided eye, and by every means possible they screamed to it. That is one reason for the India-ink silhouettes of the cops, and for convicts and prison bars and their shadows in hard sunlight, and for barefooted

husbands, in tigerish pajamas, reacting like dervishes to stepped-on tacks.

12   The early silent comedians never strove for or consciously thought of anything that could be called artistic "form," but they achieved it. For Sennett's rival, Hal Roach, Leo McCarey once devoted almost the whole of a Laurel and Hardy two-reeler to pie-throwing. The first pies were thrown thoughtfully, almost philosophically. Then innocent bystanders began to get caught into the vortex. At full pitch it was Armageddon. But everything was calculated so nicely that until late in the picture, when havoc took over, every pie made its special kind of point and piled on its special kind of laugh.

13   Sennett's comedies were just a shade faster and fizzier than life. According to legend (and according to Sennett) he discovered the sped tempo proper to screen comedy when a green cameraman, trying to save money, cranked too slow. . . . Realizing the tremendous drumlike power of mere motion to exhilarate, he gave inanimate objects a mischievous life of their own, broke every law of nature the tricked camera would serve him for and made the screen dance like a witches' Sabbath. The thing one is surest of all to remember is how toward the end of nearly every Sennett comedy, a chase (usually called the "rally") built up such a majestic trajectory of pure anarchic motion that bathing girls, cops, comics, dogs, cats, babies, automobiles, locomotives, innocent bystanders, sometimes what seemed like a whole city, an entire civilization, were hauled along head over heels in the wake of that energy like dry leaves following an express train.

14   "Nice" people, who shunned all movies in the early days, condemned the Sennett comedies as vulgar and naive. But millions of less pretentious people loved their sincerity and sweetness, their wild-animal innocence and glorious vitality. They could not put these feelings into words, but they flocked to the silents. The reader who gets back deep enough into that world will probably even remember the theater: the barefaced honky-tonk and the waltzes by Waldteufel, slammed out on a mechanical piano; the searing redolence of peanuts and demirep perfumery, tobacco and feet and sweat; the laughter of unrespectable people having a hell of a fine time, laughter as violent and steady and deafening as standing under a waterfall.

15   Sennett wheedled his first financing out of a couple of ex-bookies to whom he was already in debt. He took his comics out of music halls, burlesque, vaudeville, circuses and limbo, and through them

he tapped in on that great pipeline of horsing and miming which runs back unbroken through the fairs of the Middle Ages at least to ancient Greece. He added all that he himself had learned about the large and spurious gesture, the late decadence of the Grand Manner, as a stage-struck boy in East Berlin, Connecticut and as a frustrated opera singer and actor. The only thing he claims to have invented is the pie in the face, and he insists, "Anyone who tells you he has discovered something new is a fool or a liar or both."

16   The silent-comedy studio was about the best training school the movies have ever known, and the Sennett studio was about as free and easy and as fecund of talent as they came. All the major comedians we will mention worked there, at least briefly. So did some of the major stars of the twenties and since—notably Gloria Swanson, Phyllis Haver, Wallace Beery, Marie Dressler and Carole Lombard. Directors Frank Capra, Leo McCarey and George Stevens also got their start in silent comedy; much that remains most flexible, spontaneous and visually alive in sound movies can be traced, through them and others, to this silent apprenticeship. Everybody did pretty much as he pleased on the Sennett lot, and everybody's ideas were welcome. Sennett posted no rules, and the only thing he strictly forbade was liquor. A Sennett story conference was a most informal affair. During the early years, at least, only the most important scenario might be jotted on the back of an envelope. Mainly Sennett's men thrashed out a few primary ideas and carried them in their heads, sure the better stuff would turn up while they were shooting, in the heat of physical action. This put quite a load on the prop man; he had to have the most improbable apparatus on hand—bombs, trick telephones, what not—to implement whatever idea might suddenly turn up. All kinds of things did—and were recklessly used. Once a low-comedy auto got out of control and killed the cameraman, but he was not visible in the shot, which was thrilling and undamaged; the audience never knew the difference.

17   Sennett used to hire a "wild man" to sit in on his gag conferences, whose whole job was to think up "wildies." Usually he was an all but brainless, speechless man, scarcely able to communicate his idea; but he had a totally uninhibited imagination. He might say nothing for an hour; then he'd mutter "You take . . ." and all the relatively rational others would shut up and wait. "You take this cloud . . ." he would get out, sketching vague shapes in the air. Often he could get no further; but thanks to some kind of thought-transference,

saner men would take this cloud and make something of it. The wild man seems in fact to have functioned as the group's subconscious mind, the source of all creative energy. His ideas were so weird and amorphous that Sennett can no longer remember a one of them, or even how it turned out after rational processing. But a fair equivalent might be one of the best comic sequences in a Laurel and Hardy picture. It is simple enough—simple and real, in fact, as a nightmare. Laurel and Hardy are trying to move a piano across a narrow suspension bridge. The bridge is slung over a sickening chasm, between a couple of Alps. Midway they meet a gorilla.

18   Had he done nothing else, Sennett would be remembered for giving a start to three of the four comedians who now began to apply their sharp individual talents to this newborn language. The one whom he did not train (he was on the lot briefly but Sennett barely remembers seeing him around) wore glasses, smiled a great deal and looked like the sort of eager young man who might have quit divinity school to hustle brushes. That was Harold Lloyd. The others were grotesque and poetic in their screen characters in degrees which appear to be impossible when the magic of silence is broken. One, who never smiled, carried a face as still and sad as a daguerreotype through some of the most preposterously ingenious and visually satisfying physical comedy ever invented. That was Buster Keaton. One looked like an elderly baby and, at times, a baby dope fiend; he could do more with less than any other comedian. That was Harry Langdon. One looked like Charlie Chaplin, and he was the first man to give the silent language a soul.

19   When Charlie Chaplin started to work for Sennett he had chiefly to reckon with Ford Sterling, the reigning comedian. Their first picture together amounted to a duel before the assembled professionals. Sterling, by no means untalented, was a big man with a florid Teutonic style which, under this special pressure, he turned on full blast. Chaplin defeated him within a few minutes with a wink of the mustache, a hitch of the trousers, a quirk of the little finger.

20   With *Tillie's Punctured Romance,* in 1914, he became a major star. Soon after, he left Sennett when Sennett refused to start a landslide among the other comedians by meeting the raise Chaplin demanded. Sennett is understandably wry about it in retrospect, but he still says, "I was right at the time." Of Chaplin he says simply, "Oh well, he's just the greatest artist that ever lived." None of Chaplin's former rivals rate him much lower than that; they speak

of him no more jealously than they might of God. We will try here only to suggest the essence of his supremacy. Of all comedians he worked most deeply and most shrewdly within a realization of what a human being is, and is up against. The Tramp is as centrally representative of humanity, as many-sided and as mysterious, as Hamlet, and it seems unlikely that any dancer or actor can ever have excelled him in eloquence, variety or poignancy of motion. As for pure motion, even if he had never gone on to make his magnificent feature-length comedies, Chaplin would have made his period in movies a great one singlehanded even if he had made nothing except *The Cure,* or *One A.M.* In the latter, barring one immobile taxi driver, Chaplin plays alone, as a drunk trying to get upstairs and into bed. It is a sort of inspired elaboration on a soft-shoe dance, involving an angry stuffed wildcat, small rugs on slippery floors, a Lazy Susan table, exquisite footwork on a flight of stairs, a contretemps with a huge, ferocious pendulum and the funniest and most perverse Murphy bed in movie history—and, always made physically lucid, the delicately weird mental processes of a man ethereally sozzled.

21   Before Chaplin came to pictures people were content with a couple of gags per comedy; he got some kind of laugh every second. The minute he began to work he set standards—and continually forced them higher. Anyone who saw Chaplin eating a boiled shoe like brook trout in *The Gold Rush,* or embarrassed by a swallowed whistle in *City Lights,* has seen perfection. Most of the time, however, Chaplin got his laughter less from the gags, or from milking them in any ordinary sense, than through his genius for what may be called *inflection*—the perfect, changeful shading of his physical and emotional attitudes toward the gag. Funny as his bout with the Murphy bed is, the glances of awe, expostulation and helpless, almost whimpering desire for vengeance which he darts at this infernal machine are ever better.

22   A painful and frequent error among tyros is breaking the comic line with a too-big laugh, then a letdown; or with a laugh which is out of key or irrelevant. The masters could ornament the main line beautifully; they never addled it. In *A Night Out* Chaplin, passed out, is hauled along the sidewalk by the scruff of his coat by staggering Ben Turpin. His toes trail; he is as supine as a sled. Turpin himself is so drunk he can hardly drag him. Chaplin comes quietly to, realizes how well he is being served by his struggling pal, and with a royally delicate gesture plucks and savors a flower.

23   The finest pantomime, the deepest emotion, the richest and most poignant poetry were in Chaplin's work. He could probably pantomime Bryce's *The American Commonwealth* without ever blurring a syllable and make it paralyzingly funny into the bargain. At the end of *City Lights* the blind girl who has regained her sight, thanks to the Tramp, sees him for the first time. She has imagined and anticipated him as princely, to say the least; and it has never seriously occurred to him that he is inadequate. She recognizes who he must be by his shy, confident, shining joy as he comes silently toward her. And he recognizes himself, for the first time, through the terrible changes in her face. The camera just exchanges a few quiet close-ups of the emotions which shift and intensify in each face. It is enough to shrivel the heart to see, and it is the greatest piece of acting and the highest moment in movies.

24   Harold Lloyd worked only a little while with Sennett. During most of his career he acted for another major comedy producer, Hal Roach. He tried at first to offset Chaplin's influence and establish his own individuality by playing Chaplin's exact opposite, a character named Lonesome Luke who wore clothes much too small for him and whose gestures were likewise as unChaplinesque as possible. But he soon realized that an opposite in itself was a kind of slavishness. He discovered his own comic identity when he saw a movie about a fighting parson: a hero who wore glasses. He began to think about those glasses day and night. He decided on horn rims because they were youthful, ultravisible on the screen and on the verge of becoming fashionable (he was to make them so). Around these large lensless horn rims he began to develop a new character, nothing grotesque or eccentric, but a fresh, believable young man who could fit into a wide variety of stories.

25   Lloyd depended more on story and situation than any of the other major comedians (he kept the best stable of gagmen in Hollywood, at one time hiring six); but unlike most "story" comedians he was also a very funny man from inside. He had, as he has written, "an unusually large comic vocabulary." More particularly he had an expertly expressive body and even more expressive teeth, and out of his thesaurus of smiles he could at a moment's notice blend prissiness, breeziness and asininity, and still remain tremendously likable. His movies were more extroverted and closer to ordinary life than any others of the best comedies: the vicissitudes of a New York taxi driver; the unaccepted college boy who, by desperate courage and

inspired ineptitude, wins the Big Game. He was especially good at putting a very timid, spoiled or brassy young fellow through devastating embarrassments. He went through one of his most uproarious Gethsemanes as a shy country youth courting the nicest girl in town in *Grandma's Boy.* He arrived dressed "strictly up to date for the Spring of 1862," as a subtitle observed, and found that the ancient colored butler wore a similar flowered waistcoat and moldering cutaway. He got one wandering, nervous forefinger dreadfully stuck in a fancy little vase. The girl began cheerfully to try to identify that queer smell which dilated from him; Grandpa's best suit was rife with mothballs. A tenacious litter of kittens feasted off the goose grease on his home-shined shoes.

26   Lloyd was even better at the comedy of thrills. In *Safety Last,* as a rank amateur, he is forced to substitute for a human fly and to climb a medium-sized skyscraper. Dozens of awful things happen to him. He gets fouled up in a tennis net. Popcorn falls on him from a window above, and the local pigeons treat him like a cross between a lunch wagon and St. Francis of Assisi. A mouse runs up his britches-leg, and the crowd below salutes his desperate dance on the window ledge with wild applause of the daredevil. A good deal of this full-length picture hangs thus by its eyelashes along the face of a building. Each new floor is like a new stanza in a poem; and the higher and more horrifying it gets, the funnier it gets.

27   In this movie Lloyd demonstrates beautifully his ability to do more than merely milk a gag, but to top it. (In an old, simple example of topping, an incredible number of tall men get, one by one, out of a small closed auto. After as many have clambered out as the joke will bear, one more steps out: a midget. That tops the gag. Then the auto collapses. That tops the topper.) In *Safety Last* Lloyd is driven out to the dirty end of a flagpole by a furious dog; the pole breaks and he falls, just managing to grab the minute hand of a huge clock. His weight promptly pulls the hand down from IX to VI. That would be more than enough for any ordinary comedian, but there is further logic in the situation. Now, hideously, the whole clockface pulls loose and slants from its trembling springs above the street. Getting out of difficulty with the clock, he makes still further use of the instrument by getting one foot caught in one of these obstinate springs.

28   A proper delaying of the ultrapredictable can of course be just as funny as a properly timed explosion of the unexpected. As Lloyd

approaches the end of his horrible hegira up the side of the building in *Safety Last*, it becomes clear to the audience, but not to him, that if he raises his head another couple of inches he is going to get murderously conked by one of the four arms of a revolving wind gauge. He delays the evil moment almost interminably, with one distraction and another, and every delay is a suspense-tightening laugh; he also gets his foot nicely entangled in a rope, so that when he does get hit, the payoff of one gag sends him careening head downward through the abyss into another. Lloyd was outstanding even among the master craftsmen at setting up a gag clearly, culminating and getting out of it deftly, and linking it smoothly to the next. Harsh experience also taught him a deep and fundamental rule: never try to get "above" the audience.

29   Lloyd tried it in *The Freshman*. He was to wear an unfinished, basted-together tuxedo to a college party, and it would gradually fall apart as he danced. Lloyd decided to skip the pants, a low-comedy cliché, and lose just the coat. His gagmen warned him. A preview proved how right they were. Lloyd had to reshoot the whole expensive sequence, build it around defective pants and climax it with the inevitable. It was one of the funniest things he ever did.

30   When Lloyd was still a very young man he lost about half his right hand (and nearly lost his sight) when a comedy bomb exploded prematurely. But in spite of his artificially built-out hand he continued to do his own dirty work, like all of the best comedians. The side of the building he climbed in *Safety Last* did not overhang the street, as it appears to. But the nearest landing place was a roof three floors below him, as he approached the top, and he did everything, of course, the hard way, that is, the comic way, keeping his bottom stuck well out, his shoulders hunched, his hands and feet skidding over perdition.

31   If great comedy must involve something beyond laughter, Lloyd was not a great comedian. If plain laughter is any criterion—and it is a healthy counterbalance to the other—few people have equaled him, and nobody has ever beaten him.

32   Chaplin and Keaton and Lloyd were all more like each other, in one important way, than Harry Langdon was like any of them. Whatever else the others might be doing, they all used more or less elaborate physical comedy; Langdon showed how little of that one might use and still be a great silent-screen comedian. In his screen character he symbolized something as deeply and centrally human,

though by no means as rangily so, as the Tramp. There was, of course, an immense difference in inventiveness and range of virtuosity. It seemed as if Chaplin could do literally anything on any instrument in the orchestra. Langdon had one queerly toned, unique little reed. But out of it he could get incredible melodies.

33 Like Chaplin, Langdon wore a coat which buttoned on his wishbone and swung out wide below, but the effect was very different: he seemed like an outsized baby who had begun to outgrow his clothes. The crown of his hat was rounded and the brim was turned up all around, like a little boy's hat, and he looked as if he wore diapers under his pants. His walk was that of a child which had just gotten sure on its feet, and his body and hands fitted that age. His face was kept pale to show off, with the simplicity of a nursery-school drawing, the bright, ignorant, gentle eyes and the little twirling mouth. He had big moon cheeks, with dimples, and a Napoleonic forelock of mousy hair; the round, docile head seemed large in ratio to the cream-puff body. Twitchings of his face were signals of tiny discomforts too slowly registered by a tinier brain; quick, squirty little smiles showed his almost prehuman pleasures, his incurably premature trustfulness. He was a virtuoso of hesitations and of delicately indecisive motions, and he was particularly fine in a high wind, rounding a corner with a kind of skittering toddle, both hands nursing his hatbrim.

34 He was as remarkable a master as Chaplin of subtle emotional and mental process and operated much more at leisure. He once got a good three hundred feet of continuously bigger laughs out of rubbing his chest, in a crowded vehicle, with Limburger cheese, under the misapprehension that it was a cold salve. In another long scene, watching a brazen showgirl change her clothes, he sat motionless, back to the camera, and registered the whole lexicon of lost innocence, shock, disapproval and disgust, with the back of his neck. His scenes with women were nearly always something special. Once a lady spy did everything in her power (under the Hays Office) to seduce him. Harry was polite, willing, even flirtatious in his little way. The only trouble was that he couldn't imagine what in the world she was leering and pawing at him for, and that he was terribly ticklish. The Mata Hari wound up foaming at the mouth.

35 There was also a sinister flicker of depravity about the Langdon character, all the more disturbing because babies are premoral. He had an instinct for bringing his actual adulthood and figurative baby-

ishness into frictions as crawley as a fingernail on a slate blackboard, and he wandered into areas of strangeness which were beyond the other comedians. In a nightmare in one movie he was forced to fight a large, muscular young man; the girl Harry loved was the prize. The young man was a good boxer; Harry could scarcely lift his gloves. The contest took place in a fiercely lighted prize ring, in a prodigious pitch-dark arena. The only spectator was the girl, and she was rooting against Harry. As the fight went on, her eyes glittered ever more brightly with blood lust and, with glittering teeth, she tore her big straw hat to shreds.

36   Langdon came to Sennett from a vaudeville act in which he had fought a losing battle with a recalcitrant automobile. The minute Frank Capra saw him he begged Sennett to let him work with him. Langdon was almost as childlike as the character he played. He had only a vague idea of his story or even of each scene as he played it; each time he went before the camera Capra would brief him on the general situation and then, as this finest of intuitive improvisers once tried to explain his work, "I'd go into my routine." The whole tragedy of the coming of dialogue, as far as these comedians were concerned—and one reason for the increasing rigidity of comedy ever since—can be epitomized in the mere thought of Harry Langdon confronted with a script.

37   Langdon's magic was in his innocence, and Capra took beautiful care not to meddle with it. The key to the proper use of Langdon, Capra always knew, was "the principle of the brick." "If there was a rule for writing Langdon material," he explains, "it was this: his only ally was God. Langdon might be saved by the brick falling on the cop, but it was *verboten* that he in any way motivate the brick's fall." Langdon became quickly and fantastically popular with three pictures, *Tramp, Tramp, Tramp, The Strong Man* and *Long Pants;* from then on he went downhill even faster. "The trouble was," Capra says, "that high-brow critics came around to explain his art to him. Also he developed an interest in dames. It was a pretty high life for such a little fellow." Langdon made two more pictures with high-brow writers, one of which (*Three's a Crowd*) had some wonderful passages in it, including the prize-ring nightmare; then First National canceled his contract. He was reduced to mediocre roles and two-reelers which were more rehashes of his old gags; this time around they no longer seemed funny. "He never did really understand what hit him," says Capra. "He died broke [in 1944]. And

he died of a broken heart. He was the most tragic figure I ever came across in show business."

38   Buster Keaton started work at the age of three and one-half with his parents in one of the roughest acts in vaudeville ("The Three Keatons"); Harry Houdini gave the child the name Buster in admiration for a fall he took down a flight of stairs. In his first movies Keaton teamed with Fatty Arbuckle under Sennett. He went on to become one of Metro's biggest stars and earners; a Keaton feature cost about $200,000 to make and reliably grossed $2,000,000. Very early in his movie career friends asked him why he never smiled on the screen. He didn't realize he didn't. He had got the dead-pan habit in variety; on the screen he had merely been so hard at work it had never occurred to him there was anything to smile about. Now he tried it just once and never again. He was by his whole style and nature so much the most deeply "silent" of the silent comedians that even a smile was as deafeningly out of key as a yell. In a way his pictures are like a transcendent juggling act in which it seems that the whole universe is in exquisite flying motion and the one point of repose is the juggler's effortless, uninterested face.

39   Keaton's face ranked almost with Lincoln's as an early American archetype; it was haunting, handsome, almost beautiful, yet it was irreducibly funny; he improved matters by topping it off with a deadly horizontal hat, as flat and thin as a phonograph record. One can never forget Keaton wearing it, standing erect at the prow as his little boat is being launched. The boat goes grandly down the skids and, just as grandly, straight on to the bottom. Keaton never budges. The last you see of him, the water lifts the hat off the stoic head and it floats away.

40   No other comedian could do as much with the dead pan. He used this great, sad, motionless face to suggest various related things: a one-track mind near the track's end of pure insanity; mulish imperturbability under the wildest of circumstances; how dead a human being can get and still be alive; an awe-inspiring sort of patience and power to endure, proper to granite but uncanny in flesh and blood. Everything that he was and did bore out his rigid face and played laughs against it. When he moved his eyes, it was like seeing them move in a statue. His short-legged body was all sudden, machinelike angles, governed by a daft aplomb. When he swept a semaphorelike arm to point, you could almost hear the electrical impulse in the signal block. When he ran from a cop his transitions from accelerating

walk to easy jogtrot to brisk canter to headlong gallop to flogged-piston sprint—always floating, above this frenzy, the untroubled, untouchable face—were as distinct and as soberly in order as an automatic gearshift.

41 Keaton was a wonderfully resourceful inventor of mechanistic gags (he still spends much of his time fooling with Erector sets); as he ran afoul of locomotives, steamships, prefabricated and over-electrified houses, he put himself through some of the hardest and cleverest punishment ever designed for laughs. In *Sherlock Jr.,* boiling along on the handlebars of a motorcycle quite unaware that he has lost his driver, Keaton whips through city traffic, breaks up a tug-of-war, gets a shovelful of dirt in the fact from each of a long line of Rockette-timed ditch-diggers, approaches a log at high speed which is hinged open by dynamite precisely soon enough to let him through and, hitting an obstruction, leaves the handlebars like an arrow leaving a bow, whams through the window of a shack in which the heroine is about to be violated, and hits the heavy feet-first, knocking him through the opposite wall. The whole sequence is as clean in motion as the trajectory of a bullet.

42 Much of the charm and edge of Keaton's comedy, however, lay in the subtle leverages of expression he could work against his nominal dead pan. Trapped in the side-wheel of a ferryboat, saving himself from drowning only by walking, then desperately running, inside the accelerating wheel like a squirrel in a cage, his only real concern was, obviously, to keep his hat on. Confronted by Love, he was not as dead-pan as he was cracked up to be, either; there was an odd, abrupt motion of his head which suggested a horse nipping after a sugar lump.

43 Keaton worked strictly for laughs, but his work came from so far inside a curious and original spirit that he achieved a great deal besides, especially in his feature-length comedies. (For plain hard laughter his nineteen short comedies—the negatives of which have been lost—were even better.) He was the only major comedian who kept sentiment almost entirely out of his work, and he brought pure physical comedy to its greatest heights. Beneath his lack of emotion he was also uninsistently sardonic; deep below that, giving a disturbing tension and grandeur to the foolishness, for those who sensed it, there was in his comedy a freezing whisper not of pathos but of melancholia. With the humor, the craftsmanship and the action there was often, besides, a fine, still and sometimes dreamlike beauty. Much

of his Civil War picture *The General* is within hailing distance of Mathew Brady. And there is a ghostly, unforgettable moment in *The Navigator* when, on a deserted, softly rolling ship, all the pale doors along a deck swing open as one behind Keaton and, as one, slam shut, in a hair-raising illusion of noise.

44 Perhaps because "dry" comedy is so much more rare and odd than "dry" wit, there are people who never much cared for Keaton. Those who do cannot care mildly.

45 As soon as the screen began to talk, silent comedy was pretty well finished. The hardy and prolific Mack Sennett made the transfer; he was the first man to put Bing Crosby and W. C. Fields on the screen. But he was essentially a silent-picture man, and by the time the Academy awarded him a special Oscar for his "lasting contribution to the comedy technique of the screen" (in 1938), he was no longer active. As for the comedians we have spoken of in particular, they were as badly off as fine dancers suddenly required to appear in plays.

46 Harold Lloyd, whose work was most nearly realistic, naturally coped least unhappily with the added realism of speech; he made several talking comedies. But good as the best were, they were not so good as his silent work, and by the late thirties he quit acting. A few years ago he returned to play the lead (and play it beautifully) in Preston Sturges's *The Sin of Harold Diddlebock,* but this exceptional picture—which opened, brilliantly, with the closing reel of Lloyd's *The Freshman*—has not yet been generally released.

47 Like Chaplin, Lloyd was careful of his money; he is still rich and active. Last June, in the presence of President Truman, he became Imperial Potentate of the A.A.O.N.M.S. (Shriners). Harry Langdon, as we have said, was a broken man when sound came in.

48 Up to the middle thirties Buster Keaton made several feature-length pictures (with such players as Jimmy Durante, Wallace Beery and Robert Montgomery); he also made a couple of dozen talking shorts. Now and again he managed to get loose into motion, without having to talk, and for a moment or so the screen would start singing again. But his dark, dead voice, though it was in keeping with the visual character, tore his intensely silent style to bits and destroyed the illusion within which he worked. He gallantly and correctly refuses to regard himself as "retired." Besides occasional bits, spots and minor roles in Hollywood pictures, he has worked on summer stages, made talking comedies in France and Mexico and clowned in a French circus. This summer he has played the straw hats in *Three Men on a*

Horse. He is planning a television program. He also has a working agreement with Metro. One of his jobs there is to construct comedy sequences for Red Skelton.

49   The only man who really survived the flood was Chaplin, the only one who was rich, proud and popular enough to afford to stay silent. He brought out two of his greatest nontalking comedies, *City Lights* and *Modern Times,* in the middle of an avalanche of talk, spoke gibberish and, in the closing moments, plain English in *The Great Dictator,* and at last made an all-talking picture, *Monsieur Verdoux,* creating for that purpose an entirely new character who might properly talk a blue streak. *Verdoux* is the greatest of talking comedies though so cold and savage that it had to find its public in grimly experienced Europe.

50   Good comedy, and some that was better than good, outlived silence, but there has been less and less of it. The talkies brought one great comedian, the late, majestically lethargic W. C. Fields, who could not possibly have worked as well in silence; he was the toughest and the most warmly human of all screen comedians, and *It's a Gift* and *The Bank Dick,* fiendishly funny and incisive white-collar comedies, rank high among the best comedies (and best movies) ever made. Laurel and Hardy, the only comedians who managed to preserve much of the large, low style of silence and who began to explore the comedy of sound, have made nothing since 1945. Walt Disney, at his best an inspired comic inventor and teller of fairy stories, lost his stride during the war and has since regained it only at moments. Preston Sturges has made brilliant, satirical comedies, but his pictures are smart, nervous comedy-dramas merely italicized with slapstick. The Marx Brothers were sidesplitters but they made their best comedies years ago. Jimmy Durante is mainly a nightclub genius; Abbott and Costello are semiskilled laborers, at best; Bob Hope is a good radio comedian with a pleasing presence, but not much more, on the screen.

51   There is no hope that screen comedy will get much better than it is without new, gifted young comedians who really belong in movies, and without freedom for their experiments. For everyone who may appear we have one last, individious comparison to offer as a guidepost.

52   One of the most popular recent comedies is Bob Hope's *The Paleface.* We take no pleasure in blackening *The Paleface;* we single it out, rather, because it is as good as we've got. Anything that is

said of it here could be said, with interest, of other comedies of our time. Most of the laughs in *The Paleface* are verbal. Bob Hope is very adroit with his lines and now and then, when the words don't get in the way, he makes a good beginning as a visual comedian. But only the beginning, never the middle or the end. He is funny, for instance, reacting to a shot of violent whisky. But he does not know how to get still funnier (*i.e.,* how to build and milk) or how to be funniest last (*i.e.,* how to top or cap his gag). The camera has to fade out on the same old face he started with.

53 One sequence is promisingly set up for visual comedy. In it, Hope and a lethal local boy stalk each other all over a cow town through streets which have been emptied in fear of their duel. The gag here is that through accident and stupidity they keep just failing to find each other. Some of it is quite funny. But the fun slackens between laughs like a weak clothesline, and by all the logic of humor (which is ruthlessly logical) the biggest laugh should come at the moment, and through the way, they finally spot each other. The sequence is so weakly thought out that at that crucial moment the camera can't afford to watch them; it switches to Jane Russell.

54 Now we turn to a masterpiece. In *The Navigator* Buster Keaton works with practically the same gag as Hope's duel. Adrift on a ship which he believes is otherwise empty, he drops a lighted cigarette. A girl finds it. She calls out and he hears her; each then tries to find the other. First each walks purposefully down the long, vacant starboard deck, the girl, then Keaton, turning the corner just in time not to see each other. Next time around each of them is trotting briskly, very much in earnest; going at the same pace, they miss each other just the same. Next time around each of them is going like a bat out of hell. Again they miss. Then the camera withdraws to a point of vantage at the stern, leans its chin in its hand and just watches the whole intricate superstructure of the ship as the protagonists stroll, steal and scuttle from level to level, up, down and sidewise, always managing to miss each other by hair's-breadths, in an enchantingly neat and elaborate piece of timing. There are no subsidiary gags to get laughs in this sequence and there is little loud laughter; merely a quiet and steadily increasing kind of delight. When Keaton has got all he can out of this fine modification of the movie chase he invents a fine device to bring the two together: the girl, thoroughly winded, sits down for a breather, indoors, on a plank which workmen have left across sawhorses. Keaton pauses on an upper deck, equally

winded and puzzled. What follows happens in a couple of seconds at most: air suction whips his silk topper backward down a ventilator; grabbing frantically for it, he backs against the lip of the ventilator, jackknifes and falls in backward. Instantly the camera cuts back to the girl. A topper falls through the ceiling and lands tidily, right side up, on the plank beside her. Before she can look more than startled, its owner follows, head between his knees, crushes the topper, breaks the plank with the point of his spine and proceeds to the floor. The breaking of the plank smacks Boy and Girl together.

55   It is only fair to remember that the silent comedians would have as hard a time playing a talking scene as Hope has playing his visual ones, and that writing and directing are as accountable for the failure as Hope himself. But not even the humblest journeymen of the silent years would have let themselves off so easily. Like the masters, they knew, and sweated to obey, the laws of their craft.

A Way of Writing

WILLIAM STAFFORD

William Stafford (1914–1990) was born in Hutchinson, Kansas. He earned both a B.A. and an M.A. at the University of Kansas and a Ph.D. at Iowa State University. As a conscientious objector during World War II, he served his time working for the Church World Service and the Brethren Service. He then served for many years on the staff at Lewis and Clark College. However, he is primarily known as a poet, even though he came to poetry late. He published *West of Your City* in 1960 when he was forty-six. Subsequently, he published more than thirty books of poetry and lectured extensively throughout the country.

"A Way of Writing" was first published in *Field* magazine in 1970. In it, Stafford describes the creative process that triggers the many works of art that we find in the humanities. He first recognizes the importance of receptivity, in which the artist must wait and let the ideas come as they will. Next, he cites the need for discovery without concern for failure. Stafford emphasizes that it is the process, not the product, that must be of key importance.

1   A writer is not so much someone who has something to say as he is someone who has found a process that will bring about new

things he would not have thought of if he had not started to say them. That is, he does not draw on a reservoir; instead, he engages in an activity that brings to him a whole succession of unforeseen stories, poems, essays, plays, laws, philosophies, religions, or—but wait!

2   Back in school, from the first when I began to try to write things, I felt this richness. One thing would lead to another; the world would give and give. Now, after twenty years or so of trying, I live by that certain richness, an idea hard to pin, difficult to say, and perhaps offensive to some. For there are strange implications in it.

3   One implication is the importance of just plain receptivity. When I write, I like to have an interval before me when I am not likely to be interrupted. For me, this means usually the early morning, before others are awake. I get pen and paper, take a glance out the window (often it is dark out there), and wait. It is like fishing. But I do not wait very long, for there is always a nibble—and this is where receptivity comes in. To get started I will accept anything that occurs to me. Something always occurs, of course, to any of us. We can't keep from thinking. Maybe I have to settle for an immediate impression: it's cold, or hot, or dark, or bright, or in between! Or—well, the possibilities are endless. If I put down something, that thing will help the next thing come, and I'm off. If I let the process go on, things will occur to me that were not at all in my mind when I started. These things, odd or trivial as they may be, are somehow connected. And if I let them string out, surprising things will happen.

4   If I let them string out. . . . Along with initial receptivity, then, there is another readiness: I must be willing to fail. If I am to keep on writing, I cannot bother to insist on high standards. I must get into action and not let anything stop me, or even slow me much. By "standards" I do not mean "correctness"—spelling, punctuation, and so on. These details become mechanical for anyone who writes for a while. I am thinking about what many people would consider "important" standards, such matters as social significance, positive values, consistency, etc. I resolutely disregard these. Something better, greater, is happening! I am following a process that leads so wildly and originally into new territory that no judgment can at the moment be made about values, significance, and so on. I am making something new, something that has not been judged before. Later others—and maybe I myself—will make judgments. Now, I am headlong to discover. Any distraction may harm the creating.

5   So, receptive, careless of failure, I spin out things on the page. And a wonderful freedom comes. If something occurs to me, it is all right to accept it. It has one justification: it occurs to me. No one else can guide me. I must follow my own weak, wandering, diffident impulses.

6   A strange bonus happens. At times, without my insisting on it, my writings become coherent; the successive elements that occur to me are clearly related. They lead by themselves to new connections. Sometimes the language, even the syllables that happen along, may start a trend. Sometimes the materials alert me to something waiting in my mind, ready for sustained attention. At such times, I allow myself to be eloquent, or intentional, or for great swoops (treacherous! not to be trusted!) reasonable. But I do not insist on any of that; for I know that back of my activity there will be the coherence of my self, and that indulgence of my impulses will bring recurrent patterns and meanings again.

7   This attitude toward the process of writing creatively suggests a problem for me, in terms of what others say. They talk about "skills" in writing. Without denying that I do have experience, wide reading, automatic orthodoxies and maneuvers of various kinds, I still must insist that I am often baffled about what "skill" has to do with the precious little area of confusion when I do not know what I am going to say and then I find out what I am going to say. That precious interval I am unable to bridge by skill. What can I witness about it? It remains mysterious, just as all of us must feel puzzled about how we are so inventive as to be able to talk along through complexities with our friends, not needing to plan what we are going to say, but never stalled for long in our confident forward progress. Skill? If so, it is the skill we all have, something we must have learned before the age of three or four.

8   A writer is one who has become accustomed to trusting that grace, or luck, or—skill.

9   Yet another attitude I find necessary: most of what I write, like most of what I say in casual conversation, will not amount to much. Even I will realize, and even at the time, that it is not negotiable. It will be like practice. In conversation I allow myself random remarks—in fact, as I recall, that is the way I learned to talk—, so in writing I launch many expendable efforts. A result of this free way of writing is that I am not writing for others, mostly; they will not see the product at all unless the activity eventuates in something that

later appears to be worthy. My guide is the self, and its adventuring in the language brings about communication.

10   This process-rather-than-substance view of writing invites a final, dual reflection:

11   1. Writers may not be special—sensitive or talented in any usual sense. They are simply engaged in sustained use of a language skill we all have. Their "creations" come about through confident reliance on stray impulses that will, with trust, find occasional patterns that are satisfying.

12   2. But writing itself is one of the great, free human activities. There is scope for individuality, and elation, and discovery, in writing. For the person who follows with trust and forgiveness what occurs to him, the world remains always ready and deep, an inexhaustible environment, with the combined vividness of an actuality and flexibility of a dream. Working back and forth between experience and thought, writers have more than space and time can offer. They have the whole unexplored realm of human vision.

Tragedy and the Common Man

ARTHUR MILLER

Arthur Miller was born in 1915 in New York. He earned an A.B. degree at the University of Michigan in 1938. Thereafter, he devoted himself to writing, first with the Federal Theater Project, then as the author of radio plays, and finally as a distinguished dramatist and essayist. A few of his major works are *All My Sons* (1947), *Death of a Salesman* (1949), *The Crucible* (1953), *A View from the Bridge* (1955), and many others. He also gained fame, briefly, as the husband of Marilyn Monroe from 1956 to 1961. Miller is known best for the realism of his dramas, which examine the psychological traumas and social collapses that followed World War II. He looked critically at materialism, the decay of family values, and the search for self-respect and dignity in an indifferent world.

"Tragedy and the Common Man" was written for the *New York Times* in 1949 to respond in part to claims that Willy Loman, the protagonist of *Death of a Salesman*, could not serve as a tragic hero because he was an ordinary man, not a man of great stature or nobility. Miller responded by saying, "I believe that the common man is as apt a subject for tragedy in its highest sense as kings were." Miller's thesis is clear: "I think the tragic feeling is evoked in us when we are in the presence of a character who is ready to lay down his life, if need be, to secure one thing—his sense of personal dignity."

The spirit of the average person, according to Miller, deserves our respect.

1 In this age few tragedies are written. It has often been held that the lack is due to a paucity of heroes among us, or else that modern man has had the blood drawn out of his organs of belief by the skepticism of science, and the heroic attack on life cannot feed on an attitude of reserve and circumspection. For one reason or another, we are often held to be below tragedy—or tragedy above us. The inevitable conclusion is, of course, that the tragic mode is archaic, fit only for the very highly placed, the kings or the kingly, and where this admission is not made in so many words it is most often implied.

2 I believe that the common man is as apt a subject for tragedy in its highest sense as kings were. On the face of it this ought to be obvious in the light of modern psychiatry, which bases its analysis upon classic formulations such as the Oedipus and Orestes complexes, for instances, which were enacted by royal beings, but which apply to everyone in similar emotional situations.

3 More simply, when the question of tragedy in art is not at issue, we never hesitate to attribute to the well-placed and the exalted the very same mental processes as the lowly. And finally, if the exaltation of tragic action were truly a property of the high-bred character alone, it is inconceivable that the mass of mankind should cherish tragedy above all other forms, let alone be capable of understanding it.

4 As a general rule, to which there may be exceptions unknown to me, I think the tragic feeling is evoked in us when we are in the presence of a character who is ready to lay down his life, if need be, to secure one thing—his sense of personal dignity. From Orestes to Hamlet, Medea to Macbeth, the underlying struggle is that of the individual attempting to gain his "rightful" position in his society.

5 Sometimes he is one who has been displaced from it, sometimes one who seeks to attain it for the first time, but the fateful wound from which the inevitable events spiral is the wound of indignity, and its dominant force is indignation. Tragedy, then, is the consequence of a man's total compulsion to evaluate himself justly.

6   In the sense of having been initiated by the hero himself, the tale always reveals what has been called his "tragic flaw," a failing that is not peculiar to grand or elevated characters. Nor is it necessarily a weakness. The flaw, or crack in the character, is really nothing—and need be nothing, but his inherent unwillingness to remain passive in the face of what he conceives to be a challenge to his dignity, his image of his rightful status. Only the passive, only those who accept their lot without active retaliation, are "flawless." Most of us are in that category.

7   But there are among us today, as there always have been, those who act against the scheme of things that degrades them, and in the process of action everything we have accepted out of fear or insensitivity or ignorance is shaken before us and examined, and from this total onslaught by an individual against the seemingly stable cosmos surrounding us—from this total examination of the "unchangeable" environment—comes the terror and the fear that is classically associated with tragedy.

8   More important, from this total questioning of what has previously been unquestioned, we learn. And such a process is not beyond the common man. In revolutions around the world, these past thirty years, he has demonstrated again and again this inner dynamic of all tragedy.

9   Insistence upon the rank of the tragic hero, or the so-called nobility of his character, is really but a clinging to the outward forms of tragedy. If rank or nobility of character was indispensable, then it would follow that the problems of those with rank were the particular problems of tragedy. But surely the right of one monarch to capture the domain from another no longer raises our passions, nor are our concepts of justice what they were to the mind of an Elizabethan king.

10   The quality in such plays that does shake us, however, derives from the underlying fear of being displaced, the disaster inherent in being torn away from our chosen image of what and who we are in this world. Among us today this fear is as strong, and perhaps stronger, than it ever was. In fact, it is the common man who knows this fear best.

11   Now, if it is true that tragedy is the consequence of a man's total compulsion to evaluate himself justly, his destruction in the attempt posits a wrong or an evil in his environment. And this is precisely the morality of tragedy and its lesson. The discovery of the moral

law, which is what the enlightenment of tragedy consists of, is not the discovery of some abstract or metaphysical quantity.

12 The tragic right is a condition of life, a condition in which the human personality is able to flower and realize itself. The wrong is the condition which suppresses man, perverts the flowing out of his love and creative instinct. Tragedy enlightens—and it must, in that it points the heroic finger at the enemy of man's freedom. The thrust for freedom is the quality in tragedy which exalts. The revolutionary questioning of the stable environment is what terrifies. In no way is the common man debarred from such thoughts or such actions.

13 Seen in this light, our lack of tragedy may be partially accounted for by the turn which modern literature has taken toward the purely psychiatric view of life, or the purely sociological. If all our miseries, our indignities, are born and bred within our minds, then all action, let alone the heroic action, is obviously impossible.

14 And if society alone is responsible for the cramping of our lives, then the protagonist must needs be so pure and faultless as to force us to deny his validity as a character. From neither of these views can tragedy derive, simply because neither represents a balanced concept of life. Above all else, tragedy requires the finest appreciation by the writer of cause and effect.

15 No tragedy can therefore come about when its author fears to question absolutely everything, when he regards any institution, habit or custom as being either everlasting, immutable or inevitable. In the tragic view the need of man to wholly realize himself is the only fixed star, and whatever it is that hedges his nature and lowers it is ripe for attack and examination. Which is not to say that tragedy must preach revolution.

16 The Greeks could probe the very heavenly origin of their ways and return to confirm the rightness of laws. And Job could face God in anger, demanding his right and end in submission. But for a moment everything is in suspension, nothing is accepted, and in this stretching and tearing apart of the cosmos, in the very action of so doing, the character gains "size," the tragic stature which is spuriously attached to the royal or the high-born in our minds. The commonest of men may take on that stature to the extent of his willingness to throw all he has into the contest, the battle to secure his rightful place in his world.

17 There is a misconception of tragedy with which I have been struck in review after review, and in many conversations with writers and

readers alike. It is the idea that tragedy is of necessity allied to pessimism. Even the dictionary says nothing more about the word than that it means a story with a sad or unhappy ending. This impression is so firmly fixed that I almost hesitate to claim that in truth tragedy implies more optimism in its author than does comedy, and that its final result ought to be the reinforcement of the onlooker's brightest opinions of the human animal.

18   For, if it is true to say that in essence the tragic hero is intent upon claiming his whole due as a personality, and if this struggle must be total and without reservation, then it automatically demonstrates the indestructible will of man to achieve his humanity.

19   The possibility of victory must be there in tragedy. Where pathos rules, where pathos is finally derived, a character has fought a battle he could not possibly have won. The pathetic is achieved when the protagonist is, by virtue of his witlessness, his insensitivity or the very air he gives off, incapable of grappling with a much superior force.

20   Pathos truly is the mode for the pessimist. But tragedy requires a nicer balance between what is possible and what is impossible. And it is curious, although edifying, that the plays we revere, century after century, are the tragedies. In them, and in them alone, lies the belief—optimistic, if you will, in the perfectibility of man.

21   It is time, I think, that we who are without kings, took up this bright thread of our history and followed it to the only place it can possibly lead in our time—the heart and spirit of the average man.

To Impersonate, to Watch, and to Be Watched

ERIC BENTLEY

Eric Bentley was born in England in 1916. He earned degrees at Oxford University and Yale University. He has served the writing profession in several ways: as translator, drama critic, and professor of theater. In particular, he has written many books on various aspects of drama and the theater.

"To Impersonate, to Watch, and to Be Watched" is one chapter from his book *The Life of the Drama* (1964). In it, Bentley describes the dramatic process in which one person impersonates another while a third watches the performance. He uses the essay to distinguish between art and life. In addition, he argues that an actor performs a type of self-exhibition that is not too far removed from the striptease of the chorus girls in the Folies-Bergère in Paris. Bentley says the actor "is not exhibiting the role alone, he is exhibiting his prowess, he is exhibiting himself." At the same time, the members of the audience are voyeurs who find pleasure in looking in on sin and even damnation while escaping it at the drop of the curtain.

1   The theatrical situation, reduced to a minimum, is that A impersonates B while C looks on. Such impersonation is universal among
small children, and such playing of a part is not wholly distinct from
the other playing that children do. All play creates a world within a
world—a territory with laws of its own—and the theater might be
regarded as the most durable of the many magic palaces which infan-
tile humanity has built. The distinction between art and life begins
there.

2   Impersonation is only half of this little scheme. The other half is
watching—or, from the viewpoint of A, being watched. Even when
there is actually no spectator, an impersonator imagines that there
is, often by dividing himself into two, the actor and his audience.
That very histrionic object, the mirror, enables any actor to watch
himself and thereby to become C, the audience. And the mirror on
the wall is only one: the mirrors in the mind are many.

3   What is it to want to be watched? Impossible to ask such a
question these days without eliciting the word: exhibitionism. To
want to be watched is to be exhibitionistic. Is this merely to say:
to want to be watched is to want to be watched? Not quite.
"Exhibitionism" is a clinical phenomenon, and the word carries
a connotation of the socially inappropriate as well as the mentally
unhealthy. Which, I am afraid, only makes it the more applicable
to the theater. Wishing to be watched, sometimes and in a small
way, is one thing, but wishing to become an actor is wishing to
be watched all the time and in a big way. Such a wish would
take a lot of justifying and even more explaining. It is bizarre,
and brings to mind Thomas Mann's notion that there is a natural
affinity between art and pathology.

4   Is the Folies-Bergère the quintessence of theater? That depends,
I think, on how one takes the Folies-Bergère. Sir Kenneth Clark has
distinguished between the naked and the nude. A nude body is one
that calls for no clothing; a naked body is a clothed body temporarily
stripped of its clothing. Sir Kenneth's interest in the distinction lies
in the fact that the arts he is professionally concerned with—painting
and sculpture—deal, not with the naked, but with the nude; in fact
(so far as Europe is concerned) they invented it. Not so the theater,
however. Even in places and at times which had nothing against the
body, the method of the theater has been concealment by mask and
costume. True, one of the archetypal acts of the theater is to remove
this concealment. But one can only take off what is on. Or, in Sir

Kenneth's terms, theater can present the naked, but never the nude. When therefore the girls of the Folies-Bergère are made a highbrow tableau of in the likeness of classical nude paintings, in trying to be nude they succeed in being untheatrical. When, on the other hand, they take off their clothes for us, or parade around in *almost* no clothing, they become theatrical through the act or simulation of unmasking. In short, if these girls are nude, they are art; if they are naked, they are theater. Parts of the French audience take them to be nude, or try to. The foreign tourists take them to be naked. That is because the tourists have "dirty minds." But the tourists are right. The nudity is spurious; the nakedness, genuine.

5   Hence, theater has less in common with the tradition of the nude in painting than with the tradition of the striptease in "vulgar" entertainment. Theater is shamelessly "low"; it cannot look down on the body, because it *is* the body. If you want the soul, why pay to see chorus girls? Why pay to *see* nonchorus girls? To begin to understand and accept theatrical art, we must be willing to say, yes, it's true, we *do* wish to see, and we do wish to be stimulated by seeing bodies—we decline to say "titillated" because the word "titillate" belongs to the puritan enemy of the theater. We must be willing to aver, further, that the bodies we wish to see are not "spiritualized" as Sir Kenneth Clark says nudes are, they are "naked," their spiritual credit is nil, their appeal is "prurient." We are prying into filthy secrets: the police department and the post office can begin to shift uneasily in their shoes.

6   How indecent the theater is! Yet, for our peace of mind, the indecency is in general placed at a remove: the nakedness is usually of the soul, not the body—and it is Phaedra's nakedness we see, not Gypsy Rose Lee's. For once that we see Salome remove her seven veils in Wilde's play or Strauss's opera, we see the veils removed a thousand times in other operas and plays from the individual spirit, from society, from the universe.

7   The problem with this is that to show the naked spirit is impossible. Only the spirit's envelope can be shown, and this is the body. And though a philosopher may represent the body as a mere shadow of a more substantial spiritual reality, and a playwright may follow him in this, our crude retort is inevitably that the shadow is itself pretty substantial. "Can spirit set to a leg? No. Or an arm? No." Platonic thoughts can be entertained in the mind, but not lived by from breakfast to lunch. And though the great nakednesses of the theater

are spiritual, the immediate reality of theater is aggressively physical, corporeal.

8   The physical world is real for every artist, and is that through which even a St. John of the Cross must communicate his antiphysical philosophy. Still, literature maintains some restraint in addressing its physicalities to the mind's eye only. Even painting and sculpture maintain some restraint in that the skin tints of the one have no skin under them, and the solidities of the other have no flesh or bone. Only theater thrusts at its audience the supreme object of sensual thoughts: the human body. And while in the theater it will never be nude, and will seldom be naked, its clothing is the more erotic in its double function of concealing and revealing, canceling and enhancing, denying and affirming.

9   That clothes may be used to heighten the sexual appeal of bodies, rather than reduce it, is a familiar enough fact. The exhibitionism of the actor is not so crudely sexual. He may even make himself theatrically more interesting by being less sexual: what has more appeal than Hamlet's funereal black? At worst, an actor or actress will concentrate on secondary sexual characteristics: a sensual mouth, a soulful eye, a rich head of hair, a slim waist, a well-shaped leg. He or she exhibits the body, but not for its beauty. In this the actor is closer to the acrobat than to the artist's model, since he exhibits his body largely for what it can do. And what an actor's body can do is expressive rather than lovely, and may be expressive, indeed, in the least lovely mode, such as grotesque comedy.

10   Does an actor exhibit *himself*? There has been much discussion on this head. Educators usually tell students of theater that the actor does not exhibit himself: that would be egotistic. He submerges himself in his roles: a noble example of self-discipline, if not self-sacrifice. Louis Jouve was saying as much when he stated that to embody a role the actor disembodies himself. One knows what he meant. When Sir Laurence Olivier plays Justice Shallow, the noble Olivier face and erect body are gone. Yet the very fact that I put it this way proves that I am not looking at the performance as I would if it were played by an actor who did not have a handsome face and an erect carriage. Does this signify only that I am a gossip, unable to concentrate on the show itself? I think not. The knowledge that an acrobatic trick is difficult is not irrelevant to the experience of watching it. On the contrary. We know it is easy for many creatures to fly up and down at great speed: the interest is *only* in seeing men

and women do it, because it is not easy for them to do it. To see Olivier as Shallow is to see comparable difficulties overcome, comparable laws of nature defied by human prowess. Hence we are not enjoying the role alone, but also the actor. And he, on his side, is not exhibiting the role alone, he is exhibiting his prowess, he is exhibiting himself. Nor is the self-exhibition confined to the skill with which he portrays someone we define as "so different from himself." To wear a heavy, senile make-up and hunch the shoulders would not be enough if there were not a Justice Shallow in Olivier, if Shallow were not something he might yet become, or might have become. In such roles the actor is exhibiting the many different possibilities of being that he finds in himself.

11   No need to say anything about actors who all too evidently exhibit nothing but themselves. I am saying that even the actor who seems to be at the opposite pole from this is still exhibiting himself. Exceptional in Sir Laurence is the talent. Unexceptional is the original naïve impulse that said: Watch me!

12   What of the pleasure of watching? In some respects, there is no difference between the theater spectator and the "consumer" of other arts—the listener to music, the reader of novels. It might be imagined that his position is identical with that of the observer of painting, sculpture, and architecture: all are onlookers. But the phenomenon is less straightforward. If theater is a visual art like painting, it is also a temporal art like music. The watcher is also a listener—the voyeur is also an eavesdropper.

13   Such words as *exhibitionist* and *voyeur*—though some will discount them as jargon—add to the purely descriptive words an implication of guilt.

> I have heard
> That guilty creatures sitting at a play
> Have by the very cunning of the scene
> Been struck so to the soul that presently
> They have proclaimed their malefactions.

Literal-minded persons will find Hamlet's ideas on crime detection somewhat far-fetched, but poetic drama deals in essences, and here Shakespeare, Hamlet, and all audiences of *Hamlet* take it that the essence of theater is to strike guilty creatures to the soul—or, as we would say in prose cliché, to play on the guilt feelings of the audience. Seen in this way, the logic is good.

> The play's the thing
> Wherein I'll catch the conscience of the king. . . .

—because plays *are* things wherein consciences are caught.

14   This makes it sound as if watching were very unpleasurable
indeed—as, for King Claudius, it was. Hamlet plotted to defy the
distinction between art and life, to exploit the possibility of a leap
from art to life. When that happens we are no longer dealing with
drama but with the destruction of its main convention. If we are not
King Claudius, and have not literally killed our brother, we are also
spared his reaction. Instead of calling for lights and making our exit,
we stay on to "enjoy the show." Is our conscience *not* caught, then?
Are our withers unwrung? It is. They are. But in art, not life. Such
is the paradox of pain in drama: we do and do not suffer. We are
suffering; we are also enjoying ourselves. When we watch, though
we do not watch in the way we watch actual happenings, neither do
we watch in the spirit of "scientific detachment" but always with
some degree of emotional involvement. I am suggesting that this
involvement is not an innocent one.

15   It would be impossible to draw the line between drama and
gossip, drama and scandal, drama and the front page of the worst
newspapers—which, understandably enough, claim to be dramatic.
Even what is called pornography is by no means in any separate
realm from the realm of the tragic and comic poets. All these
things are enjoyed by human beings, and to all some measure of
guilt is attached. Perhaps if one took the guilt away, the dirty
picture, so called, would lose much of its appeal, and perhaps if
one took from theater the element of voyeurism, the occasion
would lose much of its appeal.

16   Certainly that element has been on the increase in modern times.
The Greek, Elizabethan, and Spanish theaters were less voyeuristic
because the plays were put on in broad daylight. It is the modern
age that worked out the idea of a pitch-dark auditorium. Scholars
call the modern stage the peepshow stage. The corollary is that this
is a theater for Peeping Toms. It is; and the classical criticism of it
is that, form the eighteenth century to Tennessee Williams, it has
been so too crudely. It has been, all too often, a theater of domestic
triviality.

17   The pleasure of looking on is in itself an equivocal thing. It includes
such delights as feeling one has committed the crime yet is able to

escape the penalty because the final curtain descends and one finds "it was all a dream."

18   What is pornography? One element in it is that forbidden wishes are seen gratified—the punishment being escaped because the man on the "dirty picture" is not oneself. The literature that is called pornographic often has another feature: following forbidden pleasure, condign punishment. Does not Tennessee Williams' *Sweet Bird of Youth* afford us the pleasure of being a gigolo for three quarters of the evening and then in the last part giving him the punishment that exactly fits the crime? Affords *us* the pleasure but gives *him* the punishment: which is to say, affords us the pleasure, but finds us a whipping boy. This might well be called pornography. It also has a lot in common with high tragedy which from its beginnings has presented crime and its punishment, the punished protagonist being a scapegoat for the audience. Pornography is continuous with art; and the pleasure of watching is continuous with the pleasure of peeping.

Why a Surgeon Would Write

RICHARD SELZER

Richard Selzer was born in 1928 in Troy, New York. He earned a B.S. at Union College in Schenectady, New York, a medical degree at Albany Medical College, and did postdoctoral study at Yale University. He has been in private practice as a general surgeon since 1960. He draws from his experience as a surgeon to write both stories and essays that illuminate hospital life, both from the medical point of view and that of the patients. His second work, a book of essays entitled *Mortal Lessons: Notes on the Art of Surgery* (1977), gained national attention for its ability to explain the working of the human body to the lay reader. *Confessions of a Knife* (1979) displays in essay after essay Selzer's successes and failures as a surgeon. *Letters to a Young Doctor* (1982) features both essays and short fiction that might serve as advice to a young surgeon, but his words affect all readers. Elaine Kendal of the *Los Angeles Times* says, "No one writes about the practice of medicine with Selzer's unique combination of mystery and wonder."

"Why a Surgeon Would Write" is an essay from Selzer's book *Mortal Lessons*. Here he explains that he writes in the "search for some meaning in the ritual of surgery, which is at once murderous, painful, healing, and full of love." His point is that "the truly great writing about doctors . . . must be done *by* a doctor." Selzer admits, however, that a poet may do a better job of healing our wounds and lessening the pain of sickness and death.

1   Someone asked me why a surgeon would write. Why, when the shelves are already too full? They sag under the deadweight of books. To add a single adverb is to risk exceeding the strength of the boards. A surgeon should abstain. A surgeon, whose fingers are more at home in the steamy gullies of the body than they are tapping the dry keys of a typewriter. A surgeon, who feels the slow slide of intestines against the back of his hand and is no more alarmed than were a family of snakes taking their comfort from such an indolent rubbing. A surgeon, who palms the human heart as though it were some captured bird.

2   Why should he write? Is it vanity that urges him? There is glory enough in the knife. Is it for money? One can make too much money. No. It is to search for some meaning in the ritual of surgery, which is at once murderous, painful, healing, and full of love. It is a devilish hard thing to transmit—to find, even. Perhaps if one were to cut out a heart, a lobe of the liver, a single convolution of the brain, and paste it to a page, it would speak with more eloquence than all the words of Balzac. Such a piece would need no literary style, no mass of erudition or history, but in its very shape and feel would tell all the frailty and strength, the despair and nobility of man. What? Publish a heart? A little piece of bone? Preposterous. Still I fear that is what it may require to reveal the truth that lies hidden in the body. Not all the undressings of Rabelais, Chekhov, or even William Carlos Williams have wrested it free, although God knows each one of those doctors made a heroic assault upon it.

3   I have come to believe that it is the flesh alone that counts. The rest is that with which we distract ourselves when we are not hungry or cold, in pain or ecstasy. In the recesses of the body I search for the philosophers' stone. I know it is there, hidden in the deepest, dampest cul-de-sac. It awaits discovery. To find it would be like the harnessing of fire. It would illuminate the world. Such a quest is not without pain. Who can gaze on so much misery and feel no hurt? Emerson has written that the poet is the only true doctor. I believe

him, for the poet, lacking the impediment of speech with which the rest of us are afflicted, gazes, records, diagnoses, and prophesies.

4 I invited a young diabetic woman to the operating room to amputate her leg. She could not see the great shaggy black ulcer upon her foot and ankle that threatened to encroach upon the rest of her body, for she was blind as well. There upon her foot was a Mississippi Delta brimming with corruption, sending its raw tributaries down between her toes. Gone were all the little web spaces that when fresh and whole are such a delight to loving men. She could not see her wound, but she could feel it. There is no pain like that of the bloodless limb turned rotten and festering. There is neither unguent or anodyne to kill such a pain yet leave intact the body.

5 For over a year I trimmed away the putrid flesh, cleansed, anointed, and dressed the foot, staving off, delaying. Three times each week, in her darkness, she sat upon my table, rocking back and forth, holding her extended leg by the thigh, gripping it as though it were a rocket that must be steadied lest it explode and scatter her toes about the room. And I would cut away a bit here, a bit there, of the swollen blue leather that was her tissue.

6 At last we gave up, she and I. We could not longer run ahead of the gangrene. We had not the legs for it. There must be an amputation in order that she might live—and I as well. It was to heal us both that I must take up knife and saw, and cut the leg off. And when I could feel it drop from her body to the table, see the blessed *space* appear between her and that leg, I too would be well.

7 Now it is the day of the operation. I stand by while the anesthetist administers the drugs, watch as the tense familiar body relaxes into narcosis. I turn then to uncover the leg. There, upon her kneecap, she has drawn, blindly, upside down for me to see, a face; just a circle with two ears, two eyes, a nose, and a smiling upturned mouth. Under it she has printed SMILE, DOCTOR. Minutes later I listen to the sound of the saw, until a little crack at the end tells me it is done.

8 So, I have learned that man is not ugly, but that he is Beauty itself. There is no other his equal. Are we not all dying, none faster or more slowly than any other? I have become receptive to the possibilities of love (for it is love, this thing that happens in the operating room), and each day I wait, trembling in the busy air. Perhaps today it will come. Perhaps today I will find it, take part in it, this love that blooms in the stoniest desert.

9 All through literature, the doctor is portrayed as a figure of fun. Shaw was splenetic about him; Molière delighted in pricking his pompous medicine men, and well they deserved it. The doctor is ripe for caricature. But I believe that the truly great writing about doctors has not yet been done. I think it must be done *by* a doctor, one who is through with the love affair with his technique, who recognizes that he has played Narcissus, raining kisses on a mirror, and who now, out of the impacted masses of his guilt, has expanded into self-doubt, and finally into the high state of wonderment. Perhaps he will be a nonbeliever who, after a lifetime of grand gestures and mighty deeds, comes upon the knowledge that he has done no more than meddle in the lives of his fellows, and that he has done at least as much harm as good. Yet he may continue to pretend, at least, that there is nothing to fear, that death will not come, so long as people depend on his authority. Later, after his patients have left, he may closet himself in his darkened office, sweating and afraid.

10 There is a story by Unamuno in which a priest, living in a small Spanish village, is adored by all the people for his piety, kindness, and the majesty with which he celebrates the Mass each Sunday. To them he is already a saint. It is a foregone conclusion, and they speak of him as Saint Immanuel. He helps them with their plowing and planting, tends them when they are sick, confesses them, comforts them in death, and every Sunday, in his rich, thrilling voice, transports them to paradise with his chanting. The fact is that Don Immanuel is not so much a saint as a martyr. Long ago his own faith left him. He is an atheist, a good man doomed to suffer the life of a hypocrite, pretending to a faith he does not have. As he raises the chalice of wine, his hands tremble, and a cold sweat pours from him. He cannot stop for he knows that the people need this of him, that their need is greater than his sacrifice. Still . . . still . . . could it be that Don Immanuel's whole life is a kind of prayer, a paean to God?

11 A writing doctor would treat men and women with equal reverence, for what is the "liberation" of either sex to him who knows the diagrams, the inner geographies of each? I love the solid heft of men as much as I adore the heated capaciousness of women—women in whose penetralia is found the repository of existence. I would have them glory in that. Women are physics and chemistry. They are matter. It is their bodies that tell of the frailty of men. Men have not their cellular, enzymatic wisdom. Man is albuminoid, proteinaceous, laked pearl; woman is yolky, ovoid, rich. Both are exuberant

bloody growths. I would use the defects and deformities of each for my sacred purpose of writing, for I know that it is the marred and scarred and faulty that are subject to grace. I would seek the soul in the facts of animal economy and profligacy. Yes, it is the exact location of the soul that I am after. The smell of it is in my nostrils. I have caught glimpses of it in the body diseased. If only I could tell it. Is there no mathematical equation that can guide me? So much pain and pus equals so much truth? It is elusive as the whippoorwill that one hears calling incessantly from out the night window, but which, nesting as it does low in the brush, no one sees. No one but the poet, for he sees what no one else can. He was born with the eye for it.

12   Once I thought I had it: Ten o'clock one night, the end room off a long corridor in a college infirmary, my last patient of the day, degree of exhaustion suitable for the appearance of a vision, some manifestation. The patient is a young man recently returned from Guatemala, from the excavation of Mayan ruins. His left upper arm wears a gauze dressing which, when removed, reveals a clean punched-out hole the size of a dime. The tissues about the opening are swollen and tense. A thin brownish fluid lips the edge, and now and then a lazy drop of the overflow spills down the arm. An abscess, inadequately drained. I will enlarge the opening to allow better egress of the pus. Nurse, will you get me a scalpel and some . . . ?

13   What happens next is enough to lay Francis Drake avomit in his cabin. No explorer ever stared in wilder surmise than I into that crater from which there now emerges a narrow gray head whose sole distinguishing feature is a pair of black pincers. The head sits atop a longish flexible neck arching now this way, now that, testing the air. Alternately it folds back upon itself, then advances in new boldness. And all the while, with dreadful rhythmicity, the unspeakable pincers open and close. Abscess? Pus? Never. Here is the lair of a beast at whose malignant purpose I could but guess. A Mayan devil, I think, that would soon burst free to fly about the room, with horrid blanket-wings and iridescent scales, raking, pinching, injecting God knows what acid juice. And even now the irony does not escape me, the irony of my patient as excavator excavated.

14   With all the ritual deliberation of a high priest I advance a surgical clamp toward the hole. The surgeon's heart is become a bat hanging inside down from his rib cage. The rim achieved—now thrust—and

the ratchets of the clamp close upon the empty air. The devil has retracted. Evil mocking laughter bangs back and forth in the brain. More stealth. Lying in wait. One must skulk. Minutes pass, perhaps an hour. . . . A faint disturbance in the lake, and once again the thing upraises, farther and farther, hovering. Acrouch, strung, the surgeon is one with his instrument; there is no longer any boundary between its metal and his flesh. They are joined in a single perfect tool of extirpation. It is just for this that he was born. Now—thrust—and clamp—and *yes*. Got him!

15   Transmitted to the fingers comes the wild thrashing of the creature. Pinned and wriggling, he is mine. I hear the dry brittle scream of the dragon, and a hatred seizes me, but such a detestation as would make of Iago a drooling sucktit. It is the demented hatred of the victor for the vanquished, the warden for his prisoner. It is the hatred of fear. Within the jaws of my hemostat is the whole of the evil of the world, the dark concentrate itself, and I shall kill it. For mankind. And, in so doing, will open the way into a thousand years of perfect peace. Here is Surgeon as Savior indeed.

16   Tight grip now . . . steady, relentless pull. How it scrabbles to keep its tentacle-hold. With an abrupt moist plop the extraction is complete. There, writhing in the teeth of the clamp, is a dirty gray body, the size and shape of an English walnut. He is hung everywhere with tiny black hooklets. Quickly . . . into the specimen jar of saline . . . the lid screwed tight. Crazily he swims round and round, wiping his slimy head against the glass, then slowly sinks to the bottom, the mass of hooks in frantic agonal wave.

17   "You are going to be all right," I say to my patient. "We are *all* going to be all right from now on."

18   The next day I take the jar to the medical school. "That's the larva of the botfly," says a pathologist. "The fly usually bites a cow and deposits its eggs beneath the skin. There, the egg develops into the larval form which, when ready, burrows its way to the outside through the hide and falls to the ground. In time it matures into a fullgrown botfly. This one happened to bite a man. It was about to come out on its own, and, of course, it would have died."

19   The words *imposter, sorehead, servant of Satan* sprang to my lips. But now he has been joined by other scientists. They nod in agreement. I gaze from one gray eminence to another, and know the mallet-blow of glory pulverized. I tried to save the world, but it didn't work out.

20   No, it is not the surgeon who is God's darling. He is the victim
of vanity. It is the poet who heals with his words, stanches the flow
of blood, stills the rattling breath, applies poultice to the scalded
flesh.

21   Did you ask me why a surgeon writes? I think it is because I wish
to be a doctor.

CLASSIC
ESSAYS
IN THE

Social
Sciences

Some Thoughts Concerning Education

JOHN LOCKE

John Locke (1632–1704) was born in Wrington, Somersetshire, England. He was educated at Westminster and at Christ Church, Oxford. For a time he studied medicine, but his own health prevented him from completing his studies. He worked for many years as secretary to the Earl of Shaftesbury, sharing both the Earl's prosperity and disgrace. He tutored both the Earl's son and the Earl's grandson, gaining thereby a deep interest in education. His "An Essay Concerning Human Understanding" (1687) thrust Locke into the limelight, for he gave metaphysical discourse the same attention that Newton had given physics. Locke's careful inquiry into the origin, development, and combination of our thoughts made him an early pioneer in psychology.

"Some Thoughts Concerning Education" displays Locke's thoughtful reasoning about nurturing and developing intelligence in children. He wanted young minds to think wisely in harmony with healthy bodies. He wrote, "The little or almost insensible impressions on our tender infancies have very important and lasting consequences." He also insisted on the authority of adults, a judicious response to the individual talents of every individual child, parents and instructors who set good examples, the study of English and the motivating affection that adults must display while educating the child. His thoughts are still valid today.

1   A sound mind in a sound body is a short but full description of a happy state in this world. He that has these two has little more to wish for, and he that wants either of them will be but little the better for anything else. Men's happiness or misery is most part of their own making. He whose mind directs not wisely will never take the right away, and he whose body is crazy and feeble will never be able to advance in it. I confess there are some men's constitutions of body and mind so vigorous and well framed by nature that they need not much assistance from others, but by the strength of their natural genius, they are from their cradles carried towards what is excellent; and by the privilege of their happy constitutions, are able to do wonders. But examples of this kind are but few, and I think I may say, that of all the men we meet with, nine parts of ten are what they are, good or evil, useful or not, by their education. It is that which makes the great difference in mankind. The little or almost insensible impressions on our tender infancies have very important and lasting consequences. And there it is, as in the fountains of some rivers, where a gentle application of the hand turns the flexible waters into channels, that make them take quite contrary courses; and by this little direction, given them at first in the source, they receive different tendencies, and arrive at last at very remote and distant places.

2   Those that intend ever to govern their children should begin it whilst they are very little, and look that they perfectly comply with the will of their parents. Would you have your son obedient to you when past a child, be sure then to establish the authority of a father as soon as he is capable of submission, and can understand in whose power he is. If you would have him stand in awe of you, imprint it in his infancy; and as he approaches more to a man, admit him nearer to your familiarity; so shall you have him your obedient subject (as is fit) whilst he is a child, and your affectionate friend when he is a man. For methinks they mightily misplace the treatment due to their children, who are indulgent and familiar when they are little, but

severe to them, and keep them at a distance when they are grown up. For liberty and indulgence can do no good to children; their want of judgment makes them stand in need of restraint and discipline; and, on the contrary, imperiousness and severity is but an ill way of treating men who have reason of their own to guide them, unless you have a mind to make your children, when grown up, weary of you, and secretly to say within yourselves, "When will you die, father?"

3   The child's natural genius and constitution must be considered in a right education. We must not hope wholly to change their original tempers, nor make the gay pensive and grave, nor the melancholy sportive, without spoiling them. God has stamped certain characters upon men's minds, which, like their shapes, may perhaps be a little mended, but can hardly be totally altered and transformed into the contrary. He, therefore, that is about children should well study their natures and aptitudes, and see by often trials what turn they easily take, and what becomes them, observe what their native stock is, how it may be improved, and what it is fit for. He should consider what they want, whether they be capable of having it wrought into them by industry, and incorporated there by practice, and whether it be worth while to endeavor it. For in many cases all that we can do, or should aim at, is to make the best of what nature has given, to prevent the vices and faults to which such a constitution is most inclined, and give it all the advantages it is capable of. Everyone's natural genius should be carried as far as it could; but to attempt the putting another upon him will be but labor in vain; and what is so plastered on, will at best fit but untowardly, and have always hanging to it the ungracefulness of constraint and affection.

4   Of all the ways whereby children are to be instructed and their manners formed, the plainest, easiest, and most efficacious is to set before their eyes the examples of those things you would have them do or avoid, which, when they are pointed out to them, in the practice of persons within their knowledge, with some reflections on their beauty and unbecomingness, are of more force to draw or deter their imitation, than any discourses which can be made to them. Virtues and vices can by no words be so plainly set before their understandings as the actions of other men will show them, when you direct their observation, and bid them view this or that good or bad quality in their practice. And the beauty or uncomeliness of many things, in good and ill breeding, will be better learned, and make deeper impressions on them, in the examples of others, than

from any rules or instructions which can be given about them. This is a method to be used, not only whilst they are young, but to be continued even as long as they shall be under another's tuition or conduct; nay, I know not whether it be not the best way to be used by a father, as long as he should think fit, on any occasion, to reform anything he wishes mended in his son; nothing sinking so gently, and so deep, into men's minds, as example. And what ill they either overlook or indulge in themselves they cannot but dislike, and be ashamed of, when it is set before them in another.

5   The great work of a governor is to fashion the carriage, and form the mind; to settle in his pupil good habits, and the principles of virtue and wisdom; to give him by little and little a view of mankind, and work him into a love and imitation of what is excellent and praiseworthy; and in the prosecution of it, to give him vigor, activity, and industry. The studies which he sets him upon are but as it were the exercises of his faculties and employment of his time, to keep him from sauntering and idleness, to teach him application, and accustom him to take pains, and to give him some little taste of what his own industry must perfect.

6   Latin I look upon as absolutely necessary to a gentleman; and indeed custom, which prevails over everything, has made it so much a part of education that even those children are whipped to it, and made spend many hours of their precious time uneasily in Latin, who, after they are once gone from school, are never to have more to do with it as long as they live. Can there by anything more ridiculous than that a father should waste his own money and his son's time in setting him to learn the Roman language, when at the same time he designs him for a trade, wherein he, having no use for Latin, fails not to forget that little which he brought from school, and which it is ten to one he abhors for the ill-usage it procured him?

7   The great skill of a teacher is to get and keep the attention of his scholar; whilst he has that, he is sure to advance as fast as the learner's abilities will carry him; and without that, all his bustle and pudder will be to little or no purpose. To attain this, he should make the child comprehend (as much as may be) the usefulness of what he teaches him, and let him see, by what he has learned, that he can do something which he could not before; something which gives him some power and real advantage above others who are ignorant of it. To this he should add sweetness in all his instructions, and, by

a certain tenderness in his whole carriage, make the child sensible that he loves him, and designs nothing but his good, the only way to beget love in the child, which will make him hearken to his lessons, and relish what he teaches him. Nothing but obstinacy should meet with any imperiousness, or rough usage. All other faults should be corrected with a gentle hand; and kind, engaging words will work better and more effectually upon a willing mind, and even prevent a good deal of that perverseness which rough and imperious usage often produces in well-disposed and generous minds. It is true obstinacy and wilful neglects must be mastered, even though it costs blows to do it. But I am apt to think perverseness in the pupils is often the effect of frowardness in the tutor; and that most children would seldom have deserved blows, if needless and misapplied roughness had not taught them ill-nature, and given them an aversion for their teacher, and all that comes from him.

8   To write and speak correctly gives a grace, and gains a favorable attention to what one has to say. And since it is English that an English gentleman will have constant use of, that is the language he should chiefly cultivate, and wherein most care should be taken to polish and perfect his style. To speak or write better Latin than English may make a man be talked of, but he will find it more to his purpose to express himself well in his own tongue that he uses every moment, than to have the vain commendation of others for a very insignificant quality. This I find universally neglected, nor no care taken anywhere to improve young men in their own language, that they may thoroughly understand and be masters of it. If anyone among us have a facility or purity more than ordinary in his mother tongue, it is owing to chance, or his genius, or anything, rather than to his education, or any care of his teacher. To mind what English his pupil speaks or writes is below the dignity of one bred up amongst Greek and Latin, though he have but little of them himself. These are the learned languages, fit only for learned men to meddle with and teach; English is the language of the illiterate vulgar.

from *Conservatism and Liberalism*

RALPH WALDO EMERSON

Ralph Waldo Emerson (1803–1882) was born in Boston and educated at Harvard University. He taught school for a short time, attended Harvard Divinity School, traveled to Florida for health reasons, and became, in 1829, the pastor of a Boston church. He married Ellen Tucker, but she died in 1831. In 1832, he resigned his pastorate and traveled to Europe. There he met Samuel Coleridge, William Wordsworth, and Thomas Carlyle. Stimulated by these great advocates of nature and the imagination, Emerson returned to America inflamed with the Romantic doctrine. He published *Nature* to a lukewarm response but then claimed notoriety with *The American Scholar* (1837) and *The Divinity School Address* (1838), two speeches that declared America's literary independence from Europe. After that, he was a popular figure at lecture halls, and his writings won him a wide following.

In the following excerpt from *Conservatism and Liberalism*, Emerson explores the fundamental differences between those two positions, which represent a way of life as well as political labels for today's congressional forums. His argument, however, stresses the importance of the moderate, the one who can take the best of both sides and find a reasonable answer or solution.

1   The two parties which divide the state, the party of Conservatism
and that of Innovation, are very old, and have disputed the possession
of the world ever since it was made. This quarrel is the subject of
civil history. The conservative party established the reverend hierarchies and monarchies of the most ancient world. The battle of patri-
cian and plebeian, of parent state and colony, of old usage and
accommodation to new facts, of the rich and the poor, reappears in
all countries and times. The war rages not only in battlefields, in
national councils, and ecclesiastical synods, but agitates every man's
bosom with opposing advantages every hour. On rolls the old world
meantime, and now one, now the other gets the day, and still the
fight renews itself as if for the first time, under new names and hot
personalities.

2   Such an irreconcilable antagonism, of course, must have a corre-
spondent depth of seat in the human constitution. It is the opposition
of Past and Future, of Memory and Hope, of the Understanding
and the Reason. It is the primal antagonism, the appearance in trifles
of the two poles of nature. . . .

3   There is always a certain meanness in the argument of conservatism, joined with a certain superiority in its fact. It affirms because
it holds. Its fingers clutch the fact, and it will not open its eyes
to see a better fact. The castle, which conservatism is set to defend,
is the actual state of things, good and bad. The project of innovation
is the best possible state of things. Of course, conservatism always
has the worst of the argument, is always apologizing, pleading a
necessity, pleading that to change would be to deteriorate; it must
saddle itself with the mountainous load of violence and vice of
society, must deny the possibility of good, deny ideas, and suspect
and stone the prophet; whilst innovation is always in the right,
triumphant, attacking, and sure of final success. Conservatism
stands on man's confessed limitations; reform, on his indisputable
infinitude; conservatism, on circumstance; liberalism, on power;
one goes to make an adroit member of the social frame; the other
to postpone all things to the man himself; conservatism is debonair
and social; reform is individual and imperious. We are reformers
in spring and summer; in autumn and winter we stand by the
old; reformers in the morning, conservers at night. Reform is
affirmative, conservatism negative; conservatism goes for comfort,
reform for truth. Conservatism is more candid to behold another's
worth; reform more disposed to maintain and increase its own.

Conservatism makes no poetry, breathes no prayer, has no invention; it is all memory. Reform has no gratitude, no prudence, no husbandry. It makes a great difference to your figure and to your thought, whether your foot is advancing or receding. Conservatism never puts the foot forward; in the hour when it does that, it is not establishment, but reform. Conservatism tends to universal seeming and treachery, believes in a negative fate; believes that men's temper governs them; that for me, it avails not to trust in principles; they will fail me; I must bend a little; it distrusts nature; it thinks there is a general law without a particular application,—law for all that does not include any one. Reform in its antagonism inclines to asinine resistance, to kick with hoofs; it runs to egotism and bloated self-conceit; it runs to a bodiless pretension, to unnatural refining and elevation, which ends in hypocrisy and sensual reaction.

4   And so whilst we do not go beyond general statements, it may be safely affirmed of these two metaphysical antagonists, that each is a good half, but an impossible whole. Each exposes the abuses of the other, but in a true society, in a true man, both must combine. Nature does not give the crown of its approbation, namely, beauty, to any action or emblem or actor, but to one which combines both these elements; not to the rock which resists the waves from age to age, nor to the wave which lashes incessantly the rock, but the superior beauty is with the oak which stands with its hundred arms against the storms of a century, and grows every year like a sapling; or the river which ever flowing, yet is found in the same bed from age to age; or, greatest of all, the man who has subsisted for years amid the changes of nature, yet has distanced himself, so that when you remember what he was, and see what he is, you say, what strides! what a disparity is here!

Hebraism and Hellenism

MATTHEW
ARNOLD

Matthew Arnold (1822–1888) was born in Laleham, England,
the eldest son of Dr. Thomas Arnold, the famous headmaster of
Rugby, from whom he developed his own sense of duty and
intellectual honesty. He attended Rugby and Oxford University.
Such was his intellect that he was named a Fellow of Oriel College
at Oxford. Later, he served as secretary to Lord Lansdowne, who
appointed him as an inspector of schools, a position Arnold
enjoyed until shortly before his death. Arnold was both a poet
and essayist, and in each he took a stance on the high moral
ground. Instilled with classical culture, Arnold tried to impress
upon his Victorian audience the ideals that might save society
from complacency, narrow-mindedness, and savage vulgarity. Part
of his creed was the vigorous "pursuit of our total perfection by
means of getting to know . . . the best that has been thought and
said in the world."

"Hebraism and Hellenism" is part of Arnold's long prose essay
Culture and Anarchy (1869). Here he makes crucial distinctions
between two spiritual disciplines, arguing that society swings toward
one for a time and then toward the other when, in truth, society
should maintain a balance between them. Hellenism he describes as
the objective ability "to see things as they really are"; Hebraism he
describes as "conduct and obedience." Hellenism wants humans, in

the neoclassic sense, to think properly; Hebraism, in the biblical
sense, wants humans to act well.

1   Hebraism and Hellenism,—between these two points of influence
moves our world. At one time it feels more powerfully the attraction
of one of them, at another time of the other; and it ought to be,
though it never is, evenly and happily balanced between them.

2   The final aim of both Hellenism and Hebraism, as of all great
spiritual disciplines, is no doubt the same: man's perfection or salvation. The very language which they both of them use in schooling
us to reach this aim is often identical. Even when their language
indicates by variation,—sometimes a broad variation, often a but
slight and subtle variation,—the different courses of thought which
are uppermost in each discipline, even then the unity of the final end
and aim is still apparent. To employ the actual words of that discipline
with which we ourselves are all of us most familiar, and the words
of which, therefore, come most home to us, that final end and aim
is "that we might be partakers of the divine nature." These are the
words of a Hebrew apostle, but of Hellenism and Hebraism alike
this is, I say, the aim. When the two are confronted, as they very
often are confronted, it is nearly always with what I may call a
rhetorical purpose; the speaker's whole design is to exalt and enthrone
one of the two, and he uses the other only as a foil and to enable
him the better to give effect to his purpose. Obviously, with us, it
is usually Hellenism which is thus reduced to minister to the triumph
of Hebraism. There is a sermon on Greece and the Greek spirit by
a man never to be mentioned without interest and respect, Frederick
Robertson, in which this rhetorical use of Greece and the Greek
spirit, and the inadequate exhibition of them necessarily consequent
upon this, is almost ludicrous, and would be censurable if it were
not to be explained by the exigencies of a sermon. On the other
hand, Heinrich Heine, and other writers of his sort, give us the
spectacle of the table completely turned, and of Hebraism brought
in just as a foil and contrast to Hellenism, and to make the superiority
of Hellenism more manifest. In both these cases there is injustice
and misrepresentation. The aim and end of both Hebraism and

Hellenism is, as I have said, one and the same, and this aim and end is august and admirable.

3   Still, they pursue this aim by very different courses. The uppermost idea with Hellenism is to see things as they really are; the uppermost idea with Hebraism is conduct and obedience. Nothing can do away with this ineffaceable difference. The Greek quarrel with the body and its desires is, that they hinder right thinking; the Hebrew quarrel with them is, that they hinder right acting. "He that keepeth the law, happy is he"; "Blessed is the man that feareth the Eternal, that delighteth greatly in his commandments"; that is the Hebrew notion of felicity; and, pursued with passion and tenacity, this notion would not let the Hebrew rest till, as is well known, he had at last got out of the law a network of prescriptions to enwrap his whole life, to govern every moment of it, every impulse, every action. The Greek notion of felicity, on the other hand, is perfectly conveyed in these words of a great French moralist: *"C'est le bonheur des hommes,"** — when? when they abhor that which is evil?—no; when they exercise themselves in the law of the Lord day and night?—no; when they die daily?—no; when they walk about the New Jerusalem with palms in their hands?—no; but when they think aright, when their thought hits: *"quand ils pensent juste."** At the bottom of both the Greek and the Hebrew notion is the desire, native in man, for reason and the will of God, the feeling after the universal order,—in a word, the love of God. But, while Hebraism seizes upon certain plain, capital intimations of the universal order, and rivets itself, one may say, with unequalled grandeur of earnestness and intensity on the study and observance of them, the bent of Hellenism is to follow, with flexible activity, the whole play of the universal order, to be apprehensive of missing any part of it, of sacrificing one part to another, to slip away from resting in this or that intimation of it, however capital. An unclouded clearness of mind, an unimpeded play of thought, is what this bent drives at. The governing idea of Hellenism is *spontaneity of consciousness;* that of Hebraism, *strictness of conscience.*

---

*It is happiness for men.
*When they think right.

The Shadow

CARL JUNG

Carl Jung (1875–1961) was born in Kesseil, Thurgau, Switzerland. He earned an M.D. from the University of Zurich in 1902. Jung was a student of Sigmund Freud and has gained recognition today that rivals Freud's. Jung became a master of the unconscious; indeed, he said in the prologue to his *Memories, Dreams, Reflections* that "my life is a story of the self-realization of the unconscious." His identification of the collective unconscious as a racial memory, an inherited psyche accumulated over the life of the human race, enabled him to identify universal symbols that he called *archetypes*, which echo the experiences of all humans. Jung's views alienated the Freudians, who thought Jung had ventured too far into mysticism and myth. But Jung persevered and built a dynamic following by insisting that "psychiatry must take into account all of man's experience, from the most intensely practical to the most tenuously mystical."

In "The Shadow," Jung names three archetypes that influence the human ego—shadow, anima, and animus. He examines closely the *shadow*, which requires a person to recognize "the dark aspects of the personality as present and real." He asks us to recognize that our emotional projections toward other people may lie not in the other person but in "a very long shadow" that we throw out across others. He says our shadows make it difficult for the ego to see through its illusions. The anima (the female principle) and the animus (the male principle) enter the equation when the "source of projections is no longer the shadow . . . but a contrasexual figure."

1   Whereas the contents of the *personal unconscious* are acquired during the individual's lifetime, the contents of the *collective unconscious* are invariably archetypes that were present from the beginning. Their relation to the instincts has been discussed elsewhere. The archetypes most clearly characterized from the empirical point of view are those which have the most frequent and the most disturbing influence on the ego. These are the *shadow*, the *anima*, and the *animus*. The most accessible of these, and the easiest to experience, is the shadow, for its nature can in large measure be inferred from the contents of the personal unconscious. The only exceptions to this rule are those rather rare cases where the positive qualities of the personality are repressed, and the ego in consequence plays an essentially negative or unfavorable role.

2   The shadow is a moral problem that challenges the whole ego personality, for no one can become conscious of the shadow without considerable moral effort. To become conscious of it involves recognizing the dark aspects of the personality as present and real. This act is the essential condition for any kind of self-knowledge, and it therefore, as a rule, meets with considerable resistance. Indeed, self-knowledge as a psychotherapeutic measure frequently requires much painstaking work extending over a long period.

3   Closer examination of the dark characteristics—that is, the inferiorities constituting the shadow—reveals that they have an *emotional* nature, a kind of *autonomy*, and accordingly an *obsessive* or, better, *possessive* quality. Emotion, incidentally, is not an activity of the individual but something that happens to him. Affects occur usually where adaptation is weakest, and at the same time they reveal the reason for its weakness, namely, a certain degree of inferiority and the existence of a lower level of personality. On this lower level with its uncontrolled or scarcely controlled emotions one behaves more or less like a primitive, who is not only the passive victim of his affects but also singularly incapable of moral judgment.

4   Although, with insight and good will, the shadow can to some

extent be assimilated into the conscious personality, experience shows that there are certain features which offer the most obstinate resistance to moral control and prove almost impossible to influence. These resistances are usually bound up with *projections*, which are not recognized as such, and their recognition is a moral achievement beyond the ordinary. While some traits peculiar to the shadow can be recognized without too much difficulty as one's own personal qualities, in this case both insight and good will are unavailing because the cause of the emotion appears to lie, beyond all possibility of doubt, in the *other person*. No matter how obvious it may be to the neutral observer that it is a matter of projections, there is little hope that the subject will perceive this himself. He must be convinced that he throws a very long shadow before he is willing to withdraw his emotionally toned projections from their object.

5   Let us suppose that a certain individual shows no inclination whatever to recognize his projections. The projection-making factor then has a free hand and can realize its object—if it has one—or bring about some other situation characteristic of its potency. As we know, it is not the conscious subject but the unconscious which does the projecting. *Hence one encounters projections, one does not make them.* The effect of projection is to *isolate the subject* from his environment, since instead of a real relation to it there is now only an illusory one. Projections change the world into the replica of one's own unknown face. In the last analysis, therefore, they lead to an autoerotic or autistic condition in which one dreams a world whose reality remains forever unattainable. The resultant *sentiment d'incomplétude** and the still worse feeling of sterility are in their turn explained by projection as the malevolence of the environment, and by means of this vicious circle the isolation is intensified. The more projections interpose themselves between the subject and the environment, the harder is becomes for the ego to see through its illusions. A forty-five-year-old patient who had suffered from a compulsion neurosis since he was twenty and had become completely cut off from the world once said to me: "But I can never admit to myself that I've wasted the best twenty-five years of my life!"

6   It is often tragic to see how blatantly a man bungles his own life and the lives of others yet remains totally incapable of seeing how

---

*Feeling of incompleteness.

much the whole tragedy originates in himself, and how he continually feeds it and keeps it going. Not *consciously,* of course—for consciously he is engaged in bewailing and cursing a faithless world that recedes further and further into the distance. Rather, it is an unconscious factor which spins the illusions that veil his world. And what is being spun is a cocoon, which in the end will completely envelop him.

7   One might assume that projections like these, which are so very difficult if not impossible to dissolve, would belong to the realm of the shadow—that is, to the negative side of the personality. This assumption however becomes untenable after a certain point, because the symbols that then appear no longer refer to the same but to the opposite sex, in a man's case to a woman and vice versa. The source of projections is no longer the shadow—which is always of the same sex as the subject—but a contrasexual figure. Here we meet the *animus* of a woman and the *anima* of a man, two corresponding archetypes whose autonomy and unconsciousness explain the stubbornness of their projections. Though the shadow is a motif as well known to mythology as anima and animus, it represents first and foremost the personal unconsciousness, and its content can therefore be made conscious without too much difficulty. In this it differs from anima and animus, for whereas the shadow can be seen through and recognized fairly easily, the anima and animus are much further away from consciousness and in normal circumstances are seldom if ever realized. With a little self-criticism one can see through the shadow—so far as its nature is personal. But when it appears as an archetype, one encounters the same difficulties as with anima and animus. In other words, it is quite within the bounds of possibility for a man to recognize the relative evil of his nature, but it is a rare and shattering experience for him to gaze into the face of absolute evil.

Grant and Lee: A Study in Contrasts

BRUCE CATTON

Bruce Catton (1899–1978) was born in Michigan where, as a young man, he worked at a newspaper. Later, he became one of the editors of *American Heritage* magazine. That experience instilled within him a deep, abiding love of history. His special talent enabled him to bring history to life with the style of a novelist. Indeed, his readers would await his next history in the manner that today's readers anticipate another novel by their favorite writer. Among his many historical accounts are *Mr. Lincoln's Army* (1951), *Glory Road* (1952), *A Stillness at Appomattox* (1953), *The Hallowed Ground* (1956), and *Gettysburg: The Final Fury* (1974).

"Grant and Lee: A Study in Contrasts" has become a classic example of comparison/contrast techniques. Lee represented the aristocratic patriarchy of a dying age, while Grant represented the rising age of democracy and its self-made individuals. Appomattox brought them together, so Catton wants to explain that the tenacity and fidelity of both men were ingredients that made America great. They fought with passion for their causes, and, after the battles were over, they expressed their dedication to peace for the whole nation. As Catton observes, "Two great

Americans, Grant and Lee—very different, yet under everything very much alike."

1   When Ulysses S. Grant and Robert E. Lee met in the parlor of a modest house at Appomattox Court House, Virginia, on April 9, 1865, to work out the terms for the surrender of Lee's Army of Northern Virginia, a great chapter in American life came to a close, and a great new chapter began.

2   These men were bringing the Civil War to its virtual finish. To be sure, other armies had yet to surrender, and for a few days the fugitive Confederate government would struggle desperately and vainly, trying to find some way to go on living now that its chief support was gone. But in effect it was all over when Grant and Lee signed the papers. And the little room where they wrote out the terms was the scene of one of the poignant, dramatic contrasts in American history.

3   They were two strong men, these oddly different generals, and they represented the strengths of two conflicting currents that, through them, had come into final collision.

4   Back of Robert E. Lee was the notion that the old aristocratic concept might somehow survive and be dominant in American life.

5   Lee was tidewater Virginia, and in his background were family, culture, and tradition . . . the age of chivalry transplanted to a New World which was making its own legends and its own myths. He embodied a way of life that had come down through the age of knighthood and the English country squire. America was a land that was beginning all over again, dedicated to nothing much more complicated than the rather hazy belief that all men had equal rights, and should have an equal chance in the world. In such a land Lee stood for the feeling that it was somehow of advantage to human society to have a pronounced inequality in the social structure. There should be a leisure class, backed by ownership of land; in turn, society itself should be keyed to the land as the chief source of wealth and influence. It would bring forth (according to this ideal) a class of men with a strong sense of obligation to the community; men who lived not to gain advantage for themselves, but to meet the solemn

obligations which had been laid on them by the very fact that they were privileged. From them the country would get its leadership; to them it could look for the higher values—of thought, of conduct, of personal deportment—to give it strength and virtue.

6   Lee embodied the noblest elements of this aristocratic ideal. Through him, the landed nobility justified itself. For four years, the Southern states had fought a desperate war to uphold the ideals for which Lee stood. In the end, it almost seemed as if the Confederacy fought for Lee; as if he himself was the Confederacy . . . the best thing that the way of life for which the Confederacy stood could ever have to offer. He had passed into legend before Appomattox. Thousands of tired, underfed, poorly clothed Confederate soldiers, long since past the simple enthusiasm of the early days of the struggle, somehow considered Lee the symbol of everything for which they had been willing to die. But they could not quite put this feeling into words. If the Lost Cause, sanctified by so much heroism and so many deaths, had a living justification, its justification was General Lee.

7   Grant, the son of a tanner on the Western frontier, was everything Lee was not. He had come up the hard way, and embodied nothing in particular except the eternal toughness and sinewy fiber of the men who grew up beyond the mountains. He was one of a body of men who owed reverence and obeisance to no one, who were self-reliant to a fault, who cared hardly anything for the past but who had a sharp eye for the future.

8   These frontier men were the precise opposites of the tidewater aristocrats. Back of them, in the great surge that had taken people over the Alleghenies and into the opening Western country, there was a deep, implicit dissatisfaction with a past that had settled into grooves. They stood for democracy, not from any reasoned conclusion about the proper ordering of human society, but simply because they had grown up in the middle of democracy and knew how it worked. Their society might have privileges, but they would be privileges each man had won for himself. Forms and patterns meant nothing. No man was born to anything, except perhaps to a chance to show how far he could rise. Life was competition.

9   Yet along with this feeling had come a deep sense of belonging to a national community. The Westerner who developed a farm, opened a shop or set up in business as a trader, could hope to prosper only as his own community prospered—and his community ran from

the Atlantic to the Pacific and from Canada down to Mexico. If the land was settled, with towns and highways and accessible markets, he could better himself. He saw his fate in terms of the nation's own destiny. As its horizons expanded, so did his. He had, in other words, an acute dollars-and-cents stake in the continued growth and development of his country.

10   And that, perhaps, is where the contrast between Grant and Lee becomes most striking. The Virginia aristocrat, inevitably, saw himself in relation to his own region. He lived in a static society which could endure almost anything except change. Instinctively, his first loyalty would go to the locality in which that society existed. He would fight to the limit of endurance to defend it, because in defending it he was defending everything that gave his own life its deepest meaning.

11   The Westerner, on the other hand, would fight with an equal tenacity for the broader concept of society. He fought so because everything he lived by was tied to growth, expansion, and a constantly widening horizon. What he lived by would survive or fall with the nation itself. He could not possibly stand by unmoved in the face of an attempt to destroy the Union. He would combat it with everything he had, because he could only see it as an effort to cut the ground out from under his feet.

12   So Grant and Lee were in complete contrast, representing two diametrically opposed elements in American life. Grant was the modern man emerging; beyond him, ready to come on the stage, was the great age of steel and machinery, of crowded cities and a restless, burgeoning vitality. Lee might have ridden down from the old age of chivalry, lance in hand, silken banner fluttering over his head. Each man was the perfect champion of his cause, drawing both his strengths and his weaknesses from the people he led.

13   Yet it was not all contrast, after all. Different as they were—in background, in personality, in underlying aspiration—these two great soldiers had much in common. Under everything else, they were marvelous fighters. Furthermore, their fighting qualities were really very much alike.

14   Each man had, to begin with, the great virtue of utter tenacity and fidelity. Grant fought his way down the Mississippi Valley in spite of acute personal discouragement and profound military handicaps. Lee hung on in the trenches at Petersburg after hope itself had died. In each man there was an indomitable quality . . . the born

fighter's refusal to give up as long as he can still remain on his feet and lift his two fists.

15 Daring and resourcefulness they had, too; the ability to think faster and move faster than the enemy. These were the qualities which gave Lee the dazzling campaigns of Second Manassas and Chancellorsville and won Vicksburg for Grant.

16 Lastly, and perhaps greatest of all, there was the ability, at the end, to turn quickly from war to peace once the fighting was over. Out of the way these two men behaved at Appomattox came the possibility of a peace of reconciliation. It was a possibility not wholly realized, in the years to come, but which did, in the end, help the two sections to become one nation again . . . after a war whose bitterness might have seemed to make such a reunion wholly impossible. No part of either man's life became him more than the part he played in their brief meeting in the McLean house at Appomattox. Their behavior there put all succeeding generations of Americans in their debt. Two great Americans, Grant and Lee—very different, yet under everything very much alike. Their encounter at Appomattox was one of the great moments of American history.

A Day in Samoa

MARGARET MEAD

Margaret Mead (1901–1978) served as one of America's most respected anthropologists for more than fifty years. She earned a B.A. in 1923 from Barnard College and an M.A. and Ph.D. from Columbia University. Her book *Coming of Age in Samoa* (1928), which examined the maturation of Samoans from adolescence to adulthood, won great acclaim and launched her career. She taught at Columbia University for many years, but she also served as lecturer and visiting professor at many colleges, including Stanford, Harvard, Yale, the University of Colorado, and Emory University. Among her other books are *An Anthropologist at Work* (1959), *Culture and Commitment* (1970) and *Blackberry Winter: A Memoir* (1972).

"A Day in Samoa," which is the second chapter of *Coming of Age in Samoa*, describes one day in the life of a Samoan village. Here she describes the activities that occupy the villagers from dawn to nightfall—the workers who move inland to work, the women who cluster for work and conversation, the fishermen who set sail on the ocean, the children who play, the lovers who search out places for their trysts, and the gatherings at mealtime. The society, while primitive, performs activities that occur daily in villages, cities, and metropolitan areas the world over.

1   The life of the day begins at dawn, or if the moon has shown until daylight, the shouts of the young men may be heard before

dawn from the hillside. Uneasy in the night, populous with ghosts, they shout lustily to one another as they hasten with their work. As the dawn begins to fall among the soft brown roofs and the slender palm trees stand out against a colourless, gleaming sea, lovers slip home from trysts beneath the palm trees or in the shadow of beached canoes, that the light may find each sleeper in his appointed place. Cocks crow, negligently, and a shrill-voiced bird cries from the breadfruit trees. The insistent roar of the reef seems muted to an undertone for the sounds of a waking village. Babies cry, a few short wails before sleepy mothers give them the breast. Restless little children roll out of their sheets and wander drowsily down to the beach to freshen their faces in the sea. Boys, bent upon an early fishing, start collecting their tackle and go to rouse their more laggard companions. Fires are lit, here and there, the white smoke hardly visible against the paleness of the dawn. The whole village, sheeted and frowsy, stirs, rubs its eyes, and stumbles towards the beach. "Talofa!" "Talofa!" "Will the journey start to-day?" "Is it bonito fishing your lordship is going?" Girls stop to giggle over some young ne'er-do-well who escaped during the night from an angry father's pursuit and to venture a shrewd guess that the daughter knew more about his presence than she told. The boy who is taunted by another, who has succeeded him in his sweetheart's favour, grapples with his rival, his foot slipping in the wet sand. From the other end of the village comes a long drawn-out, piercing wail. A messenger has just brought word of the death of some relative in another village. Half-clad, unhurried women, with babies at their breasts, or astride their hips, pause in their tale of Losa's outraged departure from her father's house to the greater kindness in the home of her uncle, to wonder who is dead. Poor relatives whisper their requests to rich relatives, men make plans to set a fish trap together, a woman begs a bit of yellow dye from a kinswoman, and through the village sounds the rhythmic tattoo which calls the young men together. They gather from all parts of the village, digging sticks in hand, ready to start inland to the plantation. The older men set off upon their more lonely occupations, and each household, reassembled under its peaked roof, settles down to the routine of the morning. Little children, too hungry to wait for the late breakfast, beg lumps of cold taro which they munch greedily. Women carry piles of washing to the sea or to the spring at the far end of the

village, or set off inland after weaving materials. The older girls
go fishing on the reef, or perhaps set themselves to weaving a
new set of Venetian blinds.

2   In the houses, where the pebbly floors have been swept bare with
a stiff long-handled broom, the women great with child and the
nursing mothers, sit and gossip with one another. Old men sit apart,
unceasingly twisting palm husk on their bare thighs and muttering
old tales under their breath. The carpenters begin work on the new
house, while the owner bustles about trying to keep them in a good
humour. Families who will cook to-day are hard at work; the taro,
yams and bananas have already been brought from inland; the children are scuttling back and forth, fetching sea water, or leaves to
stuff the pig. As the sun rises higher in the sky, the shadows deepen
under the thatched roofs, the sand is burning to the touch, the
hibiscus flowers wilt on the hedges, and little children bid the smaller
ones, "Come out of the sun." Those whose excursions have been
short return to the village, the women with strings of crimson jelly
fish, or baskets of shell fish, the men with cocoanuts, carried in
baskets slung on a shoulder pole. The women and children eat their
breakfasts, just hot from the oven, if this is cook day, and the young
men work swiftly in the midday heat, preparing the noon feast for
their elders.

3   It is high noon. The sand burns the feet of the little children,
who leave their palm leaf balls and their pin-wheels of frangipani
blossoms to wither in the sun, as they creep into the shade of the
houses. The women who must go abroad carry great banana leaves
as sun-shades or wind wet cloths about their heads. Lowering a few
blinds against the slanting sun, all who are left in the village wrap
their heads in sheets and go to sleep. Only a few adventurous children
may slip away for a swim in the shadow of a high rock, some industrious woman continues with her weaving, or a close little group of
women bend anxiously over a woman in labour. The village is dazzling and dead; any sound seems oddly loud and out of place. Words
have to cut through the solid heat slowly. And then the sun gradually
sinks over the sea.

4   A second time, the sleeping people stir, roused perhaps by the
cry of "a boat," resounding through the village. The fishermen beach
their canoes, weary and spent from the heat, in spite of the slaked
lime on their heads, with which they have sought to cool their brains
and redden their hair. The brightly coloured fishes are spread out

on the floor, or piled in front of the houses until the women pour water over them to free them from taboo. Regretfully, the young fishermen separate out the "Taboo fish," which must be sent to the chief, or proudly they pack the little palm leaf baskets with offerings of fish to take to their sweethearts. Men come home from the bush, grimy and heavy laden, shouting as they come, greeted in a sonorous rising cadence by those who have remained at home. They gather in the guest house for their evening kava drinking. The soft clapping of hands, the high-pitched intoning of the talking chief who serves the kava echoes through the village. Girls gather flowers to weave into necklaces; children, lusty from their naps and bound to no particular task, play circular games in the half shade of the late afternoon. Finally the sun sets, in a flame which stretches from the mountain behind to the horizon on the sea, the last bather comes up from the beach, children straggle home, dark little figures etched against the sky; lights shine in the houses, and each household gathers for its evening meal. The suitor humbly presents his offering, the children have been summoned from their noisy play, perhaps there is an honoured guest who must be served first, after the soft, barbaric singing of Christian hymns and the brief and graceful evening prayer. In front of a house at the end of the village, a father cries out the birth of a son. In some family circles a face is missing, in others little runaways have found a haven! Again quiet settles upon the village, as first the head of the household, then the women and children, and last of all the patient boys, eat their supper.

5   After supper the old people and the little children are bundled off to bed. If the young people have guests the front of the house is yielded to them. For day is the time for the councils of old men and the labours of youth, and night is the time for lighter things. Two kinsmen, or a chief and his councillor, sit and gossip over the day's events or make plans for the morrow. Outside a crier goes through the village announcing that the communal breadfruit pit will be opened in the morning, or that the village will make a great fish trap. If it is moonlight, groups of young men, women by twos and threes, wander through the village, and crowds of children hunt for land crabs or chase each other among the breadfruit trees. Half the village may go fishing by torchlight and the curving reef will gleam with wavering lights and echo with shouts of triumph or disappointment, teasing words or smothered cries of outraged modesty. Or a group of youths may dance for the pleasure of some visiting

maiden. Many of those who have retired to sleep, drawn by the merry music, will wrap their sheets about them and set out to find the dancing. A white-clad, ghostly throng will gather in a circle about the gaily lit house, a circle from which every now and then a few will detach themselves and wander away among the trees. Sometimes sleep will not descend upon the village until long past midnight; then at last there is only the mellow thunder of the reef and the whisper of lovers, as the village rests until dawn.

The Yellow Bus

LILLIAN ROSS

Lillian Ross was born in 1927 in Syracuse, New York. Beginning in 1948, she brought her special view of life to the pages of *The New Yorker* magazine. As a staff writer, she has produced essays for the "Profiles," "Reporter at Large," and "The Talk of the Town" columns, as well as short stories. Irving Wallace has said of Ross, "She is the mistress of selective listening and viewing, of capturing the one moment that entirely illumines the scene, of fastening on the one quote that Tells All. She is a brilliant interpreter of what she hears and observes. And she is the possessor of a unique writing style—spare, direct, objective, fast—a style that disarms, seemingly only full of wonder, but one that can suddenly, almost sneakily, nail a personality naked to a page." Her short stories are collected in *Vertical and Horizontal* (1963). Her essays and articles are collected in *Reporting* (1964), and *Reporting Two* (1969). Her "Talk of the Town" articles are collected in *Talk Stories* (1966).

"The Yellow Bus" first appeared in *The New Yorker* in 1960 and was reprinted in *Reporting* in 1964. Ross uses a very effective style of reporting, one in which an omniscient, third-person narrator seems to disappear. The description is direct, objective, and rendered without commentary. You will find, nevertheless, that "The Yellow Bus" uses subtle, wry humor and touches of irony to describe a group of students from Indiana—the little Bean Blossom group—on their visit to New York City. The innocence and naive attitude of the members of the group bring smiles of recognition to grizzled New Yorkers as well as the folks back home on the rolling plains of Indiana.

1   A few Sundays ago, in the late, still afternoon, a bright-yellow school bus, bearing the white-on-blue license plate of the State of Indiana and with the words "BEAN BLOSSOM TWP MONROE COUNTY" painted in black letters under the windows on each side, emerged into New York City from the Holland Tunnel. Inside the bus were eighteen members of the senior class of the Bean Blossom Township High School, who were coming to the city for their first visit. The windows of the bus, as it rolled out into Canal Street, were open, and a few of the passengers leaned out, deadpan and silent, for a look at Manhattan. The rest sat, deadpan and silent, looking at each other. In all, there were twenty-two people in the bus: eleven girls and seven boys of the senior class; their English teacher and her husband; and the driver (one of the regular bus drivers employed by the township for the school) and his wife. When they arrived, hundreds of thousands of the city's eight million inhabitants were out of town. Those who were here were apparently minding their own business; certainly they were not handing out any big hellos to the visitors. The little Bean Blossom group, soon to be lost in the shuffle of New York's resident and transient summer population, had no idea of how to elicit any hellos—or, for that matter, any goodbyes or how-are-yous. Their plan for visiting New York City was divided into three parts: one, arriving; two, staying two days and three nights; three, departing.

2   Well, they had arrived. To get here, they had driven eight hundred and forty miles in thirty-nine and a half hours, bringing with them, in addition to spending money of about fifty dollars apiece, a fund of $957.41, which the class had saved up collectively over the past six years. The money represented the profits from such enterprises as candy and ice-cream concessions at school basketball games, amusement booths at the class (junior) carnival, and ticket sales for the class (senior) play, "Mumbo-Jumbo." For six years, the members of the class had talked about how they would spend the money to celebrate their graduation. Early this year, they voted on it. Some

of the boys voted for a trip to New Orleans, but they were outvoted
by the girls, all of whom wanted the class to visit New York. The
class figured that the cost of motels and hotels—three rooms for the
boys, three rooms for the girls, one room for each of the
couples—would come to about four hundred dollars. The bus driver
was to be paid three hundred and fifty dollars for driving and given
thirty for road, bridge, and tunnel tolls. Six members of the class,
who were unable to participate in the trip, stayed home. If there
should be any money left over, it would be divided up among all
the class members when the travellers returned to Bean Blossom
Township. The names of the eighteen touring class members were:
R. Jay Bowman, Shelda Bowman (cousin of R. Jay), Robert Britton,
Mary Jane Carter, Lynn Dillon, Ina Hough, Thelma Keller, Wilma
Keller (sister of Thelma), Becky Kiser, Jeanne Molnar, Nancy Prather,
Mike Richardson, Dennis Smith, Donna Thacker, Albert Warthan,
Connie Williams, Larry Williams (not related to Connie), and Lela
Young.

3   It was also a first visit to New York for the English teacher, a
lively young lady of twenty-eight named Polly Watts, and for her
husband, Thomas, thirty-two, a graduate student in political science
at Indiana University, in Bloomington, which is about twelve miles
from the Bean Blossom Township school. The only people on the
bus who had been to New York before were the driver, a husky
uncommunicative man of forty-nine named Ralph Walls, and his
wife, Margaret, thirty-nine and the mother of his seven children,
aged twenty-one to two, all of whom were left at home. Walls was
the only adviser the others had on what to do in New York. His
advice consisted of where to stay (the Hotel Woodstock, on West
Forty-third Street, near Times Square) and where to eat (Hector's
Cafeteria, around the corner from the hotel).

4   The Bean Blossom Township school is in the village of Stinesville,
which has three hundred and fifty-five inhabitants and a town pump.
A couple of the seniors who made the trip live in Stinesville; the others
live within a radius of fifteen miles or so, on farms or in isolated houses
with vegetable gardens and perhaps a cow or two. At the start of the
trip, the travellers gathered in front of their school shortly after midnight, and by one in the morning, with every passenger occupying a
double seat in the bus (fifty-four-passenger, 1959 model), and with
luggage under the seats, and suits and dresses hung on a homemade
clothes rack in the back of the bus, they were on their way.

5   The senior-class president, R. (for Reginald) Jay Bowman, was in charge of all the voting on the trip. A wiry, energetic eighteen-year-old with a crew haircut, he had been president of the class for the past five years, and is one of two members of the class who intend to go to college. He wants to work, eventually, for the United States Civil Service, because a job with the government is a steady job. Or, in a very vague way, he thinks he may go into politics. With the help of a hundred-and-two-dollar-a-year scholarship, he plans to pay all his own expenses at Indiana University. The other student who is going to college has also chosen Indiana University. She is Nancy Prather, an outdoorsy, freckle-faced girl whose father raises dairy and beef cattle on a two-hundred-and-fifty-acre farm and who is the class salutatorian. As for the valedictorian, a heavyset, firm-mouthed girl named Connie Williams, she was planning to get married a week after returning home from New York. The other class members expected, for the most part, to get to work at secretarial or clerical jobs, or in automobile or electronic-parts factories in Bloomington. The New York trip was in the nature of a first and last fling.

6   Ralph Walls dropped the passengers and their luggage at the Woodstock and then took the bus to a parking lot on Tenth Avenue, where he was going to leave it for the duration of the visit. His job, he told his passengers, was to drive *to* New York, not *in* it. He had also told them that when he got back to the Woodstock he was going to sleep, but had explained how to get around the corner to Hector's Cafeteria. The boys and girls signed the register and went to their rooms to get cleaned up. They all felt let down. They had asked Walls whether the tall buildings they saw as they came uptown from the Holland Tunnel made up the skyline, and Walls had said he didn't know. Then they had asked him which was the Empire State Building, and he had said they would have to take a tour to find out. Thus put off, they more or less resigned themselves to saving any further questions for a tour. Jay Bowman said that he would see about tours before the following morning.

7   Mrs. Watts and her husband washed up quickly and then, notwithstanding the bus driver's advice, walked around the Times Square area to see if they could find a reasonably priced and attractive place to have supper. They checked Toffenetti's, across the street from the hotel, but they decided that it was too expensive (hamburger dinners at two dollars and ten cents, watermelon at forty cents) and too formidable. When they reconvened with the senior class in the lobby

of the Woodstock, they recommended that everybody have his first meal at Hector's. The party set out—for some reason, in Indian file—for Hector's, and the first one inside was Mike Richardson, a husky, red-haired boy with large swollen-looking hands and sunburned forearms. A stern-voiced manager near the door, shouting "Take your check! Take your check!" at all incomers, gave the Indiana group the same sightless once-over he gave everybody else. The Bean Blossom faces, which had been puzzled, fearful, and disheartened since Canal Street, now took on a look of resentment. Mike Richardson led the line to the counter. Under a sign reading "BAKED WHITEFISH," a white-aproned counterman looked at Mike and said, "Come on, fella!" Mike glumly took a plate of fish and then filled the rest of his tray with baked beans, a roll, iced tea, and strawberry shortcake (check—$1.58). The others quickly and shakily filled their trays with fish, baked beans, a roll, iced tea, and strawberry shortcake. Sweating, bumping their trays and their elbows against other trays and other elbows, they found seats in twos and threes with strangers, at tables that still had other people's dirty dishes on them. Then, in a nervous clatter of desperate and noisy eating, they stuffed their food down.

8   "My ma cooks better than this," said Albert Warthan, who was sitting with Mike Richardson and Larry Williams. Albert, the eldest of seven children of a limestone-quarry worker, plans to join the Army and become a radar technician.

9   "I took this filet de sole? When I wanted somethin' else, I don't know what?" Mike said.

10   "I like the kind of place you just set there and decide what you want," said Larry, who is going to work on his grandfather's farm.

11   "My ma and pa told me to come home when it was time to come home, and not to mess around," Albert said. "I'm ready to chuck it and go home right now."

12   "The whole idea of it is just to see it and get it over with," Mike said.

13   "You got your money divided up in two places?" Albert asked. "So's you'll have some in one place if it gets stolen in t'other?"

14   The others nodded.

15   "Man, you can keep this New York," said Larry. "This place is too hustly, with everybody pushin' and no privacy. Man, I'll take the Big Boy any old day."

16   Frisch's Big Boy is the name of an Indiana drive-in chain, where

a hamburger costs thirty cents. The general effect of Hector's Cafeteria was to give the Bean Blossom Class of 1960 a feeling of unhappiness about eating in New York and to strengthen its faith in the superiority of the Big Boys back home.

17   Jay Bowman went from table to table, polling his classmates on what they wanted to do that evening. At first, nobody wanted to do anything special. Then they decided that the only special thing they wanted to do was go to Coney Island, but they wanted to save Coney Island for the wind-up night, their last night in New York. However, nobody could think of anything to do that first night, so Jay took a re-vote, and it turned out that almost all of them wanted to go to Coney Island right away. Everybody but three girls voted to go to Coney Island straight from Hector's. Mrs. Watts was mildly apprehensive about this project, but Mike Richardson assured her it was easy; somebody at the hotel had told him that all they had to do was go to the subway and ask the cashier in the booth which train to take, and that would be that. Mrs. Watts said she was going to walk around a bit with her husband. The three girls who didn't want to go to Coney Island explained that they firmly believed the class should "have fun" on its last night in the city, and not before. The three were Ina Hough, whose father works in an R.C.A.-television manufacturing plant in Indianapolis (about fifty miles from Stinesville); Lela Young, whose foster father works in a Chevrolet-parts warehouse in Indianapolis; and Jeanne Molnar, whose father is a draftsman at the Indiana Limestone Company, in Bloomington. All three already knew that they disliked New York. People in New York, they said, were all for themselves.

18   At nine o'clock, while most of their classmates were on the Brighton B.M.T. express bound for Coney Island, the three girls walked to Sixth Avenue and Fiftieth Street with Mr. and Mrs. Watts, who left them at that point to take a walk along Fifth Avenue. The girls stood in a long line of people waiting to get into the Radio City Music Hall. After twenty minutes, they got out of the line and walked over to Rockefeller Plaza, where they admired the fountain, and to St. Patrick's Cathedral, which looked bigger to them than any church they had ever seen. The main church attended by the Bean Blossom group is the Nazarene Church. No one in the senior class had ever talked to a Jew or to more than one Catholic, or—with the exception of Mary Jane Carter, daughter of the Nazarene minister in Stinesville—had ever heard of an Episcopalian. At ten o'clock, the three girls returned to the Music Hall line,

which had dwindled, but when they got to the box office they were told that they had missed the stage show, so they decided to skip the Music Hall and take a subway ride. They took an Independent subway train to the West Fourth Street station, which a subway guard told them was where to go for Greenwich Village. They decided against getting out and looking, and in favor of going uptown on the same fare and returning to their hotel. Back at the Woodstock, where they shared a room, they locked themselves in and started putting up their hair, telling each other that everybody in New York was rude and all for himself.

19   At Coney Island, the Indiana travellers talked about how they could not get over the experience of riding for forty-five minutes, in a shaking, noisy train, to get there.

20   "The long ride was a shock to what I expected," said Albert Warthan.

21   Nancy Prather said she didn't like the looks of the subway or the people on it. "You see so many different people," she said. "Dark-complected ones one minute, light-complected ones the next."

22   "I hate New York, actually," Connie Williams said. "I'm satisfied with what we got back home."

23   "Back home, you can do anything you please in your own backyard any time you feel like it, like hootin' and hollerin' or anything," said Larry Williams. "You don't ever get to feel all cooped up."

24   "I sort of like it here in Coney Island," said Dennis Smith. "I don't feel cooped up."

25   Dennis's buddies looked at him without saying anything. His "sort of liking" Coney Island was the first sign of defection from Indiana, and the others did not seem to know what to make of it. Dennis is a broad-shouldered boy with large, beautiful, wistful blue eyes and a gold front tooth.

26   "I hate it," Connie said.

27   Jay Bowman organized as many of the group as he could to take a couple of rides on the Cyclone. Most of the boys followed these up with a ride on the parachute jump, and then complained that it wasn't what they had expected at all. Some of the boys and girls went into the Spookerama. They all rode the bobsled, and to top the evening off they rode the bumper cars. "The Spookerama was too imitation to be frightening," Albert said. Before leaving Coney Island, Jay got to work among his classmates, polling them on how much money they were prepared to spend on a tour of the city the

next day. They stayed in Coney Island about an hour. Nobody went up to the boardwalk to take a look at the ocean, which none of the class had ever seen. They didn't feel that they had to look at the ocean. "We knew the ocean was there, and anyway we aim to see the ocean on the tour tomorrow," Jay said later.

28   When Ina, Lela, and Jeanne got in line for the Music Hall, the Wattses took their stroll along Fifth Avenue and then joined a couple of friends, Mike and Ardis Cavin. Mike Cavin plays clarinet with the United States Navy Band, in Washington, D.C., and is studying clarinet—as a commuter—at the Julliard School of Music. At Madison Avenue and Forty-second Street, the two couples boarded a bus heading downtown, and while talking about where to get off they were taken in hand by an elderly gentleman sitting near them, who got off the bus when they did and walked two blocks with them, escorting them to their destination—the Jazz Gallery, on St. Mark's Place. Mike Cavin wanted to hear the tenor-saxophone player John Coltrane. The Wattses stayed at the Jazz Gallery with the Cavins for three hours, listening, with patient interest, to modern jazz. They decided that they liked modern jazz, and especially Coltrane. Leaving the Jazz Gallery after one o'clock, the two couples took buses to Times Square, walked around for twenty minutes looking for a place where they could get a snack, and finally, because every other place seemed to be closed, went to Toffenetti's. Back at the hotel, the Wattses ran into one of the Coney Island adventurers, who told them that Ina, Lela, and Jeanne were missing, or at least were not answering their telephone or knocks on their door. Mr. Watts got the room clerk, unlocked the girls' door, and found them sitting on their beds, still putting up their hair. Everybody was, more or less unaccountably, angry—the three girls who hadn't gone to Coney Island, the girls who had, the boys who had, the Wattses, and the room clerk. The Wattses got to bed at 3:30 a.m.

29   At 6:30 a.m., Mrs. Watts was called on the telephone. Message: One of the anti-Coney Island trio was lying on the floor of the room weeping and hysterical. Mrs. Watts called the room clerk, who called a doctor practicing in the Times Square area, who rushed over to the hotel, talked with the weeping girl for twenty minutes, and left her with a tranquilizing pill, which she refused to take.

30   By the time everybody had settled down enough to eat breakfast in drugstores and get ready to start out, it was after nine in the morning, half an hour behind time for the scheduled (by unanimous

vote) all-day tour of the city by chartered sightseeing bus, at six dollars per person. The tour was held up further while Mrs. Watts persuaded the weeper to take a shower, in an effort to encourage her to join the tour. After the shower, the unhappy girl stopped crying and declared that she would go along. By the time the group reached the Bowery, she felt fine, and in Chinatown, like the other boys and girls, she bought a pair of chopsticks, for thirty-five cents. The Cathedral of St. John the Divine was the highlight of the tour for many of the students, who were delighted to hear that some of the limestone used in the cathedral interior had very likely come from quarries near Stinesville. Mrs. Watts, on the other hand, who had studied art, had taught art for five years at Huntington College, in Huntington, Indiana, and had taken an accredited art tour of Europe before her marriage, indignantly considered the cathedral "an imitation of European marvels."

31 Mrs. Watts took the Bean Blossom teaching job, at thirty-six hundred dollars a year, last fall, when her husband decided to abandon a concrete-building-block business in Huntington in order to study for a Ph.D. in political science, a subject he wants to teach. Since he had decided that Indiana University was the place to do this, they moved from Huntington—where Mr. Watts had won the distinction of being the youngest man ever to hold the job of chairman of the Republican Party of Huntington County—to Bloomington. Mrs. Watts drives the twelve miles from Bloomington to Stinesville every day. She teaches English to the tenth, eleventh, and twelfth grades, and, because the school had no Spanish teacher when she signed up for the job, she teaches Spanish, too. She considers the Bean Blossom Township school the most democratic school she has ever seen. "They vote on everything," she says. "We have an average of two votes on something or other every day." Having thus been conditioned to voting as a way of life, Mrs. Watts left the voting on day-to-day plans for the group visit in the capable hands of Jay Bowman. He solved the problem of the tour's late start that morning by taking a vote on whether or not to leave out the Empire State Building. It was promptly voted out of the tour, and voted in for some later time as a separate undertaking.

32 The tour included a boat trip to the Statue of Liberty, where the group fell in with crushing mobs of people walking to the top of the torch. Mrs. Watts found the experience nightmarish, and quit at the base of the torch. Most of the boys and girls made it to the

top. "There are a hundred and sixty-eight steps up the torch, and there were forty thousand people ahead of me, but I was determined to climb up it," Jay Bowman reported to Mrs. Watts. "It took me twenty minutes, and it was worthwhile. The thing of it was I had to do it."

33   For the tour, Jay, like the other boys, had put on dress-up clothes bought specially, at a cost of about twenty-five dollars an outfit, for the trip to New York—white beachcomber pants reaching to below the knee, white cotton-knit shirt with red and blue stripes and a pocket in one sleeve, white socks with red and blue stripes, and white sneakers. The girls wore cotton skirts, various kinds of blouses, white cardigan sweaters, and low-heeled shoes. Mrs. Watts wore high-heeled pumps, even for sightseeing. Everyone else on the tour was astonished at the way New York City people dressed. "They look peculiar," Nancy Prather said. "Girls wearing high heels in the day-time, and the boys here always got a regular suit on, even to go to work in."

34   "I wouldn't trade the girls back home for any of the girls here," Jay Bowman says. "New York girls wear too much makeup. Not that my interests are centered on Nancy Glidden. She's in the junior class. I take her to shows in Bloomington. We eat pizzas, listen to Elvis Presley—things of that nature—and I always get her home by twelve. Even though my interests are centered on the junior class, I'm proud to say my classmates are the finest bunch of people in the world."

35   Jay lives with his parents and two brothers in an old nine-room house on thirty acres of land owned by Jay's father, who works in the maintenance department of the Bridgeport Brass Company, in Indianapolis. His mother works in Bloomington, on the R.C.A. color-television-set assembly line. Jay's grandfather, who has worked in limestone quarries all his life, lives across the road, on five acres of his own land, where he has a couple of cows and raises beans and corn for the use of the family. The Bowman family had no plumbing in their house while Jay was a child, and took baths in a tub in the kitchen with water from a well, but a few years ago, with their own hands, they installed a bathroom and a plumbing system, and did other work on the house, including putting in a furnace. Jay's parents get up at four in the morning to go to work. Jay, who hasn't been sick one day since he had the mumps at the age of twelve, never sleeps later than seven. He is not in the least distressed at having to

work his way through college. He plans to get to school in his own
car. This is a 1950 Chevrolet four-door sedan, which he hopes to
trade in, by paying an additional four hundred dollars, for a slightly
younger model before the end of the year.

36   "The thing of it is I feel proud of myself," Jay says. "Not to be
braggin' or anything. But I saved up better than a thousand dollars
to send myself to college. That's the way it is. I scrubbed floors, put
up hay, carried groceries, and this last winter I worked Saturdays
and Sundays in a country store on the state highway and got paid a
dollar an hour for runnin' it."

37   The Bowman family has, in addition to a kind of basic economic
ambition, two main interests—basketball and politics. Jay, like most
of the other boys on the trip, played basketball on the school basketball team, which won the first round in its section of the Wabash
Valley tournament last season. Jay talks about basketball to his classmates, but never about politics. Talk about the latter he saves for
his family. His grandfather is a Democrat. "If it was up to my grandpa,
he'd never want a single Republican in the whole country," he says.
"And my Dad agrees with him. I agree with my Dad. My Dad thinks
if Franklin D. Roosevelt was still President, this country wouldn't
be in the trouble it finds itself in."

38   At 5 p.m. of this second day in the City of New York, the
members of the Bean Blossom senior class returned to their hotel
and stood in the lobby for a while, looking from some distance
at a souvenir-and-gift stand across from the registration desk. The
stand was stocked with thermometers in the form of the Statue
of Liberty, in two sizes, priced at seventy-nine cents and ninety-
eight cents; with silver-plated charm bracelets; with pins and
compacts carrying representations of the Empire State Building;
with scarves showing the R.C.A. Building and the U.N. Building;
and with ashtrays showing the New York City skyline. Mike
Richardson edged over to the stand and picked up a wooden
plaque, costing ninety-eight cents, with the Statue of Liberty
shown at the top, American flags at the sides, and, in the middle,
a poem, inscribed "Mother" which read:

> To one who bears the sweetest name
> And adds a luster to the same
> Who shares my joys
> Who cheers when sad

The greatest friend I ever had
Long life to her, for there's no other
Can take the place of my dear mother.

39 After reading the poem, Mike smiled.

40 "Where you from?" the man behind the stand asked him.

41 "Indiana," Mike said, looking as though he were warming up. "We've been on this tour? The whole day?"

42 "Ya see everything?" the man asked.

43 "Everything except the Empire State Building," said Mike.

44 "Yeah," said the man, and looked away.

45 Mike was still holding the plaque. Carefully, he replaced it on the stand. "I'll come back for this later," he said.

46 Without looking at Mike, the man nodded.

47 Mike joined Dennis Smith and Larry Williams, who were standing with a tall, big-boned handsome girl named Becky Kiser. Becky used to be a cheerleader for the Bean Blossom Township basketball team.

48 "We was talkin' about the way this place has people layin' in the streets on that Bowery sleepin'," Larry said. "You don't see people layin' in the streets back home."

49 "I seen that in Chicago," Dennis said. "I seen *women* layin' in the streets in Chicago. That's worse."

50 The others nodded. No argument.

51 Mike took a cigarette from his sleeve pocket and lit it with a match from the same pocket. He blew out a stream of smoke with strength and confidence. "I'll be glad when we light out of here," he said. "Nothin' here feels like the farm."

52 Becky Kiser, with an expression of terrible guilt on her attractive, wide-mouthed face, said, "I bet you'd never get bored here in New York. Back home, it's the same thing all the time. You go to the skating rink. You go to the Big Boy. In the winter, there's basketball. And that's all."

53 "When I was in Chicago, I seen a man who shot a man in a bar," Dennis said. "I stood right across the street while the man who was shot the people drug him out." He looked at Becky Kiser. The other boys were also looking at her, but with condemnation and contempt. Dennis gave Becky support. "In Stinesville, they see you on the streets after eleven, they run you home," he said. "Seems like here the city never closes."

54   "Man, you're just not lookin' ahead," Mike said to Dennis, ignoring Becky.

55   "You like it here?" Larry asked, in amazement. "Taxes on candy and on everything?"

56   The Nazarene minister's daughter, Mary Jane Carter, came over with Ina Hough.

57   "Dennis, here, likes New York," Mike announced.

58   "I don't," said Ina. "I like the sights, but I think they're almost ruined by the people."

59   "The food here is expensive, but I guess that's life," said Mary Jane, in a mood of forbearance.

60   "Oh, man!" said Mike.

61   "Oh, man!" said Larry. "Cooped up in New York."

62   Ina said stiffly, "Like the guide said today, you could always tell a New Yorker from a tourist because a New Yorker never smiles, and I agree with him."

63   "After a while, you'd kinda fit in," Dennis said mildly.

64   Before dinner that night, Mr. Watts walked through the Times Square area checking prices and menus at likely restaurants. He made tentative arrangements at The Californian for a five-course steak or chicken dinner, to cost $1.95 per person, and asked Jay Bowman to go around taking a vote on the proposition. Half an hour later, Jay reported to Mr. Watts that some of the boys didn't want to go to The Californian, because they thought they'd have to do their own ordering. So Mr. Watts talked to the boys in their rooms and explained that the ordering was taken care of; all they had to say was whether they wanted steak or chicken. On the next ballot, everybody was in favor of The Californian. The class walked over. When the fifth course was finished, it was agreed that the dinner was all right, but several of the boys said they thought the restaurant was too high-class.

65   After dinner, it started to rain, and it rained hard. The Wattses and seven of the girls decided that they wanted to see "The Music Man." The four other girls wanted to see "My Fair Lady." None of the boys wanted to see a musical show. In the driving rain, the Wattses and the girls ran to the theatres of their choice, all arriving soaked to the skin. By good luck, each group was able to buy seats. At "The Music Man," the Wattses and the seven girls with them sat in the balcony, in the direct path of an air-conditioning unit [that] blew icy blasts at their legs. The girls liked their shows. The "My

Fair Lady" group was transported by the costumes. Ina Hough, who went to "The Music Man," thought that it was just like a movie, except for the way the scenes changed.

66 The boys split up, some of them taking the subway down to Greenwich Village, the others heading for the Empire State Building, where they paid a dollar-thirty for tickets to the observatory and, once up there, found that the fog and rain blotted out the view completely. "We stood there about an hour and a half messin' around, me and my buddies," Jay later told Mrs. Watts. "Wasn't no sense in leavin' at that price." In Greenwich Village, Mike Richardson, Dennis Smith, and Larry Williams walked along the narrow streets in a drizzling rain. All were still wearing their beachcomber outfits. Nobody talked to them. They didn't see anybody they wanted to talk to. They almost went into a small coffeehouse; they changed their minds because the prices looked too high. They went into one shop, a bookstore, and looked at some abstract paintings, which appealed to them. "Sort of interestin', the way they don't look like nothin'," Mike said. Then they took the subway back to Times Square, where they walked around for a while in the rain. Toward midnight, Mike and Dennis told each other they were lonesome for the smell of grass and trees, and, the rain having stopped, they walked up to Central Park, where they stayed for about an hour and got lost.

67 The next morning, a meeting of the class was held in the hotel lobby to take a vote on when to leave New York. Jay Bowman reported that they had enough money to cover an extra day in the city, plus a side trip to Niagara Falls on the way home. Or, he said, they could leave New York when they had originally planned to and go to Washington, D.C., for a day before heading home. The bus driver had told Jay that it was all one to him which they chose. The class voted for the extra day in New York and Niagara Falls.

68 "I'm glad," Becky Kiser said, with a large, friendly smile, to Dennis Smith. Several of her classmates overheard her and regarded her with a uniformly deadpan look. "I like it here," she went on. "I'd like to live here. There's so much to see. There's so much to do."

69 Her classmates continued to study her impassively until Dennis took their eyes away from her by saying, "You get a feelin' here of goin' wherever you want to. Seems the city never closes. I'd like to live here, I believe. People from everyplace are here."

70 "Limousines all over the joint," Albert Warthan said.

71 "Seems like you can walk and walk and walk," Dennis went on dreamily. "I like the way the big buildin's crowd you in. You want to walk and walk and never go to sleep."

72 "I hate it," Connie Williams said, with passion.

73 "Oh, man, you're just not lookin' ahead," Mike Richardson said to Dennis."You got a romantic notion. You're not realistic about it."

74 "This place couldn't hold me," Larry Williams said. "I like the privacy of the farm."

75 "I want to go to new places," said Becky, who had started it. "I want to go to Europe."

76 "Only place I want to go is Texas," Larry said. "I got folks in Texas."

77 "There's no place like home," Mike said. "Home's good enough for me."

78 "I believe the reason of this is we've lived all of our lives around Stinesville," Dennis said. "If you took Stinesville out of the country, you wouldn't be hurt. But if you took New York out of the country, you'd be hurt. The way the guide said, all our clothes and everything comes from New York."

79 Becky said, "In Coney Island, I saw the most handsome man I ever saw in my whole life. I think he was a Puerto Rican or something, too."

80 Albert said, "When we get back, my pa will say, 'Well, how was it!' I'll say, 'It was fine.' "

81 "I'd like to come back, maybe stay a month," Jay Bowman said diplomatically. "One thing I'd like to do is come here when I can see a major-league baseball game."

82 "I'd like to see a major-league baseball game, but I wouldn't come back just to see it," Mike said.

83 "I hate New York," Connie said.

84 "Back home, everybody says 'Excuse me,' " Nancy Prather said.

85 "I like it here," Dennis said stubbornly.

86 This day was an open one, leaving the boys and girls free to do anything they liked, without prearranged plan or vote. Mike passed close by the souvenir-and-gift stand in the hotel lobby, and the proprietor urged him to take home the Statue of Liberty.

87 "I'd like to, but it won't fit in my suitcase," Mike said, with a loud laugh.

88 A group formed to visit the zoo in Central Park, got on the

subway, had a loud discussion about where to get off, and were taken in hand by a stranger, who told them the zoo was in the Bronx. Only the boy named Lynn Dillon listened to the stranger. The others went to the zoo in Central Park. Lynn stayed on the subway till it reached the Bronx, and spent the entire day in the Bronx Zoo by himself. The rest of the zoo visitors, walking north after lunch in the cafeteria, ran into the Metropolitan Museum of Art and went in. "It was there, and it was free, so we did it," Nancy Prather said. "There were these suits of armor and stuff. Nothin' I go for myself."

89　　That morning, the Wattses had tried to get some of the boys and girls to accompany them to the Guggenheim Museum or the Museum of Modern Art, but nobody had wanted to pay the price of admission. "Why pay fifty cents to see a museum when they got them free?" the class president asked. Mrs. Watts reported afterward that the Guggenheim was the most exciting museum she had ever seen, including all the museums she had seen in Europe on her accredited art tour. "There aren't big crowds in there, for one thing," she said. "And I don't think the building overpowers the paintings at all, as I've heard." From the Guggenheim, the Wattses went to Georg Jensen's to look at silver, but didn't buy anything. Then they went to the Museum of Modern Art and had lunch in the garden. "Lovely lunch, fabulous garden, fabulous sculpture, but I'm disappointed in the museum itself," Mrs. Watts said. "Everything jammed into that small space! Impossible to get a good view of Picasso's 'Girl Before a Mirror.' "

90　　By dinnertime, more than half of the Bean Blossomers had, to their relief, discovered the Automat. Jay Bowman had a dinner consisting of a ham sandwich (forty cents), a glass of milk (ten cents), and dish of fresh strawberries (twenty cents). Then, with a couple of buddies, he bought some peanuts in their shells and some Cokes, and took them up to his room for the three of them to consume while talking about what to do that night. They decided, because they had not yet had a good view of the city from the Empire State observatory, that they would go back there. They were accompanied by most of the girls and the other boys, and this time the group got a cut rate of sixty-five cents apiece. Dennis went off wandering by himself. He walked up Fifth Avenue to Eighty-fifth Street, over to Park Avenue, down Park to Seventy-second Street, across to the West Side, down Central Park West to Sixty-sixth Street, over behind the Tavern-on-the-Green (where he watched people eating outdoors), and on down Seventh Avenue to Times Square, where he stood around on corners looking at the people who bought papers at newsstands.

91   The Wattses had arranged to meet anybody who was interested under the Washington Arch at around nine-thirty for an evening in Greenwich Village. The boys had decided to take a walk up Broadway after leaving the Empire State Building, but the girls all showed up in Washington Square, along with two soldiers and three sailors they had met in the U.S.O. across the street from the Woodstock. The Wattses led the way to a coffeehouse, where everybody had coffee or lemonade. Then the girls and the service men left the Wattses, saying they were going to take a ride on the ferry to Staten Island. The Wattses went to the Five Spot, which their jazz friend had told them had good music.

92   After breakfast the following morning, the bus driver, Ralph Walls, showed up in the hotel lobby for the first time since the group's arrival in New York and told Jay Bowman to have everyone assembled at five-forty-five the following morning for departure at six o'clock on the dot. The driver said that he was spending most of his time sleeping, and that before they left he was going to do some more sleeping. He had taken his wife on a boat trip around Manhattan, though, he said, and he had taken a few walks on the streets. After reminding Jay again about the exact time planned for the departure, he went back upstairs to his room.

93   Mrs. Watts took nine of the girls (two stayed in the hotel to sleep) for a walk through Saks Fifth Avenue, just looking. Mr. Watts took three of the boys to Abercrombie & Fitch, just looking. Everybody walked every aisle on every floor in each store, looking at everything on the counters and in the showcases. Nobody bought anything. The two groups met at noon under the clock in Grand Central; lunched at an Automat; walked over to the United Nations Building, where they decided not to take the regular tour, and took a crosstown bus to the Hudson River and went aboard the liner S.S. Independence, where they visited every deck and every lounge on the boat, and a good many of the staterooms. Then they took the bus back to Times Square and scattered to do some shopping.

94   Mike Richardson bought all his gifts—eleven dollars' worth—at the hotel stand, taking not only the plaque for his mother but a set of salt and pepper shakers, with the Statue of Liberty on the salt and the Empire State Building on the pepper, also for his mother; a

Statue of Liberty ashtray for his father; a George Washington Bridge teapot for his sister-in-law; a mechanical dog for his niece; a City Hall teapot-cup-and-saucer set for his grandparents; and a cigarette lighter stamped with the Great White Way for himself. At Macy's, Becky Kiser bought a dress, a blouse, and an ankle chain for herself, and a necklace with matching bracelet and earrings for her mother, a cuff-link-and-tie-clasp set for her father, and a bracelet for her younger sister. Albert Wall then bought a miniature camera for himself and a telephone-pad-and-pencil set stamped with the George Washington Bridge and a Statue of Liberty thermometer, large-size, as general family gifts, at the hotel stand. Jay Bowman bought an unset cultured pearl at Macy's for his girl friend in the junior class, as well as silver-looking earrings for his married sister and for his mother, and at a store called King of Slims, around the corner from the hotel, he bought four ties—a red toreador tie (very narrow) for his older brother, a black toreador tie for his younger brother, a conservative silk foulard for his father, and a white toreador tie for himself. Dennis Smith bought a Statue of Liberty ashtray for his mother and a Statue of Liberty cigarette lighter for his father. Connie Williams bought two bracelets and a Statue of Liberty pen for herself. The bus driver and his wife spent sixty dollars on clothes for their children, six of whom are girls. Nancy Prather didn't buy anything. The Wattses spent about a hundred dollars in the course of the visit, most of it on meals and entertainment.

95 On their last evening in New York, all the boys and girls, accompanied by the Wattses, went to the Radio City Music Hall, making it in time to see the stage show. Then they packed and went to bed. The bus driver, after an early dinner with his wife at Hector's Cafeteria, brought the yellow school bus over from Tenth Avenue and parked it right in front of the hotel, so that it would be there for the early start.

96 Next morning at five-forty-five, the Bean Blossomers assembled in the lobby; for the first time since the trip had started, nobody was late. The bus pulled out at exactly 6 a.m., and twenty minutes after that, heading west over the George Washington Bridge, it disappeared from the city.

CLASSIC
ESSAYS
IN THE

Physical
Sciences

The Method of Scientific Investigation

THOMAS HENRY HUXLEY

Thomas Henry Huxley (1825–1895) was a self-educated British scientist, surgeon, and writer. After medical college, he spent four years as a surgeon in the British navy on tour in the Indian Ocean and the East Indies. He wrote a scientific study of jellyfish that established his fame as a zoologist. His scientific studies drew him into the debate on evolution and the findings of Charles Darwin. Although he disagreed with Darwin on several points, he nevertheless joined the debate, defending Darwin but meeting censure by many learned people of his age. He did recognize the findings of modern science, that life in every species is the "struggle for existence" more than a gradual transmutation implied by "natural selection." He also asserted that modern humans have ended their struggle for existence and now participate in the "struggle for enjoyment." Among other words, he coined the term *agnostic* to describe a person who thinks that God's existence cannot be proved and the term *biogenesis* to argue that life develops only from previous life.

"The Method of Scientific Investigation" is an excerpt from his *Autobiography and Selected Essays* (1910). In this essay, Huxley explains the two forms of logical thinking—deduction and induction—by which we arrive at conclusions. He shows how we form various thoughts by the process of induction (sampling a number of green and hard apples) and how we use that finding to reach, through deduction, a final determination—this apple is green and hard so I will not eat it.

1   The method of scientific investigation is nothing but the expression of the necessary mode of working of the human mind. It is simply the mode at which all phenomena are reasoned about, rendered precise and exact. There is no more difference, but there is just the same kind of difference, between the mental operations of a man of science and those of an ordinary person, as there is between the operations and methods of a baker or of a butcher weighing out his goods in common scales and the operation of a chemist in performing a difficult and complex analysis by means of his balance and finely graduated weights. It is not that the action of the scales in the one case and the balance in the other differ in the principles of their construction or manner of working; but the beam of one is set on an infinitely finer axis than the other, and of course turns by the addition of a much smaller weight.

2   You will understand this better, perhaps, if I give you some familiar example. You have all heard it repeated, I dare say, that men of science work by means of induction and deduction, and that by the help of these operations, they, in a sort of sense, wring from Nature certain other things, which are called natural laws and causes, and that out of these, by some cunning skill of their own, they build up hypotheses and theories. And it is imagined by many that the operations of the common mind can be by no means compared with these processes, and that they have to be acquired by a sort of special apprenticeship to the craft. To hear all these large words, you would think that the mind of a man of science must be constituted differently from that of his fellow men; but if you will not be frightened by terms, you will discover that you are quite wrong, and that all these terrible apparatus are being used by yourselves every day and every hour of your lives.

3   There is a well-known incident in one of Molière's plays, where the author makes the hero express unbounded delight on being told that he has been talking prose during the whole of his life. In the

same way, I trust that you will take comfort, and be delighted with yourselves, on the discovery that you have been acting on the principles of inductive and deductive philosophy during the same period. Probably there is not one here who has not in the course of the day had occasion to set in motion a complex train of reasoning, of the very same kind, though differing of course in degree, as that which a scientific man goes through in tracing the causes of natural phenomena.

4   A very trivial circumstance will serve to exemplify this. Suppose you go into a fruiterer's shop, wanting an apple—you take one up, and, on biting, you find it is sour; you look at it, and see that it is hard, and green. You take up another one and that too is hard, green, and sour. The shop man offers you a third; but, before biting it, you examine it, and find that it is hard and green, and you immediately say that you will not have it, as it must be sour, like those that you have already tried.

5   Nothing can be more simple than that, you think; but if you will take the trouble to analyze and trace out into its logical elements what has been done by the mind, you will be greatly surprised. In the first place, you have performed the operation of induction. You found, that, in two experiences, hardness and greenness in apples went together with sourness. It was so in the first case, and it was confirmed by the second. True, it is a very small basis, but still it is enough to make an induction from; you generalize the facts, and you expect to find sourness in apples where you get hardness and greenness. You found upon that a general law, that all hard and green apples are sour; and that, so far as it goes, is a perfect induction. Well, having got your natural law in this way, when you are offered another apple which you find is hard and green, you say, "All hard and green apples are sour; this apple is hard and green, therefore this apple is sour." That train of reasoning is what logicians call a syllogism and has all its various parts and terms—its major premise, its minor premise, and its conclusion. And, by the help of further reasoning, which, if drawn out, would have to be exhibited in two or three other syllogisms, you arrive at your final determination: "I will not have that apple." So that, you see, you have, in the first place, established a law by induction, and upon that you have founded a deduction and reasoned out the special conclusion of the particular case. Well now, suppose, having got your law, that at some time

afterwards, you are discussing the qualities of apples with a friend; you will say to him, "It is a very curious thing—but I find that all hard and green apples are sour!" Your friend says to you, "But how do you know that?" You at once reply, "Oh, because I have tried them over and over again and have always found them to be so." Well, if we were talking science instead of common sense, we should call that an experimental verification. And, if still opposed, you go further and say, "I have heard from the people in Somersetshire and Devonshire, where a large number of apples are grown, that they have observed the same thing. It is also found to be the case in Normandy, and in North America. In short, I find it to be the universal experience of mankind wherever attention has been directed to the subject." Whereupon your friend, unless he is a very unreasonable man, agrees with you and is convinced that you are quite right in the conclusion you have drawn. He believes, although perhaps he does not know he believes it, that the more extensive verifications are—that the more frequently experiments have been made and results of the same kind arrived at—that the more varied the conditions under which the same results are attained, the more certain is the ultimate conclusion, and he disputes the question no further. He sees that the experiment has been tried under all sorts of conditions, as to time, place, and people, with the same result; and he says with you, therefore, that the law you have laid down must be a good one, and he must believe it.

6   In science we do the same thing; the philosopher exercises precisely the same faculties, though in a much more delicate manner. In scientific inquiry it becomes a matter of duty to expose a supposed law to every possible kind of verification and to take care, moreover, that this is done intentionally and not left to a mere accident, as in the case of apples. And in science, as in common life, our confidence in a law is in exact proportion to the absence of variation in the result of our experimental verifications. For instance, if you let go your grasp of an article you may have in your hand, it will immediately fall to the ground. That is a very common verification of one of the best established laws of nature—that of gravitation. The method by which men of science established the existence of that law is exactly the same as that by which we have established the trivial proposition about the sourness of hard and green apples. But we believe it in such

an extensive, thorough, and unhesitating manner because the universal experience of mankind verifies it, and we can verify it ourselves at any time; and that is the strongest possible foundation on which any natural law can rest.

Touch and Sight: The Earth and the Heavens

BERTRAND RUSSELL

Bertrand Russell (1872–1970) was born in Trelleck, Monmouthshire, England. He was educated at Trinity College, Cambridge, and became a philosopher, mathematician, and social reformer. He taught at Trinity College, Harvard, the National University of Peking, the University of Chicago, and other institutions in America and England. He was a prolific writer, and his essays and books challenged conventional thinking on many fronts. He stated, "Science is what you know, philosophy is what you don't know." Among his most well-known works are *Principia Mathematica* (1910–1913, with Alfred North Whitehead), *The ABC of Relativity* (1925), *Religion and Science* (1935), and *A History of Western Philosophy* (1945). In 1950, he was awarded the Nobel Prize in literature.

"Touch and Sight: The Earth and the Heavens" is an excerpt from *The ABC of Relativity,* in which he attempts to explain Einstein's theory of relativity for nonscientific readers. He begins with the human senses, especially sight and touch. Then he removes those sensations and moves to another dimension. His analogy of stationary positions on earth becoming moveable objects demonstrates that nothing can remain in a fixed position to anything else, yet "everything in the heavens is moving relatively to everything else."

1   Everybody knows that Einstein did something astonishing, but very few people know exactly what it was that he did. It is generally recognized that he revolutionized our conception of the physical world, but the new conceptions are wrapped up in mathematical technicalities. It is true that there are innumerable popular accounts of the theory of relativity, but they generally cease to be intelligible just at the point where they begin to say something important. The authors are hardly to blame for this. Many of the new ideas can be expressed in non-mathematical language, but they are none the less difficult on that account. What is demanded is a change in our imaginative picture of the world—a picture which has been handed down from remote, perhaps pre-human, ancestors, and has been learned by each one of us in early childhood. A change in our imagination is always difficult, especially when we are no longer young. The same sort of change was demanded by Copernicus, when he taught that the earth is not stationary and the heavens do not revolve about it once a day. To us now there is no difficulty in this idea, because we learned it before our mental habits had become fixed. Einstein's ideas, similarly, will seem easier to generations which grow up with them; but for us a certain effort of imaginative reconstruction is unavoidable.

2   In exploring the surface of the earth, we make use of all our senses, more particularly of the senses of touch and sight. In measuring lengths, parts of the human body are employed in pre-scientific ages: a "foot," a "cubit," a "span" are defined in this way. For longer distances, we think of the time it takes to walk from one place to another. We gradually learn to judge distance roughly by the eye, but we rely upon touch for accuracy. Moreover it is touch that gives us our sense of "reality." Some things cannot be touched: rainbows, reflections in looking-glasses, and so on. These things puzzle children, whose metaphysical speculations are arrested by the information that what is in the looking-glass is not "real." Macbeth's dagger was unreal because it was not "sensible to feeling as to sight." Not only

our geometry and physics, but our whole conception of what exists outside us, is based upon the sense of touch. We carry this even into our metaphors: a good speech is "solid," a bad speech is "gas," because we feel that a gas is not quite "real."

3   In studying the heavens, we are debarred from all senses except sight. We cannot touch the sun, or travel to it; we cannot walk around the moon, or apply a foot-rule to the Pleiades. Nevertheless, astronomers have unhesitatingly applied the geometry and physics which they found serviceable on the surface of the earth, and which they had based upon touch and travel. In doing so, they brought down trouble on their heads, which it was left for Einstein to clear up. It turned out that much of what we learned from the sense of touch was unscientific prejudice, which must be rejected if we are to have a true picture of the world.

4   An illustration may help us to understand how much is impossible to the astronomer as compared with the man who is interested in things on the surface of the earth. Let us suppose that a drug is administered to you which makes you temporarily unconscious, and that when you wake you have lost your memory but not your reasoning powers. Let us suppose further that while you were unconscious you were carried into a balloon, which, when you come to, is sailing with the wind on a dark night—the night of the fifth of November if you are in England, or of the fourth of July if you are in America. You can see fireworks which are being sent off from the ground, from trains, and from aeroplanes travelling in all directions, but you cannot see the ground or the trains or the aeroplanes because of the darkness. What sort of picture of the world will you form? You will think that nothing is permanent: there are only brief flashes of light, which, during their short existence, travel through the void in the most various and bizarre curves. You cannot touch these flashes of light, you can only see them. Obviously your geometry and your physics and your metaphysics will be quite different from those of ordinary mortals. If an ordinary mortal were with you in the balloon, you would find his speech unintelligible. But if Einstein were with you, you would understand him more easily than the ordinary mortal would, because you would be free from a host of preconceptions which prevent most people from understanding him.

5   The theory of relativity depends, to a considerable extent, upon getting rid of notions which are useful in ordinary life but not to our drugged balloonist. Circumstances on the surface of the earth,

for various more or less accidental reasons, suggest conceptions which turn out to be inaccurate, although they have come to seem like necessities of thought. The most important of these circumstances is that most objects on the earth's surface are fairly persistent and nearly stationary from a terrestrial point of view. If this were not the case, the idea of going on a journey would not seem so definite as it does. If you want to travel from King's Cross to Edinburgh, you know that you will find King's Cross where it has always been, that the railway line will take the course that it did when you last made the journey, and that Waverly Station in Edinburgh will not have walked up to the Castle. You therefore say and think that you have traveled to Edinburgh, not that Edinburgh has travelled to you, though the latter statement would be just as accurate. The success of this commonsense point of view depends upon a number of things which are really of the nature of luck. Suppose all the houses in London were perpetually moving about, like a swarm of bees; suppose railways moved and changed their shapes like avalanches; and finally suppose that material objects were perpetually being formed and dissolved like clouds. There is nothing impossible in these suppositions. But obviously what we call a journey to Edinburgh would have no meaning in such a world. You would begin, no doubt, by asking the taxi-driver: "Where is King's Cross this morning?" At the station you would have to ask a similar question about Edinburgh, but the booking-office clerk would reply: "What part of Edinburgh do you mean, sir? Prince's Street has gone to Glasgow, the Castle has moved up into the Highlands, and Waverly Station is under the water in the middle of the Firth of Forth." And, on the journey the stations would not be staying quiet, but some would be travelling north, some south, some east or west, perhaps much faster than the train. Under these conditions you could not say where you were at any moment. Indeed, the whole notion that one is always in some definite "place" is due to the fortunate immobility of most of the large objects on the earth's surface. The idea of "place" is only a rough practical approximation: there is nothing logically necessary about it, and it cannot be made precise.

6   If we were not much larger than an electron, we should not have this impression of stability, which is only due to the grossness of our senses. King's Cross, which to us looks solid, would be too vast to be conceived except by a few eccentric mathematicians. The bits of it that we could see would consist of little tiny points of matter,

never coming into contact with each other, but perpetually whizzing around each other in an inconceivably rapid ballet-dance. The world of our experience would be quite as mad as the one in which the different parts of Edinburgh go for walks in different directions. If—to take the opposite extreme—you were as large as the sun and lived as long, with a corresponding slowness of perception, you would again find a higgledy-piggledy universe without permanence—stars and planets would come and go like morning mists, and nothing would remain in a fixed position relative to anything else. The notion of comparative stability which forms part of our ordinary outlook is thus due to the fact that we are about the size we are, and live on a planet of which the surface is not very hot. If this were not the case, we should not find pre-relativity physics intellectually satisfying. Indeed we should never have invented such theories. We should have had to arrive at relativity physics at one bound, or remain ignorant of scientific laws. It is fortunate for us that we were not faced with this alternative, since it is almost inconceivable that one man could have done the work of Euclid, Galileo, Newton and Einstein. Yet without such an incredible genius physics could hardly have been discovered in a world where the universal flux was obvious to non-scientific observation.

7   In astronomy, although the sun, moon, and stars continue to exist year after year, yet in other respects the world we have to deal with is very different from that of everyday life. As already observed we depend exclusively on sight: the heavenly bodies cannot be touched, heard, smelt, or tasted. Everything in the heavens is moving relatively to everything else. The earth is going round the sun, the sun is moving, very much faster than an express train, towards a point in the constellation Hercules, the "fixed" stars are scurrying hither and thither like a lot of frightened hens. There are no well-marked places in the sky, like King's Cross and Edinburgh. When you travel from place to place on the earth, you say the train moves and not the stations, because the stations preserve their topographical relations to each other and the surrounding country. But in astronomy it is arbitrary which you call the train and which the station: the question is to be decided purely by convenience and as a matter of convention.

8   In this respect, it is interesting to contrast Einstein and Copernicus. Before Copernicus, people thought that the earth stood still and the heavens revolved about it once a day. Copernicus taught that "really" the earth rotates once a day, and the daily revolution of sun and

stars is only "apparent." Galileo and Newton endorsed this view, and many things were thought to prove it—for example, the flattening of the earth at the poles and the fact that bodies are heavier there than at the equator. But in the modern theory the question between Copernicus and his predecessors is merely one of convenience; all motion is relative, and there is no difference between the two statements: "The earth rotates once a day" and "the heavens revolve around the earth once a day." The two mean exactly the same thing, just as it means the same thing if I say that a certain length is six feet or two yards. Astronomy is easier if we take the sun as fixed than if we take the earth, just as accounts are easier in decimal coinage. But to say more for Copernicus is to assume absolute motion, which is a fiction. All motion is relative, and it is a mere convention to take one body as at rest. All such conventions are equally legitimate, though not all are equally convenient.

9   There is another matter of great importance, in which astronomy differs from terrestrial physics because of its exclusive dependence upon sight. Both popular thought and old-fashioned physics used the notion of "force," which seemed intelligible because it was associated with familiar sensations. When we are walking, we have sensations connected with our muscles which we do not have when we are sitting still. In the days before mechanical traction, although people could travel by sitting in their carriages, they could see the horses exerting themselves and evidently putting out "force" in the same way as human beings do. Everybody knew from experience what it is to push or pull, or to be pushed or pulled. These very familiar facts made "force" seem a natural basis for dynamics. But Newton's law of gravitation introduced a difficulty. The force between two billiard balls appeared intelligible because we know what it feels like to bump into another person; but the force between the earth and the sun, which are ninety-three million miles apart, was mysterious. Newton himself regarded this "action at a distance" as impossible, and believed that there was some hitherto undiscovered mechanism by which the sun's influence was transmitted to the planets. However, no such mechanism was discovered, and gravitation remained a puzzle. The fact is that the whole conception of "force" is a mistake. The sun does not exert any force on the planets; in Einstein's law of gravitation, the planet only pays attention to what it finds in its own neighborhood. The way in which this works will be explained in a later chapter; for the present we are only concerned with the

necessity of abandoning the notion of "force," which was due to misleading conceptions derived from the sense of touch.

10   As physics has advanced, it has appeared more and more that sight is less misleading than touch as a source of fundamental notions about matter. The apparent simplicity in the collision of billiard balls is quite illusory. As a matter of fact the two billiard balls never touch at all; what really happens is inconceivably complicated, but it is more analogous to what happens when a comet penetrates the solar system and goes away again than to what common sense supposes to happen.

11   Most of what we have said hitherto was already recognized by physicists before Einstein invented the theory of relativity. "Force" was known to be merely a mathematical fiction, and it was generally held that motion is a merely relative phenomenon—that is to say, when two bodies are changing their relative position, we cannot say that one is moving while the other is at rest, since the occurrence is merely a change in their relation to each other. But a great labor was required in order to bring the actual procedure of physics into harmony with these new convictions. Newton believed in force and in absolute space and time; he embodied these beliefs in his technical methods, and his methods remained those of later physicists. Einstein invented a new technique, free from Newton's assumptions. But in order to do so he had to change fundamentally the old ideas of space and time, which had been unchallenged from time immemorial. This is what makes both the difficulty and the interest of his theory.

What Is the Theory of Relativity?

ALBERT EINSTEIN

Albert Einstein (1879–1955) was born in Ulm, Germany. He became a naturalized Swiss citizen in 1901, immigrated to the United States in 1933, and became a naturalized citizen of the United States in 1940. He earned his undergraduate degree at the Swiss Federal Institute of Technology and a Ph.D. at the University of Zurich. Einstein earned a reputation as the preeminent scientist of the twentieth century for his theory of relativity, which changed the world's thinking about matter, space, and time. In 1921, he was awarded the Nobel Prize in physics.

"What Is the Theory of Relativity?" is Einstein's attempt to explain his concepts to a lay audience. At the invitation of the *London Times* in 1919, he addressed a general audience with this essay. Later, he published it in his 1954 book, *Ideas and Opinions*. In this essay, Einstein explains that time and space can vary with circumstances, so they must be measured relative to energy and mass. Thus we get the equation "energy equals mass times the speed of light squared." What that theory gave to scientists was a way to calculate how the masses of the universe behave.

1   I gladly accede to the request of your colleague to write something for the *Times* on relativity. After the lamentable breakdown of the old active intercourse between men of learning, I welcome this opportunity of expressing my feelings of joy and gratitude toward the astronomers and physicists of England. It is thoroughly in keeping with the great and proud traditions of scientific work in your country that eminent scientists should have spent much time and trouble, and your scientific institutions have spared no expense, to test the implications of a theory which was perfected and published during the war in the land of your enemies. Even though the investigation of the influence of the gravitational field of the sun on light rays is a purely objective matter, I cannot forbear to express my personal thanks to my English colleagues for their work; for without it I could hardly have lived to see the most important implication of my theory tested.

2   We can distinguish various kinds of theories in physics. Most of them are constructive. They attempt to build up a picture of the more complex phenomena out of the materials of a relatively simple formal scheme from which they start out. Thus the kinetic theory of gases seeks to reduce mechanical, thermal, and diffusional processes to movements of molecules—i.e., to build them up out of the hypothesis of molecular motion. When we say that we have succeeded in understanding a group of natural processes, we invariably mean that a constructive theory has been found which covers the processes in question.

3   Along with this most important class of theories there exists a second, which I will call "principle-theories." These employ the analytic, not the synthetic, method. The elements which form their basis and starting-point are not hypothetically constructed but empirically discovered ones, general characteristics of natural processes, principles that give rise to mathematically formulated criteria which the separate processes or the theoretical representations of them have to satisfy. Thus the science of thermodynamics seeks by analytical means to deduce necessary conditions, which separate events have to satisfy, from the universally experienced fact that perpetual motion is impossible.

4   The advantages of the constructive theory are completeness, adaptability, and clearness, those of the principle theory are logical perfection and security of the foundations.

5   The theory of relativity belongs to the latter class. In order to

grasp its nature, one needs first of all to become acquainted with the principles on which it is based. Before I go into these, however, I must observe that the theory of relativity resembles a building consisting of two separate stories, the special theory and the general theory. The special theory, on which the general theory rests, applies to all physical phenomena with the exception of gravitation; the general theory provides the law of gravitation and its relations to the other forces of nature.

6   It has, of course, been known since the days of the ancient Greeks that in order to describe the movement of a body, a second body is needed to which the movement of the first is referred. The movement of a vehicle is considered in reference to the earth's surface, that of a planet to the totality of the visible fixed stars. In physics the body to which events are spatially referred is called the coordinate system. The laws of the mechanics of Galileo and Newton, for instance, can only be formulated with the aid of a coordinate system.

7   The state of motion of the coordinate system may not, however, be arbitrarily chosen, if the laws of mechanics are to be valid (it must be free from rotation and acceleration). A coordinate system which is admitted in mechanics is called an "inertial system." The state of motion of an inertial system is according to mechanics not one that is determined uniquely by nature. On the contrary, the following definition holds good: a coordinate system that is moved uniformly and in a straight line relative to an inertial system is likewise an inertial system. By the "special principle of relativity" is meant the generalization of this definition to include any natural event whatever: thus, every universal law of nature which is valid in relation to a coordinate system C, must also be valid, as it stands, in relation to a coordinate system C', which is in uniform translatory motion relatively to C.

8   The second principle, on which the special theory of relativity rests, is the "principle of the constant velocity of light in vacuo." This principle asserts that light in vacuo always has a definite velocity of propagation (independent of the state of motion of the observer or of the source of the light). The confidence which physicists place in this principle springs from the successes achieved by the electrodynamics of Maxwell and Lorentz.

9   Both the above-mentioned principles are powerfully supported by experience, but appear not to be logically reconcilable. The special theory of relativity finally succeeded in reconciling them logically by

a modification of kinematics—i.e., of the doctrine of the laws relating to space and time (from the point of view of physics). It became clear that to speak of the simultaneity of two events had no meaning except in relation to a given coordinate system, and that the shape of measuring devices and the speed at which clocks move depend on their state of motion with respect to the coordinate system.

10   But the old physics, including the laws of motion of Galileo and Newton, did not fit in with the suggested relativist kinematics. From the latter, general mathematical conditions issued, to which natural laws had to conform, if the above-mentioned two principles were really to apply. To these, physics had to be adapted. In particular, scientists arrived at a new law of motion for (rapidly moving) mass points, which was admirably confirmed in the case of electrically charged particles. The most important upshot of the special theory of relativity concerned the inert masses of corporeal systems. It turned out that the inertia of a system necessarily depends on its energy-content, and this led straight to the notion that inert mass is simply latent energy. The principle of the conservation of mass lost its independence and became fused with that of the conservation of energy.

11   The special theory of relativity, which was simply a systematic development of the electrodynamics of Maxwell and Lorentz, pointed beyond itself, however. Should the independence of physical laws of the state of motion of the coordinate system be restricted to the uniform translatory motion of coordinate systems in respect to each other? What has nature to do with our coordinate systems and their state of motion? If it is necessary for the purpose of describing nature, to make use of a coordinate system arbitrarily introduced by us, then the choice of its state of motion ought to be subject to no restriction; the laws ought to be entirely independent of this choice (general principle of relativity).

12   The establishment of this general principle of relativity is made easier by a fact of experience that has long been known, namely, that the weight and the inertia of a body are controlled by the same constant (equality of inertial and gravitational mass). Imagine a coordinate system which is rotating uniformly with respect to an inertial system in the Newtonian manner. The centrifugal forces which manifest themselves in relation to this system must, according to Newton's teaching, be regarded as effects of inertia. But these centrifugal forces are, exactly like the forces of gravity, proportional to the masses of

the bodies. Ought it not to be possible in this case to regard the coordinate system as stationary and the centrifugal forces as gravitational forces? This seems the obvious view, but classical mechanics forbid it.

13 This hasty consideration suggests that a general theory of relativity must supply the laws of gravitation, and the consistent following up of the idea has justified our hopes.

14 But the path was thornier than one might suppose, because it demanded the abandonment of Euclidean geometry. This is to say, the laws according to which solid bodies may be arranged in space do not completely accord with the spatial laws attributed to bodies by Euclidean geometry. This is what we mean when we talk of the "curvature of space." The fundamental concepts of the "straight line," the "plane," etc., thereby lose their precise significance in physics.

15 In the general theory of relativity the doctrine of space and time, or kinematics, no longer figures as a fundamental independent of the rest of physics. The geometrical behavior of bodies and the motion of clocks rather depend on gravitational fields, which in their turn are produced by matter.

16 The new theory of gravitation diverges considerably, as regards principles, from Newton's theory. But its practical results agree so nearly with those of Newton's theory that it is difficult to find criteria for distinguishing them which are accessible to experience. Such have been discovered so far:

1. In the revolution of the ellipses of the planetary orbits around the sun (confirmed in the case of Mercury).
2. In the curving of light rays by the action of gravitational fields (confirmed by the English photographs of eclipses).
3. In a displacement of the spectral lines toward the red end of the spectrum in the case of light transmitted to us from stars of considerable magnitude (unconfirmed so far).

17 The chief attraction of the theory lies in its logical completeness. If a single one of the conclusions drawn from it proves wrong, it must be given up; to modify it without destroying the whole structure seems to be impossible.

18 Let no one suppose, however, that the mighty work of Newton can really be superseded by this or any other theory. His great and lucid ideas will retain their unique significance for all time as the

foundation of our whole modern conceptual structure in the sphere of natural philosophy.

19   *Note:* Some of the statements in your paper concerning my life and person owe their origin to the lively imagination of the writer. Here is yet another application of the principle of relativity for the delectation of the reader: today I am described in Germany as a "German savant," and in England as a "Swiss Jew." Should it ever be my fate to be represented as a *bête noire,* I should, on the contrary, become a "Swiss Jew" for the Germans and a "German savant" for the English.

"But a Watch in the Night": A Scientific Fable

JAMES C. RETTIE

James C. Rettie (1904–1969) was a quiet, somewhat reclusive economist who preserved his privacy, so the biographical facts about his life are obscure. He did work for a time at an experimental station of the National Forest Service in Upper Darby, Pennsylvania, and he served as an advisor to the U.S. Department of the Interior during the administrations of John F. Kennedy and Lyndon B. Johnson. He authored numerous articles and government reports, but he is best remembered for the essay reprinted here.

" 'But a Watch in the Night': A Scientific Fable" first appeared in a collection of essays on the environment, *Forever the Land* (1950). Rettie wrote of the fictional planet of Copernicus, where the Copernicans have been photographing Earth in time-lapse photography for 757 million years, one photograph per year. His hypothesis was that the Copernicans were traveling to the United States to show their photos, in which the history of Earth becomes a movie, and the life of humans on Earth is shown as one very small but significant bleep on Earth's surface. The essay really has two messages: one containing factual information on soil erosion and the other outlining the destructive effect of human beings on Earth's environment.

1   Out beyond our solar system there is a planet called Copernicus. It came into existence some four or five billion years before the birth of our Earth. In due course of time it became inhabited by a race of intelligent men.

2   About 750 million years ago the Copernicans had developed the motion picture machine to a point well in advance of the stage that we have reached. Most of the cameras that we now use in motion picture work are geared to take twenty-four pictures per second on a continuous strip of film. When such film is run through a projector, it throws a series of images on the screen and these change with a rapidity that gives the visual impression of normal movement. If a motion is too swift for the human eye to see it in detail, it can be captured and artificially slowed down by means of the slow-motion camera. This one is geared to take many more shots per second—ninety-six or even more than that. When the slow-motion film is projected at the normal speed of twenty-four pictures per second, we can see just how the jumping horse goes over a hurdle.

3   What about motion that is too slow to be seen by the human eye? That problem has been solved by the use of the time-lapse camera. In this one, the shutter is geared to take only one shot per second, or one per minute, or even one per hour—depending upon the kind of movement that is being photographed. When the time-lapse film is projected at the normal speed of twenty-four pictures per second, it is possible to see a bean sprout growing up out of the ground. Time-lapse films are useful in the study of many types of motion too slow to be observed by the unaided, human eye.

4   The Copernicans, it seems, had time-lapse cameras some 757 million years ago and they also had superpowered telescopes that gave them a clear view of what was happening upon this Earth. They decided to make a film record of the life history of Earth and to make it on the scale of one picture per year. The photography has been in progress during the last 757 million years.

5   In the near future, a Copernican interstellar expedition will arrive upon our Earth and bring with it a copy of the time-lapse film. Arrangements will be made for showing the entire film in one continuous run. This will begin at midnight of New Year's Eve and continue day and night without a single stop until midnight of December 31. The rate of projection will be twenty-four pictures per second. Time on the screen will thus seem to move at the rate of twenty-four years per second; 1440 years per minute; 86,400 years per hour; approximately two million years per day; and sixty-two million years per month. The normal lifespan of individual man will occupy about three seconds. The full period of earth history that will be unfolded on the screen (some 757 million years) will extend from what the geologists call Precambrian times up to the present. This will, by no means, cover the full time-span of the earth's geological history but it will embrace the period since the advent of living organisms.

6   During the months of January, February, and March the picture will be desolate and dreary. The shape of the land masses and the oceans will bear little or no resemblance to those that we know. The violence of geological erosion will be much in evidence. Rains will pour down on the land and promptly go booming down to the seas. There will be no clear streams anywhere except where the rains fall upon hard rock. Everywhere on the steeper ground the stream channels will be filled with boulders hurled down by rushing waters. Raging torrents and dry stream beds will keep alternating in quick succession. High mountains will seem to melt like so much butter in the sun. The shifting of land into the seas, later to be thrust up as new mountains, will be going on at a grand scale.

7   Early in April there will be some indication of the presence of single-celled living organisms in some of the warmer and sheltered coastal waters. By the end of the month it will be noticed that some of these organisms have become multicellular. A few of them, including the Trilobites, will be encased in hard shells.

8   Toward the end of May, the first vertebrates will appear, but they will still be aquatic creatures. In June about 60 percent of the land area that we know as North America will be under water. One broad channel will occupy the space where the Rocky Mountains now stand. Great deposits of limestone will be forming under some of the shallower seas. Oil and gas deposits will be in process of formation—also under shallow seas. On land there will still be no sign of vegetation. Erosion will be rampant, tearing loose particles and

chunks of rock and grinding them into sand and silt to be spewed out by the streams into bays and estuaries.

9   About the middle of July the first land plants will appear and take up the tremendous job of soil building. Slowly, very slowly, the mat of vegetation will spread, always battling for its life against the power of erosion. Almost foot by foot, the plant life will advance, lacing down with its root structures whatever pulverized rock material it can find. Leaves and stems will be giving added protection against the loss of the soil foothold. The increasing vegetation will pave the way for the land animals that will live upon it.

10   Early in August the seas will be teeming with fish. This will be what geologists call the Devonian period. Some of the races of these fish will be breathing by means of lung tissue instead of through gill tissues. Before the month is over, some of the lung fish will go ashore and take on a crude lizardlike appearance. Here are the first amphibians.

11   In early September the insects will put in their appearance. Some will look like huge dragonflies and will have a wing spread of 24 inches. Large portions of the land masses will now be covered with heavy vegetation that will include the primitive spore-propagating trees. Layer upon layer of this plant growth will build up, later to appear as the coal deposits. About the middle of this month, there will be evidence of the first seed-bearing plants and the first reptiles. Heretofore, the land animals will have been amphibians that could reproduce their kind only by depositing a soft egg mass in quiet waters. The reptiles will be shown to be freed from the aquatic bond because they can reproduce by means of a shelled egg in which the embryo and its nurturing liquids are sealed and thus protected from destructive evaporation. Before September is over, the first dinosaurs will be seen—creatures destined to dominate the animal realm for about 140 million years and then to disappear.

12   In October there will be a series of mountain uplifts along what is now the eastern coast of the United States. A creature with feathered limbs—half bird and half reptile in appearance—will take itself into the air. Some small and rather unpretentious animals will be seen to bring forth their young in a form that is a miniature replica of the parents and to feed these young on milk secreted by mammary glands in the female parent. The emergence of this mammalian form of animal life will be recognized as one of the great events in geologic time. October will also witness the high

water mark of the dinosaurs—creatures ranging in size from that of the modern goat to monsters like Brontosaurus that weighed some 40 tons. Most of them will be placid vegetarians, but a few will be hideous-looking carnivores, like Allosaurus and Tyrannosaurus. Some of the herbivorous dinosaurs will be clad in bony armor for protection against their flesh-eating comrades.

13   November will bring pictures of a sea extending from the Gulf of Mexico to the Arctic in space now occupied by the Rocky Mountains. A few of the reptiles will take to the air on batlike wings. One of these, called Pteranodon, will have a wingspread of 15 feet. There will be a rapid development of the modern flowering plants, modern trees, and modern insects. The dinosaurs will disappear. Toward the end of the month there will be a tremendous land disturbance in which the Rocky Mountains will rise out of the sea to assume a dominating place in the North American landscape.

14   As the picture runs on into December it will show the mammals in command of the animal life. Seed-bearing trees and grasses will have covered most of the land with a heavy mantle of vegetation. Only the areas newly thrust up from the sea will be barren. Most of the streams will be crystal clear. The turmoil of geologic erosion will be confined to localized areas. About December 25 will begin the cutting of the Grand Canyon of the Colorado River. Grinding down through layer after layer of sedimentary strata, this stream will finally expose deposits laid down in Precambrian times. Thus in the walls of that canyon will appear geological formations dating from recent times to the period when the Earth had no living organisms upon it.

15   The picture will run on through the latter days of December and even up to its final day with still no sign of mankind. The spectators will become alarmed in the fear that man has somehow been left out. But not so; sometime about noon on December 31 (one million years ago) will appear a stooped, massive creature of manlike proportions. This will be Pithecanthropus, the Java ape man. For tools and weapons he will have nothing but crude stone and wooden clubs. His children will live a precarious existence threatened on the one side by hostile animals and on the other by tremendous climatic changes. Ice sheets—in places 4000 feet deep—will form in the northern parts of North America and Eurasia. Four times this glacial ice will push southward to cover half the continents. With each advance the plant and animal life will be swept under or pushed

southward. With each recession of the ice, life will struggle to reestablish itself in the wake of the retreating glaciers. The woolly mammoth, the musk ox, and the caribou all will fight to maintain themselves near the ice line. Sometimes they will be caught and put into cold storage—skin, flesh, blood, bones and all.

16   The picture will run on through supper time with still very little evidence of man's presence on the earth. It will be about 11 o'clock when Neanderthal man appears. Another half hour will go by before the appearance of Cro-Magnon man living in caves and painting crude animal pictures on the walls of his dwelling. Fifteen minutes more will bring Neolithic man, knowing how to chip stone and thus produce sharp cutting edges for spears and tools. In a few minutes more it will appear that man has domesticated the dog, the sheep, and, possibly, other animals. He will then begin the use of milk. He will also learn the arts of basket weaving and the making of pottery and dugout canoes.

17   The dawn of civilization will not come until about five or six minutes before the end of the picture. The story of the Egyptians, the Babylonians, the Greeks, and the Romans will unroll during the fourth, the third, and the second minute before the end. At 58 minutes and 43 seconds past 11:00 P.M. (just 1 minute and 17 seconds before the end) will come the beginning of the Christian era. Columbus will discover the New World 20 seconds before the end. The Declaration of Independence will be signed just 7 seconds before the final curtain comes down.

18   In those few moments of geologic time will be the story of all that has happened since we became a nation. And what a story it will be! A human swarm will sweep across the face of the continent and take it away from the . . . red men. They will change it far more radically than it has ever been changed before in a comparable time. The great virgin forests will be seen going down before ax and fire. The soil, covered for eons by its protective mantle of trees and grasses, will be laid bare to the ravages of water and wind erosion. Streams that had been flowing clear will, once again, take up a load of silt and push it toward the seas. Humus and mineral salts, both vital elements of productive soil, will be seen to vanish at a terrifying rate. The railroads and highways and cities that will spring up may divert attention, but they cannot cover up the blight of man's recent activities. In great sections of Asia, it will be seen that man must utilize cow dung and every scrap of available straw or grass for fuel to cook

his food. The forests that once provided wood for this purpose will be gone without a trace. The use of these agricultural wastes for fuel, in place of returning them to the land, will be leading to increasing soil impoverishment. Here and there will be seen a dust storm darkening the landscape over an area a thousand miles across. Man-creatures will be shown counting their wealth in terms of bits of printed paper representing other bits of a scarce but comparatively useless yellow metal that is kept buried in strong vaults. Meanwhile, the soil, the only real wealth that can keep mankind alive on the face of this earth is savagely being cut loose from its ancient moorings and washed into the seven seas.

19   We have just arrived upon this earth. How long will we stay?

The Moving Tides

RACHEL CARSON

Rachel Carson (1907–1964) was born in Springfield, Pennsylvania. She earned her A.B. at the Pennsylvania College for Women and her A.M. at Johns Hopkins University; she did additional graduate study at the Marine Biological Laboratory in Woods Hole, Massachusetts. She combined her deep and abiding interest in nature with a desire to write. Her first book, *Under the Sea-Wind: A Naturalist's Picture of Ocean Life* (1941), established her reputation, and *The Sea Around Us* (1950) confirmed it. Scientifically accurate but written in a fluent style, *The Sea Around Us* climbed to first place on the nonfiction bestseller lists, a rare feat for a scientific book. Carson's most famous work is *Silent Spring* (1962), a controversial book attacking the use of dangerous chemical fertilizers that destroy animals and birds and threaten to destroy humans. The book prompted President John F. Kennedy to launch an investigation that ultimately confirmed her findings and to set stricter controls on the indiscriminate use of pesticides.

"The Moving Tides" first appeared in *The Sea Around Us*. In it, Carson explains that the sun and moon, constantly changing, affect the tides in different places in different ways. As she explains it, the tides are a local matter "with astonishing differences occurring within a very short geographic distance." She explains that "heavenly bodies set the water in motion," but the depth of the tide is determined by topography—that is, the slope of the ocean floor, the width and depth of a bay, and other factors in the land mass. Carson also presents a catalog of special places where the tides create havoc in various ways.

In every country the moon keeps ever the rule of alliance with the sea which it once for all has agreed upon.

THE VENERABLE BEDE

1　　There is no drop of water in the ocean, not even in the deepest parts of the abyss, that does not know and respond to the mysterious forces that create the tide. No other force that affects the sea is so strong. Compared with the tide the wind-created waves are surface movements felt, at most, no more than a hundred fathoms below the surface. So, despite their impressive sweep, are the planetary currents, which seldom involve more than the upper several hundred fathoms. The masses of water affected by the tidal movement are enormous, as will be clear from one example. Into one small bay on the east coast of North America—Passamaquoddy—2 billion tons of water are carried by the tidal current twice each day; into the whole Bay of Fundy, 100 billion tons.

2　　Here and there we find dramatic illustration of the fact that the tides affect the whole ocean, from its surface to its floor. The meeting of opposing tidal currents in the Strait of Messina creates whirlpools (one of them is Charybdis of classical fame) which so deeply stirs the waters of the strait that fish bearing all the marks of abyssal existence, their eyes atrophied or abnormally large, their bodies studded with phosphorescent organs, frequently are cast up on the lighthouse beach, and the whole area yields a rich collection of deep-sea fauna for the Institute of Marine Biology at Messina.

3　　The tides are a response of the mobile waters of the ocean to the pull of the moon and the more distant sun. In theory, there is a gravitational attraction between every drop of sea water and even the outermost star of the universe. In practice, however, the pull of the remote stars is so slight as to be obliterated in the vaster move-

ments by which the ocean yields to the moon and the sun. Anyone
who has lived near tidewater knows that the moon, far more than
the sun, controls the tides. He has noticed that, just as the moon
rises later each day by fifty minutes, on the average, than the day
before, so, in most places, the time of high tide is correspondingly
later each day. And as the moon waxes and wanes in its monthly
cycle, so the height of the tide varies. Twice each month, when the
moon is a mere thread of silver in the sky, and again when it is full,
we have the strongest tidal movements—the highest flood tides and
the lowest ebb tides of the lunar month. These are called the spring
tides. At these times sun, moon, and earth are directly in line and
the pull of the two heavenly bodies is added together to bring the
water high on the beaches, and send its surf leaping upward against
the sea cliffs, and draw a brimming tide into the harbors so that the
boats float high beside their wharfs. And twice each month, at the
quarters of the moon, when sun, moon, and earth lie at the apexes
of a triangle, and the pull of sun and moon are opposed, we have the
moderate tidal movements called the neap tides. Then the difference
between high and low water is less than at any other time during
the month.

4   That the sun, with a mass 27 million times that of the moon,
should have less influence over the tides than a small satellite of the
earth is at first surprising. But in the mechanics of the universe,
nearness counts for more than distant mass, and when all the mathematical calculations have been made we find that the moon's power
over the tides is more than twice that of the sun.

5   The tides are enormously more complicated than all this would
suggest. The influence of sun and moon is constantly changing,
varying with the phases of the moon, with the distance of moon and
sun from the earth, and with the position of each to north or south
of the equator. They are complicated further by the fact that every
body of water, whether natural or artificial, has its own period of
oscillation. Disturb its waters and they will move with a seesaw or
rocking motion, with the most pronounced movement at the ends
of the container, the least motion at the center. Tidal scientists now
believe that the ocean contains a number of "basins," each with its
own period of oscillation determined by its length and depth. The
disturbance that sets the water in motion is the attracting force of
the moon and sun. But the kind of motion, that is, the period of
the swing of the water, depends upon the physical dimensions of the

basin. What this means in terms of actual tides we shall presently see.

6   The tides present a striking paradox, and the essence of it is this: the force that sets them in motion is cosmic, lying wholly outside the earth and presumably acting impartially on all parts of the globe, but the nature of the tide at any particular place is a local matter, with astonishing differences occurring within a very short geographic distance. When we spend a long summer holiday at the seashore we may become aware that the tide in our cove behaves very differently from that at a friend's place twenty miles up the coast, and is strikingly different from what we may have known in some other locality. If we are summering on Nantucket Island our boating and swimming will be little disturbed by the tides, for the range between high water and low is only about a foot or two. But if we choose to vacation near the upper part of the Bay of Fundy, we must accommodate ourselves to a rise and fall of 40 to 50 feet, although both places are included within the same body of water—the Gulf of Maine. Or if we spend our holiday on Chesapeake Bay we may find that the time of high water each day varies by as much as 12 hours in different places on the shores of the same bay.

7   The truth of the matter is that local topography is all-important in determining the features that to our minds make "the tide." The attractive force of the heavenly bodies sets the water in motion, but how, and how far, and how strongly it will rise depend on such things as the slope of the bottom, the depth of a channel, or the width of a bay's entrance.

8   The United States Coast and Geodetic Survey has a remarkable, robotlike machine with which it can predict the time and height of the tide on any past or future date, for any part of the world, on one essential condition. This is that at some time local observations must have been made to show how the topographic features of the place modify and direct the tidal movements.

9   Perhaps the most striking differences are in the range of tide, which varies tremendously in different parts of the world, so that what the inhabitants of one place might consider disastrously high water might be regarded as no tide at all by coastal communities only a hundred miles distant. The highest tides in the world occur in the Bay of Fundy, with a rise of about 50 feet in Minas Basin near the head of the Bay at the spring tides. At least half a dozen other places scattered around the world have a tidal range of more than

30 feet—Puerto Gallegos in Argentina and Cook Inlet in Alaska, Frobisher Bay in Davis Strait, the Koksoak River emptying into Hudson Strait, and the Bay of St. Malo in France come to mind. At many other places "high tide" may mean a rise of only a foot or so, perhaps only a few inches. The tides of Tahiti rise and fall in a gentle movement, with a difference of no more than a foot between high water and low. On most oceanic islands the range of the tide is slight. But it is never safe to generalize about the kinds of places that have high or low tides, because two areas that are not far apart may respond in very different ways to the tide-producing forces. At the Atlantic end of the Panama Canal the tidal range is not more than 1 or 2 feet, but at the Pacific end, only 40 miles away, the range is 12 to 16 feet. The Sea of Okhotsk is another example of the way the height of the tide varies. Throughout much of the Sea the tides are moderate—only about 2 feet—but in some parts of the Sea there is a 10-foot rise, and at the head of one of its arms—the Gulf of Penjinsk—the rise is 37 feet.

10   What is it about one place that will bring 40 or 50 feet of water rising about its shores, while at another place, lying under the same moon and sun, the tide will rise only a few inches? What, for example, can be the explanation of the great tides on the Bay of Fundy, while only a few hundred miles away at Nantucket Island, on the shores of the same ocean, the tide range is little more than a foot?

11   The modern theory of tidal oscillation seems to offer the best explanation of such local differences—the rocking up and down of water in each natural basin about a central, virtually tideless node. Nantucket is located near the node of its basin, where there is little motion, hence a small tide range. Passing northeastward along the shores of this basin, we find the tides becoming progressively higher, with a 6-foot range at Nauset Harbor on Cape Cod, 8.9 feet at Gloucester, 15.7 feet at West Quoddy Head, 20.9 feet at St. John, and 39.4 feet at Folly Point. The Nova Scotia shore of the Bay of Fundy has somewhat higher tides than the corresponding points on the New Brunswick shore, and the highest tides of all are in Minas Basin at the head of the Bay. The immense movements of water in the Bay of Fundy result from a combination of circumstances. The Bay lies at the end of an oscillating basin. Furthermore, the natural period of oscillation of the basin is approximately 12 hours. This very nearly coincides with the period of the ocean tide. Therefore the water movement within the bay is sustained and enormously

increased by the ocean tide. The narrowing and shallowing of the bay in its upper reaches, compelling the huge masses of water to crowd into a constantly diminishing area, also contribute to the great heights of the Fundy tides.

12 The tidal rhythms, as well as the range of tide, vary from ocean to ocean. Flood tide and ebb succeed each other around the world, as night follows day, but as to whether there shall be two high tides and two low in each lunar day, or only one, there is no unvarying rule. To those who know best the Atlantic Ocean—either its eastern or western shores—the rhythm of two high tides and two low tides in each day seems "normal." Here, on each flood tide, the water advances about as far as on the preceding high; and succeeding ebb tides fall about equally low. But in that great inland sea of the Atlantic, the Gulf of Mexico, a different rhythm prevails around most of its borders. At best the tidal rise here is but a slight movement, of no more than a foot or two. At certain places on the shores of the Gulf it is a long, deliberate undulation—one rise and one fall in the lunar day of 24 hours plus 50 minutes—resembling the untroubled breathing of that earth monster to whom the ancients attributed all tides. This "diurnal rhythm" is found in scattered places about the earth— such as at Saint Michael, Alaska, and at Do Son in French Indo-China—as well as in the Gulf of Mexico. By far the greater part of the world's coasts—most of the Pacific basin and the shores of the Indian Ocean—display a mixture of the diurnal and semidiurnal types of tides. There are two high and two low tides in a day, but the succeeding floods may be so unequal that the second scarcely rises to mean sea level; or it may be the ebb tides that are of extreme inequality.

13 There seems to be no simple explanation of why some parts of the ocean should respond to the pull of sun and moon with one rhythm and other parts with another, although the matter is perfectly clear to tidal scientists on the basis of mathematical calculations. To gain some inkling of the reasons, we must recall the many separate components of the tide-producing force, which in turn result from the changing relative positions of sun, moon, and earth. Depending on local geographic features, every part of earth and sea, while affected in some degree by each component, is more responsive to some than to others. Presumably the shape and depths of the Atlantic basin cause it to respond most strongly to the forces that produce a semidiurnal rhythm. The Pacific and Indian oceans, on the other hand, are

affected by both diurnal and semidiurnal forces, and a mixed tide results.

14   The island of Tahiti is a classic example of the way even a small area may react to one of the tide-producing forces to the virtual exclusion of the others. On Tahiti, it is sometimes said, you can tell the time of day by looking out at the beach and noticing the stage of the tide. This is not strictly true, but the legend has a certain basis. With slight variations, high tide occurs at noon and at midnight; low water, at six o'clock morning and evening. The tides thus ignore the effect of the moon, which is to advance the time of the tides by 50 minutes each day. Why should the tides of Tahiti follow the sun instead of the moon? The most favored explanation is that the island lies at the axis or node of one of the basins set in oscillation by the moon. There is very little motion in response to the moon at this point, and the waters are therefore free to move in the rhythm induced by the sun.

15   If the history of the earth's tides should one day be written by some observer of the universe, it would no doubt be said that they reached their greatest grandeur and power in the younger days of Earth, and that they slowly grew feebler and less imposing until one day they ceased to be. For the tides were not always as they are today, and as with all that is earthly, their days are numbered.

16   In the days when the earth was young, the coming in of the tide must have been a stupendous event. If the moon was, as we have supposed in an earlier chapter, formed by the tearing away of a part of the outer crust of the earth, it must have remained for a time very close to its parent. Its present position is the consequence of being pushed farther and farther away from the earth for some 2 billion years. When it was half its present distance from the earth, its power over the ocean tides was eight times as great as now, and the tidal range may even then have been several hundred feet on certain shores. But when the earth was only a few million years old, assuming that the deep ocean basins were then formed, the sweep of the tides must have been beyond all comprehension. Twice each day, the fury of the incoming waters would inundate all the margins of the continents. The range of the surf must have been enormously extended by the reach of the tides, so that the waves would batter the crests of high cliffs and sweep inland to erode the continents. The fury of such tides would contribute not a little to the general bleakness and grimness and uninhabitability of the young earth.

17   Under such conditions, no living thing could exist on the shores or pass beyond them, and, had conditions not changed, it is reasonable to suppose that life would have evolved no further than the fishes. But over the millions of years the moon has receded, driven away by the friction of the tide it creates. The very movement of the water over the bed of the ocean, over the shallow edges of the continents, and over the inland seas carries within itself the power that is slowly destroying the tides, for tidal friction is gradually slowing down the rotation of the earth. In those early days we have spoken of, it took the earth a much shorter time—perhaps only about 4 hours—to make a complete rotation on its axis. Since then, the spinning of the globe has been so greatly slowed that a rotation now requires, as everyone knows, about 24 hours. This retarding will continue, according to mathematicians, until the day is about 50 times as long as it is now.

18   And all the while the tidal friction will be exerting a second effect, pushing the moon farther away, just as it has already pushed it out more than 200,000 miles. (According to the laws of mechanics, as the rotation of the earth is retarded, that of the moon must be accelerated, and centrifugal force will carry it farther away.) As the moon recedes, it will, of course, have less power over the tides and they will grow weaker. It will also take the moon longer to complete its orbit around the earth. When finally the length of the day and of the month coincide, the moon will no longer rotate relatively to the earth, and there will be no lunar tides.

19   All this, of course, will require time on a scale the mind finds it difficult to conceive, and before it happens it is quite probable that the human race will have vanished from the earth. This may seem, then, like a Wellsian fantasy of a world so remote that we may dismiss it from our thoughts. But already, even in our allotted fraction of earthly time, we can see some of the effects of these cosmic processes. Our day is believed to be several seconds longer than that of Babylonian times. Britain's Astronomer Royal recently called the attention of the American Philosophical Society to the fact that the world will soon have to choose between two kinds of time. The tide-induced lengthening of the day has already complicated the problems of human systems of keeping time. Conventional clocks, geared to the earth's rotation, do not show the effect of the lengthening days. New atomic clocks now being constructed will show actual time and will differ from other clocks.

20   Although the tides have become tamer, and their range is now measured in tens instead of hundreds of feet, mariners are nevertheless greatly concerned not only with the stages of the tide and the set of the tidal currents, but with the many violent movements and disturbances of the sea that are indirectly related to the tides. Nothing the human mind has invented can tame a tide rip or control the rhythm of the water's ebb and flow, and the most modern instruments cannot carry a vessel over a shoal until the tide has brought a sufficient depth of water over it. Even the *Queen Mary* waits for slack water to come to her pier in New York; otherwise the set of the tidal current might swing her against the pier with enough force to crush it. On the Bay of Fundy, because of the great range of tide, harbor activities in some of the ports follow a pattern as rhythmic as the tides themselves, for vessels can come to the docks to take on or discharge cargo during only a few hours on each tide, leaving promptly to avoid being stranded in mud at low water.

21   In the confinement of narrow passages or when opposed by contrary winds and swells, the tidal currents often move with uncontrollable violence, creating some of the most dangerous waterways of the world. It is only necessary to read the Coast Pilots and Sailing Directions for various parts of the world to understand the menace of such tidal currents to navigation.

22   "Vessels around the Aleutians are in more danger from tidal currents than from any other cause, save the lack of surveys," says the postwar edition of the *Alaska Pilot*. Through Unalga and Akutan Passes, which are among the most-used routes for vessels entering Bering Sea from the Pacific, strong tidal currents pour, making their force felt well offshore and setting vessels unexpectedly against the rocks. Through Akun Strait the flood tide has the velocity of a mountain torrent, with dangerous swirls and overfalls. In each of these passes the tide will raise heavy, choppy seas if opposed by wind or swells. "Vessels must be prepared to take seas aboard," warns the *Pilot*, for a 15-foot wave of a tide rip may suddenly rise and sweep across a vessel, and more than one man has been carried off to his death in this way.

23   On the opposite side of the world, the tide setting eastward from the open Atlantic presses between the islands of the Shetlands and Orkneys into the North Sea, and on the ebb returns through the same narrow passages. At certain stages of the tide these waters are dotted with dangerous eddies, with strange upward domings, or with

sinister pits or depressions. Even in calm weather boats are warned to avoid the eddies of Pentland Firth, which are known as the Swilkie; and with an ebb tide and a northwest wind the heavy breaking seas of the Swilkie are a menace to vessels "which few, having once experienced, would be rash enough to encounter a second time."

24 Edgar Allan Poe, in his "Descent into the Maelstrom," converted one of the more evil manifestations of the tide into literature. Few who have read the story will forget its drama—how the old man led his companion to a mountain cliff high above the sea and let him watch the water far below in the narrow passageway between the islands, with its sinister foam and scum, its uneasy bubbling and boiling, until suddenly the whirlpool was formed before his eyes and rushed with an appalling sound through the narrow waterway. Then the old man told the story of his own descent into the whirlpool and of his miraculous escape. Most of us have wondered how much of the story was fact, how much the creation of Poe's fertile imagination. There actually is a Maelstrom and it exists where Poe placed it, between two of the islands of the Lofoten group off the west coast of Norway. It is, as he described it, a gigantic whirlpool or series of whirlpools, and men with their boats have actually been drawn down into these spinning funnels of water. Although Poe's account exaggerates certain details, the essential facts on which he based his narrative are verified in the *Sailing Directions for the Northwest and North Coasts of Norway,* a practical and circumstantial document:

25 "Though rumor has greatly exaggerated the importance of the Malström, or more properly Moskenstraumen, which runs between Mosken and Lofotodden, it is still the most dangerous tideway in Lofoten, its violence being due, in great measure, to the irregularity of the ground . . . As the strength of the tide increases the sea becomes heavier and the current more irregular, forming extensive eddies or whirlpools (Malström). During such periods no vessel should enter the Moskenstraumen.

26 "These whirlpools are cavities in the form of an inverted bell, wide and rounded at the mouth and narrowed toward the bottom; they are largest when first formed and are carried along with the current, diminishing gradually until they disappear; before the extinction of one, two or three more will appear, following each other like so many pits in the sea . . . Fishermen affirm that if they are aware of their approach to a whirlpool and have time to throw an oar or any other bulky body into it they will get over it safely; the reason

is that when the continuity is broken and the whirling motion of the sea interrupted by something thrown into it the water must rush suddenly in on all sides and fill up the cavity. For the same reason, in strong breezes, when the waves break, though there may be a whirling round, there can be no cavity. In the Maltström boats and men have been drawn down by these vortices, and much loss of life has resulted."

27   Among unusual creations of the tide, perhaps the best known are the bores. The world possesses half a dozen or more famous ones. A bore is created when a great part of the flood tide enters a river as a single wave, or at most two or three waves, with a steep and high front. The conditions that produce bores are several: there must be a considerable range of tide, combined with sand bars or other obstructions in the mouth of the river, so that the tide is hindered and held back, until it finally gathers itself together and rushes through. The Amazon is remarkable for the distance its bore travels upstream—some 200 miles—with the result that the bores of as many as five flood tides may actually be moving up the river at one time.

28   On the Tsientang River, which empties into the China Sea, all shipping is controlled by the bore—the largest, most dangerous, and best known in the world. The ancient Chinese used to throw offerings into the river to appease the angry spirit of this bore, whose size and fury appear to have varied from century to century, or perhaps even from decade to decade, as the silting of the estuary has shifted and changed. During most of the month the bore now advances up river in a wave 8 to 11 feet high, moving at a speed of 12 or 13 knots, its front "a sloping cascade of bubbling foam, falling forward and pounding on itself and on the river." Its full ferocity is reserved for the spring tides of the full moon and the new moon, at which times the crest of the advancing wave is said to rise 25 feet above the surface of the river.

29   There are bores, though none so spectacular, in North America. There is one at Moncton, on New Brunswick's Petitcodiac River, but it is impressive only on the spring tides of the full or new moon. At Turnagain Arm in Cook Inlet, Alaska, where the tides are high and the currents strong, the flood tide under certain conditions comes in as a bore. Its advancing front may be four to six feet high and is recognized as being so dangerous to small craft that boats are beached well above the level of the flats when the bore is approaching.

It can be heard about half an hour before its arrival at any point, traveling slowly with a sound as of breakers on a beach.

30   The influence of the tide over the affairs of sea creatures as well as men may be seen all over the world. The billions upon billions of sessile animals, like oysters, mussels, and barnacles, owe their very existence to the sweep of the tides, which brings them the food which they are unable to go in search of. By marvelous adaptations of form and structure, the inhabitants of the world between the tide lines are enabled to live in a zone where the danger of being dried up is matched against the danger of being washed away, where for every enemy that comes by sea there is another that comes by land, and where the most delicate of living tissues must somehow withstand the assault of storm waves that have power to shift tons of rock or to crack the hardest granite.

31   The most curious and incredibly delicate adaptations, however, are the ones by which the breeding rhythm of certain marine animals is timed to coincide with phases of the moon and the stages of the tide. In Europe it has been well established that the spawning activities of oysters reach their peak on the spring tides, which are about two days after the full or the new moon. In the waters of northern Africa there is a sea urchin that, on the nights when the moon is full and apparently only then, releases its reproductive cells into the sea. And in tropical waters in many parts of the world there are small marine worms whose spawning behavior is so precisely adjusted to the tidal calendar that, merely from observing them, one could tell the month, the day, and often the time of day as well.

32   Near Samoa in the Pacific, the palolo worm lives out its life on the bottom of the shallow sea, in holes in the rocks and among the masses of corals. Twice each year, during the neap tides of the moon's last quarter in October and November, the worms forsake their burrows and rise to the surface in swarms that cover the water. For this purpose, each worm has literally broken its body in two, half to remain in its rock tunnel, half to carry the reproductive products to the surface and there to liberate the cells. This happens at dawn on the day before the moon reaches its last quarter, and again on the following day; on the second day of the spawning the quantity of eggs liberated is so great that the sea is discolored.

33   The Fijians, whose waters have a similar worm, call them "Mbalolo" and have designated the periods of their spawning "Mbalolo lailai" (little) for October and "Mbalolo levu" (large) for November.

Similar forms near the Gilbert Islands respond to certain phases of the moon in June and July; in the Malay Archipelago a related worm swarms at the surface on the second and third night after the full moon of March and April, when the tides are running highest. A Japanese palolo swarms after the new moon and again after the full moon in October and November.

34   Concerning each of these, the question recurs but remains unanswered: is it the state of the tides that in some unknown way supplies the impulse from which springs this behavior, or is it, even more mysteriously, some other influence of the moon? It is easier to imagine that it is the press and the rhythmic movement of the water that in some way brings about this response. But why is it only certain tides of the year, and why for some species is it the fullest tides of the month and for others the least movements of the waters that are related to the perpetuation of the race? At present, no one can answer.

35   No other creature displays so exquisite an adaptation to the tidal rhythm as the grunion—a small, shimmering fish about as long as a man's hand. Through no one can say what processes of adaptation, extending over no one knows how many millennia, the grunion has come to know not only the daily rhythm of the tides, but the monthly cycle by which certain tides sweep higher on the beaches than others. It has so adapted its spawning habits to the tidal cycle that the very existence of the race depends on the precision of this adjustment.

36   Shortly after the full moon of the months from March to August, the grunion appear in the surf on the beaches of California. The tide reaches flood stage, slackens, hesitates, and begins to ebb. Now on these waves of the ebbing tide the fish begin to come in. Their bodies shimmer in the light of the moon as they are borne up the beach on the crest of a wave, they lie glittering on the wet sand for a perceptible moment of time, then fling themselves into the wash of the next wave and are carried back to sea. For about an hour after the turn of the tide this continues, thousands upon thousands of grunion coming up onto the beach, leaving the water, returning to it. This is the spawning act of the species.

37   During the brief interval between successive waves, the male and female have come together in the wet sand, the one to shed her eggs, the other to fertilize them. When the parent fish return to the

water, they have left behind a mass of eggs buried in the sand. Succeeding waves on that night do not wash out the eggs because the tide is already ebbing. The waves of the next high tide will not reach them, because for a time after the full of the moon each tide will halt its advance a little lower on the beach than the preceding one. The eggs, then, will be undisturbed for at least a fortnight. In the warm, damp, incubating sand they undergo their development. Within two weeks the magic change from fertilized eggs to larval fishlet is completed, the perfectly formed little grunion still confined within the membranes of the egg, still buried in the sand, waiting for release. With the tides of the new moon it comes. Their waves wash over the places where the little masses of the grunion eggs were buried, the swirl and rush of the surf stirring the sand deeply. As the sand is washed away, and the eggs feel the touch of the cool sea water, the membranes rupture, the fishlets hatch, and the waves that released them bear them away to the sea.

38   But the link between tide and living creature I like best to remember is that of a very small worm, flat of body, with no distinction of appearance, but with one unforgettable quality. The name of this worm is *Convoluta roscoffensis* and it lives on the sandy beaches of northern Brittany and the Channel Islands. Convoluta has entered into a remarkable partnership with a green alga, whose cells inhabit the body of the worm and lend to its tissues their own green color. The worm lives entirely on the starchy products manufactured by its plant guest, having become so completely dependent upon this means of nutrition that its digestive organs have degenerated. In order that the algal cells may carry on their function of photosynthesis (which is dependent upon sunlight) Convoluta rises from the damp sands of the intertidal zone as soon as the tide has ebbed, the sand becoming spotted with large green patches composed of thousands of the worms. For the several hours while the tide is out, the worms lie thus in the sun, and the plants manufacture their starches and sugars; but when the tide returns, the worms must again sink into the sand to avoid being washed away, out into deep water. So the whole lifetime of the worm is a succession of movements conditioned by the stages of the tide—upward into sunshine on the ebb, downward on the flood.

39   What I find most unforgettable about Convoluta is this: sometimes it happens that a marine biologist, wishing to study some related problem, will transfer a whole colony of the worms into the labora-

tory, there to establish them in an aquarium, where there are no tides. But twice each day Convoluta rises out of the sand on the bottom of the aquarium, into the light of the sun. And twice each day it sinks again into the sand. Without a brain, or what we would call a memory, or even any very clear perception, Convoluta continues to live out its life in this alien place, remembering, in every fiber of its small green body, the tidal rhythm of the distant sea.

The Bird and the Machine

LOREN EISELEY

Loren Eiseley (1907–1977) was born in Lincoln, Nebraska. He attended the University of Nebraska, where he developed a deep and abiding interest in both anthropology and writing. He contributed essays to numerous magazines. His primary work, however, was in anthropology at the University of Pennsylvania, where he served as professor and provost for many years. A Guggenheim Foundation Fellow, he sponsored various anthropological expeditions for several universities and for the Smithsonian Institute.

He earned his reputation as a writer in 1957 with the publication of *The Immense Journey*, a collection of his essays about evolution. He also wrote *Darwin's Century* (1958), *The Firmament of Time* (1960), *The Unexpected Universe* (1969), and *The Night Country* (1971).

"The Bird and the Machine" appeared in *The Immense Journey*. Here Eiseley speculates as he reads a *New York Times* piece in which some journalists report that machines are getting smarter and smarter. He meditates on the human body as a machine and the individual cell as a machine. But he knows from experience that life, throbbing and robust, cannot be duplicated by a machine. He then tells a story about his capture of a sparrow hawk and his subsequent release of the hawk so that it could rejoin its mate. Thereafter, it could "cry out with joy" and "dance in the air with the fierce passion of a bird."

1   I suppose their little bones have years ago been lost among the stones and winds of those high glacial pastures. I suppose their feathers blew eventually into the piles of tumbleweed beneath the straggling cattle fences and rotted there in the mountain snows, along with dead steers and all the other things that drift to an end in the corners of the wire. I do not quite know why I should be thinking of birds over the *New York Times* at breakfast, particularly the birds of my youth half a continent away. It is a funny thing what the brain will do with memories and how it will treasure them and finally bring them into odd juxtapositions with other things, as though it wanted to make a design, or get some meaning out of them, whether you want it or not, or even see it.

2   It used to seem marvelous to me, but I read now that there are machines that can do these things in a small way, machines that can crawl about like animals, and that it may not be long now until they do more things—maybe even make themselves—I saw that piece in the *Times* just now. And then they will, maybe—well, who knows—but you read about it more and more with no one making any protest, and already they can add better than we and reach up and hear things through the dark and finger the guns over the night sky.

3   This is the new world that I read about at breakfast. This is the world that confronts me in my biological books and journals, until there are times when I sit quietly in my chair and try to hear the little purr of the cogs in my head and the tubes flaring and dying as the messages go through them and the circuits snap shut or open. This is the great age, make no mistake about it; the robot has been born somewhat appropriately along with the atom bomb, and the brain they say now is just another type of more complicated feedback system. The engineers have its basic principles worked out; it's mechanical, you know; nothing to get superstitious about; and man can always improve on nature once he gets the idea. Well, he's got it all right and that's why, I guess, that I sit here in my chair, with the article crunched in my hand, remembering those two birds and

that blue mountain sunlight. There is another magazine article on my desk that reads "Machines Are Getting Smarter Every Day." I don't deny it, but I'll still stick with the birds. It's life I believe in, not machines.

4   Maybe you don't believe there is any difference. A skeleton is all joints and pulleys, I'll admit. And when man was in his simpler stages of machine building in the eighteenth century, he quickly saw the resemblances. "What," wrote Hobbes, "is the heart but a spring, and the nerves but so many strings, and the joints but so many wheels, giving motion to the whole body?" Tinkering about in their shops it was inevitable in the end that men would see the world as a huge machine "subdivided into an infinite number of lesser machines."

5   The idea took on with a vengeance. Little automatons toured the country—dolls controlled by clockwork. Clocks described as little worlds were taken on tours by their designers. They were made up of moving figures, shifting scenes and other remarkable devices. The life of the cell was unknown. Man, whether he was conceived as possessing a soul or not, moved and jerked about like these tiny puppets. A human being thought of himself in terms of his own tools and implements. He had been fashioned like the puppets he produced and was only a more clever model made by a greater designer.

6   Then in the nineteenth century, the cell was discovered, and the single machine in its turn was found to be the product of millions of infinitesimal machines—the cells. Now, finally, the cell itself dissolves away into an abstract chemical machine—and that into some intangible, inexpressible flow of energy. The secret seems to lurk all about, the wheels get smaller and smaller, and they turn more rapidly, but when you try to seize it the life is gone—and so, by popular definition, some would say that life was never there in the first place. The wheels and the cogs are the secret and we can make them better in time—machines that will run faster and more accurately than real mice to real cheese.

7   I have no doubt it can be done, though a mouse harvesting seeds on an autumn thistle is to me a fine sight and more complicated, I think, in his multiform activity, than a machine "mouse" running a maze. Also, I like to think of the possible shape of the future brooding in mice, just as it brooded once in a rather ordinary mousy insectivore who became a man. It leaves a nice fine indeterminate sense of

wonder that even an electronic brain hasn't got, because you know perfectly well that if the electronic brain changes, it will be because of something man has done to it. But what man will do to himself he doesn't really know. A certain scale of time and a ghostly intangible thing called change are ticking in him. Powers and potentialities like the oak in the seed, or a red and awful ruin. Either way, it's impressive; and the mouse has it, too. Or those birds, I'll never forget those birds—yet before I measured their significance, I learned the lesson of time first of all. I was young then and left alone in a great desert—part of an expedition that had scattered its men over several hundred miles in order to carry on research more effectively. I learned there that time is a series of planes existing superficially in the same universe. The tempo is a human illusion, a subjective clock ticking in our own kind of protoplasm.

8   As the long months passed, I began to live on the slower planes and to observe more readily what passed for life there. I sauntered, I passed more and more slowly up and down the canyons in the dry baking heat of midsummer. I slumbered for long hours in the shade of huge brown boulders that had gathered in tilted companies out on the flats. I had forgotten the world of men and the world had forgotten me. Now and then I found a skull in the canyons, and these justified my remaining there. I took a serene cold interest in these discoveries. I had come, like many a naturalist before me, to view life with a wary and subdued attention. I had grown to take pleasure in the divested bone.

9   I sat once on a high ridge that fell away before me into a waste of sand dunes. I sat through hours of a long afternoon. Finally, as I glanced beside my boot an indistinct configuration caught my eye. It was a coiled rattlesnake, a big one. How long he had sat with me I do not know. I had not frightened him. We were both locked in the sleep-walking tempo of the earlier world, baking in the same high air and sunshine. Perhaps he had been there when I came. He slept on as I left, his coils, so ill discerned by me, dissolving once more among the stones and gravel from which I had barely made him out.

10   Another time I got on a higher ridge, among some tough little wind-warped pines half covered over with sand in a basin-like depression that caught everything carried by the air up to those heights. There were a few thin bones of birds, some cracked shells of indeter-

minable age, and the knotty fingers of pine roots bulged out of shape from their long and agonizing grasp upon the crevices of the rock. I lay under the pines in the sparse shade and went to sleep once more.

11   It grew cold finally, for autumn was in the air by then, and the few things that lived thereabouts were sinking down into an even chillier scale of time. In the moments between sleeping and waking I saw the roots about me and slowly, slowly, a foot in what seemed many centuries, I moved my sleep-stiffened hands over the scaling bark and lifted my numbed face after the vanishing sun. I was a great awkward thing of knots and aching limbs, trapped up there in some long, patient endurance that involved the necessity of putting living fingers into rock and by slow, aching expansion bursting those rocks asunder. I suppose, so thin and slow was the time of my pulse by then, that I might have stayed on to drift still deeper into the lower cadences of the frost, or the crystalline life that glisters in pebbles, or shines in a snowflake, or dreams in the meteoric iron between the worlds.

12   It was a dim descent, but time was present in it. Somewhere far down in that scale the notion struck me that one might come the other way. Not many months thereafter I joined some colleagues heading higher into a remote windy tableland where huge bones were reputed to protrude like boulders from the turf. I had drowsed with reptiles and moved with the century-long pulse of trees; now, lethargically, I was climbing back up some invisible ladder of quickening hours. There had been talk of birds in connection with my duties. Birds are intense, fast-living creatures—reptiles, I suppose one might say, that have escaped out of the heavy sleep of time, transformed fairy creatures dancing over sunlit meadows. It is a youthful fancy, no doubt, but because of something that happened up there among the escarpments of that range, it remains with me a lifelong impression. I can never bear to see a bird imprisoned.

13   We came into that valley through the trailing mists of a spring night. It was a place that looked as though it might never have known the foot of man, but our scouts had been ahead of us and we knew all about the abandoned cabin of stone that lay far up on one hillside. It had been built in the land rush of the last century and then lost to the cattlemen again as the marginal soils failed to take the plow.

14   There were spots like this all over that country. Lost graves marked by unlettered stones and old corroding rim-fire cartridge cases lying

where somebody had made a stand among the boulders that rimmed the valley. They are all that remain of the range wars; the men are under the stones now. I could see our cavalcade winding in and out through the mist below us: torches, the reflection of the truck lights on our collecting tins, and the far-off bumping of a loose dinosaur thigh bone in the bottom of a trailer. I stood on a rock a moment looking down and thinking what it cost in money and equipment to capture the past.

15   We had, in addition, instructions to lay hands on the present. The word had come through to get them alive—birds, reptiles, anything. A zoo somewhere abroad needed restocking. It was one of those reciprocal matters in which science involves itself. Maybe our museum needed a stray ostrich egg and this was the payoff. Anyhow, my job was to help capture some birds and that was why I was there before the trucks.

16   The cabin had not been occupied for years. We intended to clean it out and live in it, but there were holes in the roof and the birds had come in and were roosting in the rafters. You could depend on it in a place like this where everything blew away, and even a bird needed some place out of the weather and away from coyotes. A cabin going back to nature in a wild place draws them till they come in, listening at the eaves, I imagine, pecking softly among the shingles till they find a hole and then suddenly the place is theirs and man is forgotten.

17   Sometimes of late years I find myself thinking the most beautiful sight in the world might be the birds taking over New York after the last man has run away to the hills. I will never live to see it, of course, but I know just how it will sound because I've lived up high and I know the sort of watch birds keep on us. I've listened to sparrows tapping tentatively on the outside of air conditioners when they thought no one was listening, and I know how other birds test the vibrations that come up to them through the television aerials.

18   "Is he gone?" they ask, and the vibrations come up from below, "Not yet, not yet."

19   Well, to come back, I got the door open softly and I had the spotlight all ready to turn on and blind whatever birds there were so they couldn't see to get out through the roof. I had a short piece of ladder to put against the far wall where there was a shelf on which I expected to make the biggest haul. I had all the information I

needed just like any skilled assassin. I pushed the door open, the hinges squeaking only a little. A bird or two stirred—I could hear them—but nothing flew and there was a faint starlight through the holes in the roof.

20　　I padded across the floor, got the ladder up and the light ready, and slithered up the ladder till my head and arms were over the shelf. Everything was dark as pitch except for the starlight at the little place back of the shelf near the eaves. With the light to blind them, they'd never make it. I had them. I reached my arm carefully over in order to be ready to seize whatever was there and I put the flash on the edge of the shelf where it would stand by itself when I turned it on. That way I'd be able to use both hands.

21　　Everything worked perfectly except for one detail—I didn't know what kind of birds were there. I never thought about it at all, and it wouldn't have mattered if I had. My orders were to get something interesting. I snapped on the flash and sure enough there was a great beating and feathers flying, but instead of my having them, they, or rather he, had me. He had my hand, that is, and for a small hawk not much bigger than my fist he was doing all right. I heard him give one short metallic cry when the light went on and my hand descended on the bird beside him; after that he was busy with his claws and his beak was sunk in my thumb. In the struggle I knocked the lamp over on the shelf, and his mate got her sight back and whisked neatly through the hole in the roof and off among the stars outside. It all happened in fifteen seconds and you might think I would have fallen down the ladder, but no, I had a professional assassin's reputation to keep up, and the bird, of course, made the mistake of thinking the hand was the enemy and not the eyes behind it. He chewed my thumb up pretty effectively and lacerated my hand with his claws, but in the end I got him, having two hands to work with.

22　　He was a sparrow hawk and a fine young male in the prime of life. I was sorry not to catch the pair of them, but as I dripped blood and folded his wings carefully, holding him by the back so that he couldn't strike again, I had to admit the two of them might have been more than I could have handled under the circumstances. The little fellow had saved his mate by diverting me, and that was that. He was born to it, and made no outcry now, resting in my hand hopelessly, but peering toward me in the shadows behind the lamp with a fierce, almost indifferent glance. He neither gave nor expected mercy and something out of the high air passed from him to me, stirring a faint embarrassment.

23   I quit looking into that eye and managed to get my huge carcass with its fist full of prey back down the ladder. I put the bird in a box too small to allow him to injure himself by struggle and walked out to welcome the arriving trucks. It had been a long day, and camp still to make in the darkness. In the morning that bird would be just another episode. He would go back with the bones in the truck to a small cage in a city where he would spend the rest of his life. And a good thing, too. I sucked my aching thumb and spat out some blood. An assassin has to get used to these things. I had a professional reputation to keep up.

24   In the morning, with the change that comes on suddenly in that high country, the mist that had hovered below us in the valley was gone. The sky was a deep blue, and one could see for miles over the high outcroppings of stone. I was up early and brought the box in which the little hawk was imprisoned out onto the grass where I was building a cage. A wind as cool as a mountain spring ran over the grass and stirred my hair. It was a fine day to be alive. I looked up and all around and at the hole in the cabin roof out of which the other little hawk had fled. There was no sign of her anywhere that I could see.

25   "Probably in the next county by now," I thought cynically, but before beginning work I decided I'd have a look at my last night's capture.

26   Secretively, I looked again all around the camp and up and down and opened the box. I got him right out in my hand with his wings folded properly and I was careful not to startle him. He lay limp in my grasp and I could feel his heart pound under the feathers but he only looked beyond me and up.

27   I saw him look that last look away beyond me into a sky so full of light that I could not follow his gaze. The little breeze flowed over me again, and nearby a mountain aspen shook all its tiny leaves. I suppose I must have had an idea then of what I was going to do, but I never let it come up into consciousness. I just reached over and laid the hawk on the grass.

28   He lay there a long minute without hope, unmoving, his eyes still fixed on the blue vault above him. It must have been that he was already so far away in heart that he never felt the release from my

hand. He never even stood. He just lay with his breast against the grass.

29   In the next second after that long minute he was gone. Like a flicker of light, he had vanished with my eyes full on him, but without actually seeing even a premonitory wing beat. He was gone straight into that towering emptiness of light and crystal that my eyes could scarcely bear to penetrate. For another long moment there was silence. I could not see him. The light was too intense. Then from far up somewhere a cry came ringing down.

30   I was young then and had seen little of the world, but when I heard that cry my heart turned over. It was not the cry of the hawk I had captured; for, by shifting my position against the sun, I was now seeing further up. Straight out of the sun's eye, where she must have been soaring restlessly above us for untold hours, hurtled his mate. And from far up, ringing from peak to peak of the summits over us, came a cry of such unutterable and ecstatic joy that it sounds down across the years and tingles among the cups on my quiet breakfast table.

31   I saw them both now. He was rising fast to meet her. They met in a great soaring gyre that turned to a whirling circle and a dance of wings. Once more, just once, their two voices, joined in a harsh wild medley of question and response, struck and echoed against the pinnacles of the valley. Then they were gone forever somewhere into those upper regions beyond the eyes of men.

32   I am older now, and sleep less, and have seen most of what there is to see and am not very much impressed any more, I suppose, by anything. "What Next in the Attributes of Machines?" my morning headline runs. "It Might Be the Power to Reproduce Themselves."

33   I lay the paper down and across my mind a phrase floats insinuatingly: "It does not seem that there is anything in the construction, constituents, or behavior of the human being which it is essentially impossible for science to duplicate and synthesize. On the other hand . . ."

34   All over the city the cogs in the hard, bright mechanisms have begun to turn. Figures move through computers, names are spelled out, a thoughtful machine selects the fingerprints of a wanted criminal from an array of thousands. In the laboratory an electronic mouse runs swiftly through a maze toward the cheese it can neither taste nor enjoy. On the second run it does better than a living mouse.

35   "On the other hand . . ." Ah, my mind takes up, on the other
       hand the machine does not bleed, ache, hang for hours in the empty
       sky in a torment of hope to learn the fate of another machine, nor
       does it cry out with joy nor dance in the air with the fierce passion
       of a bird. Far off, over a distance greater than space, that remote cry
       from the heart of heaven makes a faint buzzing among my breakfast
       dishes and passes on and away.

The Long Habit

LEWIS
THOMAS

Lewis Thomas, who was born in 1913, is a physician, professor, and award-winning essayist. He taught medicine at the University of Minnesota, served as dean of the Yale Medical School, and now serves as chancellor of the Memorial Sloan-Kettering Cancer Center. In 1970, he began contributing a column to the *New England Journal of Medicine* entitled "Notes of a Biology Watcher." These essays examined scientific topics, but they were couched in the language of the humanities. Thomas makes highly personal explorations of biological and sociological issues in a graceful, relaxed style.

"The Long Habit" first appeared in the *New England Journal of Medicine* and was reprinted in a collection of Thomas's essays entitled *The Lives of the Cell*. In this essay, Thomas offers the plaintive cry that living "has become an addiction" to the point that the approach of death has become "unmentionable" and "unthinkable." However, he argues the scientific fact that aging and dying are natural processes coordinated and integrated into the physiologic procedures of the human body. Here we have the classic conflict of the scientist and humanist; one side of Thomas argues the biological facts and the other side wonders how to account for "that permanent vanishing of consciousness."

1   We continue to share with our remotest ancestors the most tangled and evasive attitudes about death, despite the great distance we have come in understanding some of the profound aspects of biology. We have as much distaste for talking about personal death as for thinking about it; it is an indelicacy, like talking in mixed company about venereal disease or abortion in the old days. Death on a grand scale does not bother us in the same special way: we can sit around a dinner table and discuss war, involving 60 million volatilized human deaths, as though we were talking about bad weather; we can watch abrupt bloody death every day, in color, on films and television, without blinking back a tear. It is when the numbers of dead are very small, and very close, that we begin to think in scurrying circles. At the very center of the problem is the naked cold deadness of one's own self, the only reality in nature of which we can have absolute certainty, and it is unmentionable, unthinkable. We may be even less willing to face the issue at first hand than our predecessors because of a secret new hope that maybe it will go away. We like to think, hiding the thought, that with all the marvelous ways in which we seem now to lead nature around by the nose, perhaps we can avoid the central problem if we just become, next year, say, a bit smarter.

2   "The long habit of living," said Thomas Browne, "indisposeth us to dying." These days, the habit has become an addiction: we are hooked on living; the tenacity of its grip on us, and ours on it, grows in intensity. We cannot think of giving it up, even when living loses its zest—even when we have lost the zest for zest.

3   We have come a long way in our technologic capacity to put death off, and it is imaginable that we might learn to stall it for even longer periods, perhaps matching the life-spans of the Abkhasian Russians, who are said to go on, springily, for a century and a half. If we can rid ourselves of some of our chronic, degenerative diseases, and cancer, strokes, and coronaries, we might go on and on. It sounds attractive and reasonable, but it is no certainty. If we became free of disease, we would make a much better run of it for the last decade or so, but might still terminate on about the same schedule as now. We may be like the genetically different lines of mice, or like Hayflick's different tissue-culture lines, programmed to die after a predeter-mined number of days, clocked by their genomes. If this is the way it is, some of us will continue to wear out and come unhinged in the sixth decade, and some much later, depending on genetic timetables.

4   If we ever do achieve freedom from most of today's diseases, or even complete freedom from disease, we will perhaps terminate by drying out and blowing away on a light breeze, but we will still die.

5   Most of my friends do not like this way of looking at it. They prefer to take it for granted that we only die because we get sick, with one lethal ailment or another, and if we did not have our diseases we might go on indefinitely. Even biologists choose to think this about themselves, despite the evidences of the absolute inevitability of death that surround their professional lives. Everything dies, all around, trees, plankton, lichens, mice, whales, flies, mitochondria. In the simplest creatures it is sometimes difficult to see it as death, since the strands of replicating DNA they leave behind are more conspicuously the living parts of themselves than with us (not that it is fundamentally any different, but it seems so). Flies do not develop a ward round of diseases that carry them off, one by one. They simply age, and die like flies.

6   We hanker to go on, even in the face of plain evidence that long, long lives are not necessarily pleasurable in the kind of society we have arranged thus far. We will be lucky if we can postpone the search for new technologies for a while, until we have discovered some satisfactory things to do with the extra time. Something will surely have to be found to take the place of sitting on the porch re-examining one's watch.

7   Perhaps we would not be so anxious to prolong life if we did not detest so much the sickness of withdrawal. It is astonishing how little information we have about this universal process, with all the other dazzling advances in biology. It is almost as though we wanted not to know about it. Even if we could imagine the act of death in isolation, without any preliminary stage of being struck down by disease, we would be fearful of it.

8   There are signs that medicine may be taking a new interest in the process, partly from curiosity, partly from an embarrassed realization that we have not been handling this aspect of disease with as much skill as physicians once displayed, back in the days before they became convinced that disease was their solitary and sometimes defeatable enemy. It used to be the hardest and most important of all the services of a good doctor to be on hand at the time of death and to provide comfort, usually in the home. Now it is done in hospitals, in secrecy (one of the reasons for the increased fear of death these days may be that so many people are totally unfamiliar with it; they

never actually see it happen in real life). Some of our technology permits us to deny its existence, and we maintain flickers of life for long stretches in one community of cells or another, as though we were keeping a flag flying. Death is not a sudden-all-at-once affair; cells go down in sequence, one by one. You can, if you like, recover great numbers of them many hours after the lights have gone out, and grow them out in cultures. It takes hours, even days, before the irreversible word finally gets around to all the provinces.

9   We may be about to rediscover that dying is not such a bad thing to do after all. Sir William Osler took this view: he disapproved of people who spoke of the agony of death, maintaining that there was no such thing.

10   In a nineteenth-century memoir on an expedition in Africa, there is a story by David Livingston about his own experience of near-death. He was caught by a lion, crushed across the chest in the animal's great jaws, and saved in the instant by a lucky shot from a friend. Later, he remembered the episode in clear detail. He was so amazed by the extraordinary sense of peace, calm, and total pain-lessness associated with being killed that he constructed a theory that all creatures are provided with a protective physiologic mechanism, switched on at the verge of death, carrying them through in a haze of tranquillity.

11   I have seen agony in death only once, in a patient with rabies; he remained acutely aware of every stage in the process of his own disintegration over a twenty-four-hour period, right up to his final moment. It was as though, in the special neuropathology of rabies, the switch had been prevented from turning.

12   We will be having new opportunities to learn more about the physiology of death at first hand, from the increasing numbers of cardiac patients who have been through the whole process and then back again. Judging from what has been found out thus far, from the first generation of people resuscitated from cardiac standstill (already termed the Lazarus syndrome), Osler seems to have been right. Those who remember parts or all of their episodes do not recall any fear, or anguish. Several people who remained conscious throughout, while appearing to have been quite dead, could only describe a remarkable sensation of detachment. One man underwent coronary occlusion with cessation of the heart and dropped for all practical purposes dead, in front of a hospital; within a few minutes his heart had been restarted by electrodes and he breathed his way

back into life. According to his account, the strangest thing was that there were so many people around him, moving so urgently, handling his body with such excitement, while all his awareness was of quietude.

13   In a recent study of the reaction to dying in patients with obstructive disease of the lungs, it was concluded that the process as considerably more shattering for the professional observers than the observed. Most of the patients appeared to be preparing themselves with equanimity for death, as though intuitively familiar with the business. One elderly woman reported that the only painful and distressing part of the process was in being interrupted; on several occasions she was provided with conventional therapeutic measures to maintain oxygenation or restore fluids and electrolytes, and each time she found the experience of coming back harrowing; she deeply resented the interference with her dying.

14   I find myself surprised by the thought that dying is an all-right thing to do, but perhaps it should not surprise. It is, after all, the most ancient and fundamental of biologic functions, with its mechanisms worked out with the same attention to detail, the same provision for the advantage of the organism, the same abundance of genetic information for guidance through the stages, that we have long since become accustomed to finding in all the crucial acts of living.

15   Very well. But even so, if the transformation is a coordinated, integrated physiologic process in its initial, local stages, there is still that permanent vanishing of consciousness to be accounted for. Are we to be stuck forever with this problem? Where on earth does it go? Is it simply stopped dead in its tracks, lost in humus, wasted? Considering the tendency of nature to find uses for complex and intricate mechanisms, this seems to me unnatural. I prefer to think of it as somehow separated off at the filaments of its attachment, and then drawn like an easy breath back into the membrane of its origin, a fresh memory for a biospherical nervous system, but I have no data on the matter.

16   This is for another science, another day. It may turn out, as some scientists suggest, that we are forever precluded from investigating consciousness by a sort of indeterminacy principle that stipulates that the very act of looking will make it twitch and blur out of sight. If this is true, we will never learn. I envy some of my friends who are convinced about telepathy; oddly enough, it is my European scientist

acquaintances who believe it most freely and take it most lightly. All their aunts have received Communications, and there they sit, with proof of the motility of consciousness at their fingertips, and the making of a new science. It is discouraging to have had the wrong aunts, and never the ghost of a message.

Pain Is Not the Ultimate Enemy

NORMAN COUSINS

Norman Cousins (1915–1990) was born in Union Hill, New Jersey. He attended the Teachers College of Columbia University. Cousins started his career writing for the *New York Evening Post*. He proved his skills quickly and, at age twenty-five, became editor of the *Saturday Review of Literature*, a post he held for many years. He also served his country as a diplomat for three different presidents. Cousins produced many essays and books during his long career, many on political issues, such as *The Good Inheritance: The Democratic Chance* (1942). Other works touched on social issues, such as *Modern Man Is Obsolete* (1945). Later, after an illness, he wrote several significant works on health, such as *Anatomy of an Illness as Perceived by the Patient* (1979) and *Healing and Belief* (1982). Cousins battled and overcame a degenerative disease and later healed himself after a heart attack.

"Pain Is Not the Ultimate Enemy" is an excerpt from *Anatomy of an Illness*. Here he describes how two physicians used deductive reasoning to cure some of the problems associated with leprosy. As Cousins explains, the doctors were "determined to pit the scientific method against the old mysteries of leprosy."

1   If an account is ever written about the attempts of the medical profession to understand pain, the name of Paul Brand may have an honored place. Dr. Brand has worked with lepers for most of his medical career. He is an English orthopedic surgeon, recognized throughout world medical circles for his work in restoring crippled or paralyzed hands to productive use. His principal work at Medical College at Vellore, India, was as director of orthopedic surgery.

2   Paul Brand went to Vellore as a young man in 1947. His wife, also a surgeon, joined him at Vellore a year later. Together, they constituted one of the most remarkable husband-and-wife medical teams in the world. Paul Brand restored to thousands of lepers the use of their hands and arms. Margaret Brand saved thousands of lepers from blindness. Both of them taught at the medical college, undertook important research, and worked at the hospital and in field clinics.

3   Paul Brand's main purpose in coming to the Christian Medical College and Hospital at Vellore was to see whether he might be able to apply his highly developed skills in reconstructive surgery to the special problems of lepers. Commonly, lepers' fingers tend to "claw" or partially close up because of the paralysis of vital nerves controlling the muscles of the hand. Brand wanted to try to reactivate the fingers by connecting them to healthy nerve impulses in the leper's forearm. This would require, of course, reeducating the patient so that his brain could transmit orders to the lower forearm instead of the hand for activating the fingers.

4   He wasn't at Vellore very long, however, before he realized he couldn't confine himself to problems caused by the clawish hands of lepers. He would have to deal with the total problem of leprosy—what it was, how it took hold in the human body, how it might be combated. He immersed himself in research. The more he learned, the greater was his awareness that most of the attitudes toward leprosy he had carried with him to Vellore were outmoded to the point of being medieval. He became determined to pit the scientific method against the old mysteries of leprosy.

5   He was to discover that the prevailing ideas about "leprous tissue" were mistaken. Wrong, too, was the notion that missing toes or fingers or atrophy of the nose were direct products or manifestations of the disease. Most significant of all perhaps was his awareness that leprosy was a disease of painlessness.

6   As head of the research section, Paul Brand first needed to find out as much as he could about tissue from the affected parts of lepers. Medicine had long known that leprosy was produced by a bacillus somewhat similar to the organism that causes tuberculosis. This discovery had been made by Gerhard Henrik Hansen almost a century and a half ago; the term "Hansen's disease" became synonymous with leprosy. As in the case of tuberculosis, the *bacillus leprae* produced tubercles. The leprosy tubercles varied in size from a small pea to a large olive. They appeared on the face, ears, and bodily extremities. It was commonly thought that the bacillus was responsible in some way for the sloughing-off of fingers and toes, and even of hands and feet. Yet very little had been done in actual tissue research. Was there anything in the flesh of finger stumps or toes that differentiated this tissue from healthy cells? Was the *bacillus leprae* an active agent in the atrophy? Dr. Brand put the pathologists to work. Through research, they came up with the startling finding that there was no difference between healthy tissue and the tissue of a leper's fingers or toes.

7   One point, however, was scientifically certain: the *bacillus leprae* killed nerve endings. This meant that the delicate sense of touch was missing or seriously injured. But the flesh itself, Dr. Brand ascertained, was otherwise indistinguishable from normal tissue.

8   As is often the case in medical research, some of Paul Brand's most important discoveries about leprosy came about not as the result of systematic pursuit but through accident. Soon after arriving in Vellore he observed the prodigious strength in lepers' hands. Even a casual handshake with a leper was like putting one's fingers in a vise. Was this because something in the disease released manual strength not known to healthy people?

9   The answer came one day when Paul Brand was unable to turn a key in a large rusty lock. A leprous boy of twelve observed Dr. Brand's difficulty and asked to help. Dr. Brand was astonished at the ease with which the youngster turned the key. He examined the boy's thumb and forefinger of the right hand. The key had cut the flesh to the bone. The boy had been completely unaware of what was happening to his fingers while turning the key.

10   Dr. Brand had his answer at once. The desensitized nerve endings had made it possible for the child to keep turning the key long past the point where a healthy person would have found it painful to continue. Healthy people possess strength they never use precisely

because resistant pressure causes pain. A leper's hands are not more powerful, he reasoned; they just lack the mechanism of pain to tell them when to stop applying pressure. In this way serious damage could be done to flesh and bone.

11   Was it possible, Dr. Brand asked himself, that the reason lepers lost fingers and toes was not because of leprosy itself but because they were insensitive to injury? In short, could a person be unaware that, in the ordinary course of a day's activity, he might be subjecting his body to serious physical damage? Paul Brand analyzed all the things he himself did in the course of a day—turning faucets and doorknobs, operating levers, dislodging or pulling or pushing things, using utensils of all kinds. In most of these actions, pressure was required. And the amount of pressure was determined both by the resistance of the object and the ability of his fingers and hands to tolerate stress. Lacking the sensitivity, he knew, he would continue to exert pressure even though damage to his hands might be incurred in the process.

12   He observed lepers as they went about their daily tasks and was convinced he was correct. He began to educate lepers in stress toler-ance; he designed special gloves to protect their hands; and he set up daily examinations so that injuries would not lead to ulceration and to disfigurement, as had previously occurred. Almost miracu-lously, the incidence of new injuries was sharply reduced. Lepers became more productive. Paul Brand began to feel he was making basic progress.

13   Some mysteries, however, persisted. How to account for the con-tinuing disappearance of fingers, in part or whole? Why was it that parts of fingers would vanish from one day to the next? Were they knocked off? There was nothing to indicate that bones of lepers were any more brittle than the bones of normal people. If a leper cut off a finger while using a saw, or if a finger were somehow broken off, it should be possible to produce the missing digit. But no one ever found a finger after it had been lost. Why?

14   Paul Brand thought about the problem. Then, suddenly, the answer flashed through his mind. It had to be rats. And it would happen at night, while the lepers were asleep. Since the hands of lepers were desensitized, they wouldn't know they were being attacked and so would put up no resistance.

15   Paul Brand set up observation posts at night in the huts and wards. It was just as he had thought. The rats climbed the beds of lepers,

sniffed carefully, and, when they encountered no resistance, went to work on fingers and toes. The fingers hadn't been dropping off; they were being eaten. This didn't mean that all "lost" fingers had disappeared in this way. They could be knocked off through accidents and then carried away by rats or other animals before the loss would be observed. But a major cause of the disappearance had now been identified.

16   Paul Brand and his staff went to work, mounting a double-pronged attack against the invaders. The program for rodent control was stepped up many times. Barriers were built around the legs of beds. The beds themselves were raised. The results were immediately apparent. There was a sharp drop in the disappearance of fingers and toes.

17   All this time, Paul Brand kept up his main work—reconstructing hands, rerouting muscles, straightening out fingers. Where fingers were shortened or absent, the remaining digits had to be made fully operative. Thousands of lepers were restored to manual productivity.

18   One of the grim but familiar marks of many lepers is the apparent decay of their noses. What caused the shrinkage? It was highly unlikely that the nose suffered from the kind of persistent injury that frequently affected the desensitized hands and feet. What about rats? This, too, seemed unlikely. Enough sensitivity existed in a leper's face, especially around the mouth, to argue strongly against the notion of rodent assault.

19   As Paul Brand pursued the riddle, he became convinced that neither injuries nor rats were involved. Finally, he found his answer in his research on the effect of *bacillus leprae* on the delicate membranes inside the nose. These membranes would contract severely in lepers. This meant that the connecting cartilage would be yanked inward. What was happening, therefore, was not decay or loss of nasal structure through injury. The nose was being drawn into the head.

20   It was a startling discovery, running counter to medical ideas that had lasted for centuries. Could Brand prove it? The best way of proceeding, he felt, was by surgery that would push the nose back into the face. He therefore reconstructed the nose from the inside. It was a revolutionary approach.

21   He knew that the operation couldn't work in all cases. Where the leprosy was so far advanced that membrane shrinkage left little to work with, it was doubtful that the operation would be successful. But there was a good chance that, in those cases where the disease

could be arrested and where the shrinkage was not extreme, noses could be pushed back into place.

22   The theory worked. As a result, the nose restorative operation developed at Vellore has been used for the benefit of large numbers of lepers at hospitals throughout the world.

23   Next, blindness. Of all the afflictions of leprosy, perhaps none is more serious or characteristic than blindness. Here, too, it had been assumed for many centuries that loss of sight was a specific manifestation of advanced leprosy. At Vellore, this assumption was severely questioned. Intensive study of the disease convinced Paul Brand and his fellow researchers that blindness was not a direct product of leprosy but a by-product. A serious vitamin A deficiency, for example, could be a major contributing cause of cataracts and consequent blindness. Where cataracts were already formed, it was possible to remove them by surgery.

24   It was in this field that Dr. Margaret Brand became especially active and effective. On some days she would perform as many as a hundred cataract operations. This number would seem high to the point of absurdity to many European and American eye surgeons for whom twelve such operations in a single day would be considered formidable. But the eye surgeons at Vellore have to contend with literally thousands of people waiting in line to be saved from blindness. They often work fourteen to sixteen hours a day, using techniques that facilitate rapid surgery.

25   Dr. Margaret Brand was part of a medical and surgical field team that would make regular rounds among villages far removed from the hospital. Surgical tents would be set up. Electricity would be supplied by power take-off devices from the jeep motors.

26   Cataracts, however, were not the whole story in blindness among lepers. Many lepers at Vellore didn't suffer from cataracts, yet were losing their sight from eye ulcerations. Did the *bacillus leprae* produce the infection and the resultant ulcerations and blindness? Or, as in the case of fingers and toes, was the loss of function a by-product in which other causes had to be identified and eliminated?

27   The latter line of reasoning proved to be fruitful. Human eyes are constantly exposed to all sorts of irritations from dust and dirt in the air. The eyes deal with these invasions almost without a person being aware of the process. Thousands of times a day the eyelids close and open, washing the surface of the eye with soothing saline fluid released by the tear ducts.

28   Paul Brand and his colleagues believed this washing process didn't take place in lepers because there was a loss of sensation on the eye surface caused by the atrophy of nerve endings. This hypothesis was easily and readily confirmed. They observed the eyes of lepers when subjected to ordinary irritations. There was, as they had suspected, no batting of the eyelids; therefore, there could be no washing process. The big problem, then, was to get the eyelids working again.

29   Why not educate lepers to make a conscious effort to bat their eyes? There being no impairment of a leper's ability to close his eyes at will, it ought to be possible to train lepers to be diligent in this respect. But experiments quickly demonstrated the disadvantages of this approach. Unless a leper concentrated on the matter constantly, it wouldn't work. And if he did concentrate, he could think of almost nothing else. No; what was needed was a way of causing eyelid action that would clean the eyes automatically.

30   In the case of fingers or toes, it was possible to educate lepers in stress tolerances and to give them protective gloves or shoes. How to keep dirt and foreign objects from getting into the eye? Eye goggles might be one answer but they were not airtight, were cumbersome, would fog up because of the high humidity, and were too easily lost. Something more basic would have to be found.

31   The answer, again, was found in reconstructive surgery. Paul Brand and his team devised a way of hooking up the muscles of the jaw to the eyelid. Every time a leper opened his mouth the new facial muscles would pull the eyelids and cause them to close, thus washing the eyeball. In this way, a leper could literally talk and eat his way out of oncoming blindness. Countless numbers of lepers have their sight today because of this ingenious use of surgery in facilitating the use of nature's mechanism to get rid of dirt and dust in the eyes.

CLASSIC
ESSAYS
IN

Business
and
Economics

Division of Labour

ADAM SMITH

Adam Smith (1723–1790) was born in Kirkcaldy, a small Scottish fishing village. At age four, he was kidnapped by a band of gypsies, but his parents and friends soon recovered him. He studied at the University of Glasgow and Oxford University. In 1751, he accepted a post at Glasgow University. While there, he wrote *Theory of Moral Sentiments* (1759). A position with the Duke of Buccleuch enabled him to travel to Europe and, later, back in Scotland, to develop the book that was one of the earliest explorations of economic theory: *An Inquiry into the Nature and Cause of the Wealth of Nations* (1776). Smith supported an open marketplace of free trade, where buyers and sellers could meet to develop a pattern of social as well as economic harmony. His economic liberalism meant few government regulations, no tariffs, and individual freedom in trade.

"Division of Labour" examines how the workforce was divided for mass production (before the Industrial Revolution). Smith argues that the division of labor offers three advantages: (1) it improves the dexterity of each individual worker who can concentrate on one skill, (2) it saves time, and (3) it motivates the invention of new machinery to increase efficiency. Smith concludes that workers supply the capitalist and society with a product, and they, in turn, "accommodate him as amply with what he has occasion for, and a general plenty diffuses itself through all the different ranks of the society."

1   The greatest improvement in the productive powers of labour, and the greater part of the skill, dexterity, and judgment with which it is any where directed, or applied, seem to have been the effects of the division of labour.

2   The effects of the division of labour, in the general business of society, will be more easily understood, by considering in what manner it operates in some particular manufactures. It is commonly supposed to be carried furthest in some very trifling ones; not perhaps that it really is carried further in them than in others of more importance: but in those trifling manufactures which are destined to supply the small wants of but a small number of people, the whole number of workmen must necessarily be small; and those employed in every different branch of the work can often be collected into the same workhouse, and placed at once under the view of the spectator. In those great manufactures, on the contrary, which are destined to supply the great wants of the great body of the people, every different branch of the work employs so great a number of workmen, that it is impossible to collect them all into the same workhouse. We can seldom see more, at one time, than those employed in one single branch. Though in such manufactures, therefore, the work may really be divided into a much greater number of parts, than in those of a more trifling nature, the division is not near so obvious, and has accordingly been much less observed.

3   To take an example, therefore, from a very trifling manufacture; but one in which the division of labour has been very often taken notice of, the trade of the pin-maker; a workman not educated to this business (which the division of labour has rendered a distinct trade), nor acquainted with the use of the machinery employed in it (to the invention of which the same division of labour has probably given occasion), could scarce, perhaps, with his utmost industry, make one pin in a day, and certainly could not make twenty. But in the way in which this business is now carried on, not only the whole work is a peculiar trade, but it is divided into a number of branches,

of which the greater part are likewise peculiar trades. One man draws out the wire, another straights it, a third cuts it, a fourth points it, a fifth grinds it at the top for receiving the head; to make the head requires two or three distinct operations; to put it on, is a peculiar business, to whiten the pins is another; it is even a trade by itself to put them into the paper; and the important business of making a pin is, in this manner, divided into about eighteen distinct operations, which, in some manufactories, are all performed by distinct hands, though in others the same man will sometimes perform two or three of them. I have seen a small manufactory of this kind where ten men only were employed, and where some of them consequently performed two or three distinct operations. But though they were very poor, and therefore but indifferently accommodated with the necessary machinery, they could, when they exerted themselves, make among them about twelve pounds of pins in a day. There are in a pound upwards of four thousand pins of a middling size. Those ten persons, therefore, could make among them upwards of forty-eight thousand pins in a day. Each person, therefore, making a tenth part of forty-eight thousand pins, might be considered as making four thousand eight hundred pins in a day. But if they had all wrought separately and independently, and without any of them having been educated to this peculiar business, they certainly could not each of them have made twenty, perhaps not one pin in a day; that is, certainly, not the two hundred and fortieth, perhaps not the four thousand eight hundredth part of what they are at present capable of performing, in consequence of a proper division and combination of their different operations.

4   In every other art and manufacture, the effects of the division of labour are similar to what they are in this very trifling one; though, in many of them, the labour can neither be so much subdivided, nor reduced to so great a simplicity of operation. The division of labour, however, so far as it can be introduced, occasions, in every art, a proportionable increase of the productive powers of labour. The separation of different trades and employments from one another, seems to have taken place, in consequence of this advantage. This separation too is generally carried furthest in those countries which enjoy the highest degree of industry and improvement; what is the work of one man in a rude state of society, being generally that of several in an improved one. In every improved society, the farmer is generally nothing but a farmer; the manufacturer, nothing but a

manufacturer. The labour too which is necessary to produce any
one complete manufacture, is almost always divided among a great
number of hands. How many different trades are employed in each
branch of the linen and woollen manufactures, from the growers of
the flax and the wool, to the bleachers and smoothers of the linen,
or to the dyers and dressers of the cloth!

5   This great increase of the quantity of work, which, in consequence
of the division of labour, the same number of people are capable of
performing, is owing to three different circumstances; first, to the
increase of dexterity in every particular workman; secondly, to the
saving of the time which is commonly lost in passing from one species
of work to another; and lastly, to the invention of a great number
of machines which facilitate and abridge labour, and enable one man
to do the work of many.

6   First, the improvement of the dexterity of the workman necessarily
increases the quantity of the work he can perform; and the division
of labour, by reducing every man's business to some one simple
operation, and by making this operation the sole employment of his
life, necessarily increases very much the dexterity of the workman.
A common smith, who, though accustomed to handle the hammer,
has never been used to make nails, if upon some particular occasion
he is obliged to attempt it, will scarce, I am assured, be able to make
above two or three hundred nails in a day, and those too very bad
ones. A smith who has been accustomed to make nails, but whose
sole or principal business has not been that of a nailer, can seldom
with his utmost diligence make more than eight hundred or a thousand nails in a day. I have seen several boys under twenty years of
age who had never exercised any other trade but that of making
nails, and who, when they exerted themselves, could make, each of
them, upwards of two thousand three hundred nails in a day. The
making of a nail, however, is by no means one of the simplest operations. The same person blows the bellows, stirs or mends the fire as
there is occasion, heats the iron, and forges every part of the nail:
In forging the head too he is obliged to change his tools. The
different operations into which the making of a pin, or of a metal
button, is subdivided, are all of them much more simple, and the
dexterity of the person, of whose life it has been the sole business
to perform them, is usually much greater. The rapidity with which
some of the operations of those manufactures are performed, exceeds

what the human hand could, by those who had never seen them, be supposed capable of acquiring.

7 Secondly, the advantage which is gained by saving the time commonly lost in passing from one sort of work to another, is much greater than we should at first view be apt to imagine it. It is impossible to pass very quickly from one kind of work to another, that is carried on in a different place, and with quite different tools. A country weaver, who cultivates a small farm, must lose a good deal of time in passing from his loom to the field, and from the field to his loom. When the two trades can be carried on in the same workhouse, the loss of time is no doubt much less. It is even in this case, however, very considerable. A man commonly saunters a little in turning his hand from one sort of employment to another. When he first begins the new work he is seldom very keen and hearty; his mind, as they say, does not go to it, and for some time he rather trifles than applies to good purpose. The habit of sauntering and of indolent careless application, which is naturally, or rather necessarily acquired by every country workman who is obliged to change his work and his tools every half hour, and to apply his hand in twenty different ways almost every day of his life; renders him almost always slothful and lazy, and incapable of any vigorous application even on the most pressing occasions. Independent, therefore, of his deficiency in point of dexterity, this cause alone must always reduce considerably the quantity of work which he is capable of performing.

8 Thirdly, and lastly, every body must be sensible how much labour is facilitated and abridged by the application of proper machinery. It is unnecessary to give any example. I shall only observe, therefore, that the invention of all those machines by which labour is so much facilitated and abridged, seems to have been originally owing to the division of labour. Men are much more likely to discover easier and readier methods of attaining any object, when the whole attention of their minds is directed towards that single object, than when it is dissipated among a great variety of things. But in consequence of the division of labour, the whole of every man's attention comes naturally to be directed towards some one very simple object. It is naturally to be expected, therefore, that some one or other of those who are employed in each particular branch of labour should soon find out easier and readier methods of performing their own particular work, wherever the nature of it admits of such improvement. A great part of the machines made use of in those manufactures in which

labour is most subdivided, were originally the inventions of common workmen, who, being each of them employed in some very simple operation, naturally turned their thoughts towards finding out easier and readier methods of performing it. Whoever has been much accustomed to visit such manufactures, must frequently have been shown very pretty machines, which were the inventions of such workmen, in order to facilitate and quicken their own particular part of the work. In the first fire-engines, a boy was constantly employed to open and shut alternately the communication between the boiler and the cylinder, according as the piston either ascended or descended. One of those boys, who loved to play with his companions, observed that, by tying a string from the handle of the valve which opened this communication to another part of the machine, the valve would open and shut without his assistance, and leave him at liberty to divert himself with his play-fellows. One of the greatest improvements that has been made upon this machine, since it was first invented, was in this manner the discovery of a boy who wanted to save his own labour.

9   All the improvements in machinery, however, have by no means been the inventions of those who had occasion to use the machines. Many improvements have been made by the ingenuity of the makers of the machines, when to make them became the business of a peculiar trade; and some by that of those who are called philosophers or men of speculation, whose trade it is not to do any thing, but to observe every thing; and who, upon that account, are often capable of combining together the powers of the most distant and dissimilar objects. In the progress of society, philosophy or speculation becomes, like every other employment, the principal or sole trade and occupation of a particular class of citizens. Like every other employment too, it is subdivided into a great number of different branches, each of which affords occupation to a peculiar tribe or class of philosophers; and this subdivision of employment in philosophy, as well as in every other business, improves dexterity, and saves time. Each individual becomes more expert in his own peculiar branch, more work is done upon the whole, and the quantity of science is considerably increased by it.

10   It is the great multiplication of the productions of all the different arts, in consequence of the division of labour, which occasions, in a well-governed society, that universal opulence which extends itself to the lowest ranks of people. Every workman has a great quantity

of his own work to dispose of beyond what he himself has occasion for; and every other workman being exactly in the same situation, he is enabled to exchange a great quantity of his own goods for a great quantity, or, what comes to the same thing, for the price of a great quantity of theirs. He supplies them abundantly with what they have occasion for, and they accommodate him as amply with what he has occasion for, and a general plenty diffuses itself through all the different ranks of the society.

11   Observe the accommodation of the most common artificer or day-labourer in a civilized and thriving country, and you will perceive that the number of people of whose industry a part, though but a small part, has been employed in procuring him this accommodation, exceeds all computation. The woollen coat, for example, which covers the day-labourer, as coarse and rough as it may appear, is the produce of the joint labour of a great multitude of workmen. The shepherd, the sorter of the wool, the wool-comber or carder, the dyer, the scribbler, the spinner, the weaver, the fuller, the dresser, with many others, must all join their different arts in order to complete even this homely production. How many merchants and carriers, besides, must have been employed in transporting the materials from some of those workmen to others who often live in a very distant part of the country! How much commerce and navigation in particular, how many ship-builders, sailors, sail-makers, rope-makers, must have been employed in order to bring together the different drugs made use of by the dyer, which often come from the remotest corners of the world! What a variety of labour too is necessary in order to produce the tools of the meanest of those workmen! To say nothing of such complicated machines as the ship of the sailor, the mill of the fuller, or even the loom of the weaver, let us consider only what a variety of labour is requisite in order to form that very simple machine, the shears with which the shepherd clips the wool. The miner, the builder of the furnace for smelting the ore, the feller of the timber, the burner of the charcoal to be made use of in the smelting-house, the brick-maker, the brick-layer, the workmen who attend the furnace, the mill-wright, the forger, the smith, must all of them join their different arts in order to produce them. Were we to examine, in the same manner, all the different parts of his dress and household furniture, the coarse linen shirt which he wears next his skin, the shoes which cover his feet, the bed which he lies on, and all the different parts which compose it, the kitchen-grate at which he pre-

pares his victuals, the coals which he makes use of for that purpose, dug from the bowels of the earth, and brought to him perhaps by a long sea and a long land carriage, all the other utensils of his kitchen, all the furniture of his table, the knives and forks, the earthen or pewter plates upon which he serves up and divides his victuals, the different hands employed in preparing his bread and his beer, the glass window which lets in the heat and the light, and keeps out the wind and the rain, with all the knowledge and art requisite for preparing that beautiful and happy invention, without which these northern parts of the world could scarce have afforded a very comfortable habitation, together with the tools of all the different workmen employed in producing those different conveniences; if we examine, I say, all these things, and consider what a variety of labour is employed about each of them, we shall be sensible that without the assistance and cooperation of many thousands, the very meanest person in a civilized country could not be provided, even according to, what we very falsely imagine, the easy and simple manner in which he is commonly accommodated. Compared, indeed, with the more extravagant luxury of the great, his accommodation must no doubt appear extremely simple and easy; and yet it may be true, perhaps, that the accommodation of an European prince does not always so much exceed that of an industrious and frugal peasant, as the accommodation of the latter exceeds that of many an African king, the absolute master of the lives and liberties of ten thousand naked savages.

Alienated Labor

KARL MARX

Karl Marx (1818–1883) was born in Trier, Prussia (now Germany). He studied history, law, and philosophy at the Universities of Bonn and Berlin, where he examined the ideas of Aristotle, Hume, Kant, and especially Hegel. He served as the editor of a radically liberal newspaper in Cologne, *Die Rheinische Zeitung*. The paper was soon blacklisted, so he moved to Paris. It was there that he developed his belief that people can gain true democracy only in a classless society. In November 1847, the Communist League, based in London, commissioned Marx and Friedrich Engels to write the league's political statement. The result was *The Communist Manifesto* (1848). Because of his revolutionary ideas and activities, Marx was forced to live mainly outside of Germany. It was in London that he finished his life's primary work, *Das Kapital* (1864), translated as *Capital: A Critique of Capitalist Production*. Acting against the principle of other economists, such as the bourgeois ideas of Adam Smith, Marx argued against exploitation of workers by the capitalist system. He believed that at some point the workers would take control of the government, abolish private property, and install socialism.

Marx wrote "Alienated Labor" in 1848, but it remained unpublished until 1927. In it, Marx explains that most workers become alienated from the products they produce, so the more a worker produces, the "more pointless his life becomes." Marx clarifies this idea by saying, "The life which he has conferred on the object confronts him in the end as a hostile and alien force." Ultimately, the worker becomes "a slave of things."

1   We shall begin with a contemporary economic fact. The worker becomes all the poorer the more wealth he produces, the more his production increases in power and volume. The worker becomes an ever cheaper commodity the more commodities he creates. As the world of things increases in value, the human world becomes devalued. For labor not only produces commodities; it makes a commodity of the work process itself, as well as the worker—and indeed at the same rate as it produces goods.

2   This means simply that the object produced by man's labor—its product—now confronts him in the shape of an alien thing, a power independent of the producer. The product of labor is labor given embodiment in a material form; this product is the objectification of labor. The performance of work is thus at the same time its objectification. In the sphere of political economy, the performance of work appears as a material loss, a departure from reality for the worker; objectification appears both as deprivation of the object and enslavement to it; and appropriation of the product by others as alienation.

3   The reduction of labor to a mere commodity—in short, the dehumanization of work—goes so far that the worker is reduced to the point of starving to death. So remote from life has work become that the worker is robbed of the real things essential not only for his existence but for his work. Indeed, work itself becomes something which he can obtain only with the greatest difficulty and at intervals. And so much does appropriation of his product by others appear as alienation that the more things the worker produces, the fewer can he possess and the more he falls under the domination of the wealth he produces but cannot enjoy—capital.

4   All these consequences flow from the fact that the worker is related to the product of his labor as to an alien thing. From this premise it is clear that the more the worker exerts himself, the more powerful becomes the world of things which he creates and which confront him as alien objects; hence the poorer he becomes in his inner life,

and the less belongs to him as his own. It is the same with religion. The more man puts into God, the less he retains in himself. The worker puts his life into the things he makes; and his life then belongs to him no more, but to the product of his labor. The greater the worker's activity, therefore, the more pointless his life becomes. Whatever the product of his labor, it is no longer his own. Therefore, the greater this product, the more he is diminished. The alienation of the worker from his product means not only that his labor becomes an impersonal object and takes on its own existence, but that it exists outside himself, independently, and alien to him, and that it opposes itself to him as an autonomous power. The life which he has conferred on the object confronts him in the end as a hostile and alien force.

5   Let us now look more closely at the phenomenon of objectification and its result for the worker: alienation and, in effect, divorce from the product of his labor. To understand this, we must realize that the worker can create nothing without nature, without the sensuous, external world which provides the raw material for his labor. But just as nature provides labor with means of existence in the sense of furnishing raw material which labor processes, so also does it provide means for the worker's physical subsistence. Thus the more the worker by his labor appropriates the external, sensuous world of nature, the more he deprives himself of the means of life in two respects: first, that the sensuous external world becomes progressively detached from him as the medium necessary to his labor; and secondly, that nature becomes increasingly remote from him as the medium through which he gains his physical subsistence.

6   In both respects, therefore, the worker becomes a slave of things; first, in that labor itself is something he obtains—that is, he gets work; and secondly, in that he obtains thereby the physical means of subsistence. Thus, things enable him to exist, first as a worker, and secondly, as one in bondage to physical objects. The culmination of this process of enslavement is that only as a worker can he maintain himself in his bondage and only as a bondsman to things can he find work.

7   In the laws of political economy, the alienation of the worker from his product is expressed as follows: the more the worker produces, the less he has to consume; the more value he creates, the more valueless, the more unworthy he becomes; the better formed is his product, the more deformed becomes the worker; the more civilized his product, the more brutalized becomes the worker; the mightier the work,

the more powerless the worker; the more ingenious the work, the duller becomes the worker and the more he becomes nature's bondsman.

8   Political economy conceals the alienation inherent in labor by avoiding any mention of the evil effects of work on those who work. Thus, whereas labor produces miracles for the rich, for the worker it produces destitution. Labor produces palaces, but for the worker, hovels. It produces beauty, but it cripples the worker. It replaces labor by machines, but how does it treat the worker? By throwing some workers back into a barbarous kind of work, and by turning the rest into machines. It produces intelligence, but for the worker, stupidity and cretinism.

9   Fundamentally, the relationship of labor to the product of labor is the relationship of the worker to the object of his production. The relationship of property owners to the objects of production and to production itself is only a consequence of his primary relationship, and simply confirms it. We shall consider this other aspect later. When we ask, then, what is the essential relationship of labor, we are concerned with the relationship of the worker to production.

10   Thus far we have considered only one aspect of the alienation of the worker, namely, his relationship to the product of his labor. But his estrangement is manifest not only in the result, but throughout the work process—within productive activity itself. How could the worker stand in an alien relationship to the product of his activity if he were not alienated in the very act of production? The product after all is but the résumé of his activity, of production. Hence if the product of labor is alienation, production itself must be active alienation—the alienation of the product of labor merely sums up the alienation in the work process itself.

11   What then do we mean by the alienation of labor? First, that the work he performs is extraneous to the worker, that is, it is not personal to him, is not part of his nature; therefore he does not fulfill himself in work, but actually denies himself; feels miserable rather than content, cannot freely develop his physical and mental powers, but instead becomes physically exhausted and mentally debased. Only while not working can the worker be himself; for while at work he experiences himself as a stranger. Therefore only during leisure hours does he feel at home, while at work he feels homeless. His labor is not voluntary, but coerced, forced labor. It satisfies no spontaneous cre-

ative urge, but is only a means for the satisfaction of wants which have nothing to do with work. Its alien character therefore is revealed by the fact that when no physical or other compulsion exists, work is avoided like the plague. Extraneous labor, labor in which man alienates himself, is a labor of self-sacrifice, of mortification. Finally, the alienated character of work for the worker is shown by the fact that the work he does is not his own, but another's, and that at work he belongs not to himself, but to another. Just as in religion the spontaneous activity of human imagination, of the human brain and heart, is seen as a force from outside the individual reacting upon him as the alien activity of gods or devils, so the worker's labor is no more his own spontaneous activity; but is something impersonal, inhuman and belonging to another. Through his work the laborer loses his identity.

12   As a result, man—the worker—feels freely active only in his animal functions—eating, drinking, procreating, or at most in his dwelling and personal adornment—while in his human and social functions he is reduced to an animal. The animal becomes human, and the human becomes animal. Certainly eating, drinking and procreating are also genuinely human functions; but abstractly considered, apart from all other human activities and regarded as ultimate ends in themselves, they are merely animal functions.

13   We have considered the alienation of practical human activity or labor from two aspects. First, the relationship of the worker is the product of labor as an alien object which dominates him. This relationship implies at the same time a relationship to the sensuous external world of nature as an alien and hostile world. Second the relationship of labor to the act of production within the work process. This is the relationship of the worker to his own activity as something alien, and not belonging to him; it is activity as misery, strength as weakness, creation as emasculation; it is the worker's own physical and mental energy, his personal life (for what is life but activity?) as an activity which is turned against himself, which neither depends on nor belongs to him. Here we have self-alienation as opposed to alienation from things.

14   And now we see that yet a third aspect of alienated labor can be deduced from the two already considered. For man is a creature of his species [*Gattungswesen*] not only because in practice and in theory he adopts mankind as the object of his creation—indeed his field is the whole of nature—but also because within himself he, one man,

represents the whole of mankind and therefore he is a universal and a free being.

15   The life of the species, for man as for animals, has its physical basis in the fact that man, like animals, lives on nature; and since man is more universal than animals, so too the realm of nature on which he lives is more universal. Just as plants, animals, stones, the air, light, etc. theoretically form a part of human consciousness, as subjects for natural science and art, providing man with intellectual and spiritual nourishment from the non-human world—nourishment which he must first prepare and transform before he can enjoy and absorb it—so too this non-human world is a practical part of human life and activity, since man also subsists physically on nature's products in the form of food, heat, clothing, shelter, etc. The universality of man in practice is seen in the universality which makes the whole of nature conceivable as man's inorganic body, since nature is first, his direct means of existence, and second, the raw material, the field, the instrument of his vital activity. Nature is man's inorganic body, that is, nature apart from the human body itself. To say that man lives on nature means that nature is his body with which he must remain in constant and vital contact in order not to die. And to say that man's physical and spiritual life is linked to nature is simply an expression of the interdependence of all natural forces, for man himself is part of nature.

16   Just as alienated labor separates man from nature and from himself—his own active functions and life activity—so too it alienates him from the species, from other men. It degrades all the life of the species and makes some cold and abstract notion of individual life and toil into the goal of the entire species, whose common life also then becomes abstract and alienated.

17   What happens in the end is that man regards his labor—his life-activity, his productive life—merely as a means of satisfying his drive for physical existence. Yet productive life is the real life of the species. We live in order to create more living things. The whole character of a species is evident in its particular type of life-activity; and free, conscious activity is the generic character of human beings. But alienated labor reduces this area of productive life to a mere means of existence.

18   Among animals there is no question of regarding one part of life as cut off from the rest; the animal is one with its life-activity. Man, on the other hand, makes his life-activity the object of his conscious

will; and this is what distinguishes him from animals. It is because of this free, conscious activity that he is a creature of his species. Or perhaps it is because he is a creature of his species that he is a conscious being, that he is able to direct his life-activity; and that he treats his own life as subject matter and as an object of his own determination. Alienated labor reverses this relationship: man, the self-conscious being, turns his chief activity—labor, which should express his profound essence—into a mere means of physical existence.

19 In manipulating inorganic nature and creating an objective world by his practical activity, man confirms himself as a conscious creature of his species, that is, as a member of his whole species, a being who regards the whole of mankind as involved in himself, and himself as part of mankind. Admittedly animals also produce, building, as do bees, ants or beavers, their nests or dens. But animals produce only for their own immediate needs or for those of their young. Animal production is limited, while man's production is universal. The animal produces only under compulsion of direct physical need, while man produces even when free from physical need, and only truly produces or creates when truly free from such need. Animals produce or reproduce only themselves, while man reproduces the whole of nature. Whatever animals produce—nests or food—is only for their own bodies; but man's creations supply the needs of many species. And whereas animals construct only in accordance with the standards and needs of their kind, man designs and produces in accordance with the standards of all known species and can apply the standards appropriate to the subject. Man therefore designs in accordance with the laws of beauty.

20 Thus it is precisely in shaping the objective world that man really proves himself as a creature of his species; for in this handiwork resides his active species-life. By means of man's productivity, nature appears to him as his work and his reality. The true object of man's labor therefore is the objectification of man's species-life—his profound essence; for in his labor man duplicates himself not merely intellectually, in consciousness, but also actively, in reality; and in the world that he has made man contemplates his own image. When, therefore, alienated labor tears away from man the object of his production, it snatches from his species-life—the essence of his being—and transforms his advantage over animals into a disadvantage, insofar as his inorganic body, nature, is withdrawn from him.

21 Hence, in degrading labor—which should be man's free, sponta-

neous activity—to a mere means of physical subsistence, alienated labor degrades man's essential life to a mere means to an end. The awareness which man should have of his relationship to the rest of mankind is reduced to a state of detachment in which he and his fellows become simply unfeeling objects. Thus alienated labor turns man's essential humanity into a non-human property. It estranges man from his own human body, and estranges him from nature and from his own spiritual essence—his human being.

22 An immediate consequence of man's estrangement from the product of his labor is man's estrangement from man. When man confronts himself, he confronts other men. What characterizes his relationship to his work, to the product of his labor, and to himself also characterizes his relationship to other men, their work, and the products of their labor.

23 In general, the statement that man is alienated from the larger life of his species means that men are alienated from each other and from human nature. Man's self-estrangement—and indeed all his attitudes to himself—first finds expression in his relationship to other men. Thus in the relationship of alienated labor each man's view of his fellows is determined by the narrow standards and activities of the work place.

24 We started with an economic fact, the separation of the worker from the means of production. From this fact flows our concept of alienated or estranged labor; and in analyzing this concept, we merely analyzed a fact of political economy.

25 Let us now see how alienated labor appears in real life. If the product of my labor is alien to me, if it confronts me as an alien power, to whom then does it belong? If my own activity belongs not to me, but is an alien, forced activity, to whom does it then belong? It must belong to a being other than me. Who then is this being?

26 Is it the gods? In ancient times the major productive effort was evidently in the service of the gods—for example, temple building in Egypt, India, Mexico; and the product of that effort belonged to the gods. But the gods were never the lords of labor. Neither was nature ever man's taskmaster. What a contradiction it would be if man—as he more and more subjugated nature by his labor, rendering divine miracles superfluous by the wonders of industry—if man were then to renounce his pleasure in producing and his enjoyment of the product merely in order to continue serving the gods.

27   Hence, the alien being to whom labor and the product of labor belong, in whose service labor is performed and for whose enjoyment the product of labor serves—this being can only be man himself. So, if the product of labor does not belong to the worker, if it confronts him as an alien power, this must mean that it belongs to a man other than the worker. If the worker's activity is a torment to him, it must be a source of enjoyment and pleasure to another man. Neither the gods nor nature but only man himself can be this alien power over men.

28   Let us consider our earlier statement that man's relation to himself first becomes objectified, embodied and real through his relation to other men. Therefore, if he is related to the product of his objectified labor as to an alien, hostile, powerful and independent object, then he is related in such a way that someone else is master of this object—someone who is alien, hostile, powerful and independent of him. If his own activity is not free, then he is related to it as an activity in the service, and under the domination, coercion and yoke, of another man.

29   The alienation of man from himself and from nature appears in his relationships with other men. Thus religious self-alienation necessarily appears in the relationship between laymen and priest—or—since we are here dealing with the spiritual world—between laymen and intercessor. In the everyday, practical world, however, self-alienation manifests itself only through real, practical relationships between men. The medium through which alienation occurs is itself a practical one. As alienated laborer, man not only establishes a certain relationship to the object and process of production as to alien and hostile powers; he also fixes the relationship of other men to his production and to his product; and the relationship between himself and other men. Just as he turns his own product into something not belonging to him; so he brings about the domination of the non-producer over production and its product. In becoming alienated from his own activity, he surrenders power over that activity to a stranger.

30   So far we have considered this alienated relationship only from the worker's standpoint. Later we shall also consider it from the standpoint of the nonworker, since through the process of alienating his labor the worker brings forth another man who stands outside the work process. The relationship of the worker to work also determines the relationship of the capitalist—or whatever one chooses to

call the master of labor—to work. Private property thus is essentially the result, the necessary consequence of alienated labor and of the extraneous relationship of the worker to nature and to himself. Hence private property results from the phenomenon of alienated labor—that is, alienated labor alienated life and alienated man.

The Gospel of Wealth

ANDREW CARNEGIE

Andrew Carnegie (1835–1919) was born in Dunfermline, Scotland, but his family moved to the United States when he was thirteen. They settled in Allegheny City, Pennsylvania, near Pittsburgh. He worked in the mills and as a telegraph operator, a railroad clerk, a train dispatcher, and, at twenty-four, a division manager. Eventually he entered the steel manufacturing business, where he was enormously successful. At retirement, his fortune exceeded $500,000,000. Carnegie used his immense wealth to support libraries, education, and the movement for world peace.

"The Gospel of Wealth" is Carnegie's defense of his great wealth. He argues a theory in which the wealthy pass down to the laboring class the refinements that will improve them culturally—libraries, scholarships for advanced studies, public buildings, works of art, and so forth. He says that the division between the poor and the very rich is not something to deplore but to welcome "as highly beneficial." He sees the progress of the human race depending upon industrial progress so that each succeeding generation will have more comforts than the previous one. To him, competition "insures the survival of the fittest in every department," so it is good for the human race, even though some individuals might suffer.

1   The problem of our age is the proper administration of wealth, that the ties of brotherhood may still bind together the rich and poor in harmonious relationship. The conditions of human life have not only been changed, but revolutionized, within the past few hundred years. In former days there was little difference between the dwelling, dress, food, and environment of the chief and those of his retainers. The Indians are today where civilized man then was. When visiting the Sioux, I was led to the wigwam of the chief. It was like the others in external appearance, and even within the difference was trifling between it and those of the poorest of his braves. The contrast between the palace of the millionaire and the cottage of the laborer with us today measures the change which has come with civilization. This change, however, is not to be deplored, but welcomed as highly beneficial. It is well, nay, essential, for the progress of the race that the houses of some should be homes for all that is highest and best in literature and the arts, and for all the refinements of civilization, rather than that none should be so. Much better this great irregularity than universal squalor. Without wealth there can be no Mæcenas. The "good old times" were not good old times. Neither master nor servant was as well situated then as today. A relapse to old conditions would be disastrous to both—not the least so to him who serves—and would sweep away civilization with it. But whether the change be for good or ill, it is upon us, beyond our power to alter, and, therefore, to be accepted and made the best of it. It is a waste of time to criticize the inevitable.

2   It is easy to see how the change has come. One illustration will serve for almost every phase of the cause. In the manufacture of products we have the whole story. It applies to all combinations of human industry, as stimulated and enlarged by the inventions of this scientific age. Formerly, articles were manufactured at the domestic hearth, or in small shops which formed part of the household. The master and his apprentices worked side by side, the latter living with the master, and therefore subject to the same conditions. When these apprentices rose to be masters, there was little or no change in their mode of life, and they, in turn, educated succeeding apprentices in the same routine. There was, substantially, social equality, and even political equality, for those engaged in industrial pursuits had then little or no voice in the State.

3   The inevitable result of such a mode of manufacture was crude articles at high prices. Today the world obtains commodities of excel-

lent quality at prices which even the preceding generation would have deemed incredible. In the commercial world similar causes have produced similar results, and the race is benefited thereby. The poor enjoy what the rich could not before afford. What were the luxuries have become the necessaries of life. The laborer has now more comforts than the farmer had a few generations ago. The farmer has more luxuries than the landlord had, and is more richly clad and better housed. The landlord has books and pictures rarer and appointments more artistic than the king could then obtain.

4   The price we pay for this salutary change is, no doubt, great. We assemble thousands of operatives in the factory, and in the mine, of whom the employer can know little or nothing, and to whom he is little better than a myth. All intercourse between them is at an end. Rigid castes are formed, and, as usual, mutual ignorance breeds mutual distrust. Each caste is without sympathy with the other, and ready to credit anything disparaging in regard to it. Under the law of competition, the employer of thousands is forced into the strictest economies, among which the rates paid to labor figure prominently, and often there is friction between the employer and the employed, between capital and labor, between rich and poor. Human society loses homogeneity.

5   The price which society pays for the law of competition, like the price it pays for cheap comforts and luxuries, is also great; but the advantages of this law are also greater still than its cost—for it is to this law that we owe our wonderful material development, which brings improved conditions in its train. But, whether the law be benign or not, we must say of it, as we say of the change in the conditions of men to which we have referred: it is here; we cannot evade it; no substitutes for it have been found; and while the law may be sometimes hard for the individual, it is best for the race, because it insures the survival of the fittest in every department. We accept and welcome, therefore, as conditions to which we must accommodate ourselves, great inequality of environment; the concentration of business, industrial and commercial, in the hands of a few; and the law of competition between these, as being not only beneficial, but essential to the future progress of the race. Having accepted these, it follows that there must be great scope for the exercise of special ability in the merchant and in the manufacturer who has to conduct affairs upon a great scale. That this talent for organization and management is rare among men is proved by the

fact that it invariably secures enormous rewards for its possessor, no matter where or under what laws or conditions. The experienced in affairs always rate the MAN whose services can be obtained as a partner as not only the first consideration, but such as render the question of his capital scarcely worth considering: for able men soon create capital; in the hands of those without the special talent required, capital soon takes wings. Such men become interested in firms or corporations using millions; and, estimating only simple interest to be made upon the capital invested, it is inevitable that their income must exceed their expenditure and that they must, therefore, accumulate wealth. Nor is there any middle ground which such men can occupy, because the great manufacturing or commercial concern which does not earn at least interest upon its capital soon becomes bankrupt. It must either go forward or fall behind; to stand still is impossible. It is a condition essential to its successful operation that it should be thus far profitable, and even that, in addition to interest on capital, it should make profit. It is a law, as certain as any of the others named, that men possessed of this peculiar talent for affairs, under the free play of economic forces must, of necessity, soon be in receipt of more revenue than can be judiciously expended upon themselves; and this law is as beneficial for the race as the others.

6   Objections to the foundations upon which society is based are not in order, because the condition of the race is better with these than it has been with any other which has been tried. Of the effect of any new substitutes proposed we cannot be sure. The Socialist or Anarchist who seeks to overturn present conditions is to be regarded as attacking the foundation upon which civilization itself rests, for civilization took its start from the day when the capable, industrious workman said to his incompetent and lazy fellow, "If thou dost not sow, thou shalt not reap," and thus ended primitive Communism by separating the drones from the bees. One who studies this subject will soon be brought face to face with the conclusion that upon the sacredness of property civilization itself depends—the right of the laborer to his hundred dollars in the savings bank, and equally the legal right of the millionaire to his millions. Every man must be allowed "to sit under his own vine and fig-tree, with none to make afraid," if human society is to advance, or even to remain so far advanced as it is. To those who propose to substitute Communism for this intense Individualism, the answer therefore is: The race has

tried that. All progress from that barbarous day to the present time has resulted from its displacement. Not evil, but good, has come to the race from the accumulation of wealth by those who have had the ability and energy to produce it. But even if we admit for a moment that it might be better for the race to discard its present foundation, Individualism—that it is a nobler ideal that man should labor, not for himself alone, but in and for a brotherhood of his fellows, and share with them all in common . . . even admit all this, and a sufficient answer is, This is not evolution, but revolution. It necessitates the changing of human nature itself—a work of eons, even if it were good to change it, which we cannot know.

7   It is not practicable in our day or in our age. Even if desirable theoretically, it belongs to another and long-succeeding sociological stratum. Our duty is with what is practicable now—with the next step possible in our day and generation. It is criminal to waste our energies in endeavoring to uproot, when all we can profitably accomplish is to bend the universal tree of humanity a little in the direction most favorable to the production of good fruit under existing circumstances. We might as well urge the destruction of the highest existing type of man because he failed to reach our ideal as to favor the destruction of Individualism, Private Property, the Law of Accumulation of Wealth, and the Law of Competition; for these are the highest result of human experience, the soil in which society, so far, has produced the best fruit. Unequally or unjustly, perhaps, as these laws sometimes operate, and imperfect as they appear to the Idealist, they are, nevertheless, like the highest type of man, the best and most valuable of all that humanity has yet accomplished.

8   We start, then, with a condition of affairs under which the best interests of the race are promoted, but which inevitably gives wealth to the few. Thus far, accepting conditions as they exist, the situation can be surveyed and pronounced good. The question then arises—and if the foregoing be correct, it is the only question with which we have to deal—What is the proper mode of administering wealth after the laws upon which civilization is founded have thrown it into the hands of the few? And it is of this great question that I believe I offer the true solution. It will be understood that fortunes are here spoken of, not moderate sums saved by many years of effort, the returns from which are required for the comfortable maintenance and education of families. This is not wealth, but only competence,

which it should be the aim of all to acquire, and which it is for the best interests of society should be acquired.

9   This, then, is held to be the duty of the man of wealth: to set an example of modest, unostentatious living, shunning display or extravagance; to provide moderately for the legitimate wants of those dependent upon him; and, after doing so, to consider all surplus revenues which come to him simply as trust funds, which he is called upon to administer, and strictly bound as a matter of duty to administer in the manner which, in his judgment, is best calculated to produce the most beneficial results for the community—the man of wealth thus becoming the mere trustee and agent for his poorer brethren, bringing to their service his superior wisdom, experience, and ability to administer, doing for them better than they would or could do for themselves.

10   . . . Those who would administer wisely must, indeed, be wise; for one of the serious obstacles to the improvement of our race is indiscriminate charity. It were better for mankind that the millions of the rich were thrown into the sea than so spent as to encourage the slothful, the drunken, the unworthy. Of every thousand dollars spent in so-called charity today, it is probable that nine hundred and fifty dollars is unwisely spent—so spent, indeed, as to produce the very evils which it hopes to mitigate or cure. A well-known writer of philosophic books admitted the other day that he had given a quarter of a dollar to a man who approached him as he was coming to visit the house of his friend. He knew nothing of the habits of this beggar, knew not the use that would be made of this money, although he had every reason to suspect that it would be spent improperly. This man professed to be a disciple of Herbert Spencer; yet the quarter-dollar given that night will probably work more injury than all the money will do good which its thoughtless donor will ever be able to give in true charity. He only gratified his own feelings, saved himself from annoyance—and this was probably one of the most selfish and very worst actions of his life, for in all respects he is most worthy.

11   In bestowing charity, the main consideration should be to help those who will help themselves; to provide part of the means by which those who desire to improve may do so; to give those who desire to rise the aids by which they may rise; to assist, but rarely or never to do all. Neither the individual nor the race is improved by

almsgiving. Those worthy of assistance, except in rare cases, seldom require assistance. . . .

12   The best means of benefiting the community is to place within its reach the ladders upon which the aspiring can rise—free libraries, parks, and means of recreation, by which men are helped in body and mind; works of art, certain to give pleasure and improve the public taste; and public institutions of various kinds, which will improve the general condition of the people; in this manner returning their surplus wealth to the mass of their fellows in the forms best calculated to do them lasting good.

13   Thus is the problem of rich and poor to be solved. The laws of accumulation will be left free, the laws of distribution free. Individualism will continue, but the millionaire will be but a trustee for the poor, intrusted for a season with a great part of the increased wealth of the community, but administering it for the community far better than it could or would have done for itself. The best minds will thus have reached a stage in the development of the race in which it is clearly seen that there is no mode of disposing of surplus wealth creditable to thoughtful and earnest men into whose hands it flows, save by using it year by year for the general good. This day already dawns. Men may die without incurring the pity of their fellows, still sharers in great business enterprises from which their capital cannot be or has not been withdrawn, and which is left chiefly at death for public uses; yet the day is not far distant when the man who dies leaving behind him millions of available wealth, which was free to him to administer during life, will pass away "unwept, unhonored, and unsung," no matter to what uses he leaves the dross which he cannot take with him. Of such as these the public verdict will then be: "The man who dies thus rich dies disgraced."

14   Such, in my opinion is the true gospel concerning wealth, obedience to which is destined some day to solve the problem of the rich and the poor, and to bring "Peace on earth, among men good will."

The Peter Principle

LAURENCE J. PETER
AND RAYMOND HULL

Laurence J. Peter (1919–1990) was an educator at the University of Southern California, and Raymond Hull (1919–1985) was principally a dramatist. Together they produced an immensely popular book, *The Peter Principle: Why Things Always Go Wrong* (1969), which analyzed the manner in which businesses promote perfectly good workers into management positions where they cannot do their best work. Thus the system fosters and rewards ineptitude. Peter published two sequels. *Why Things Go Wrong: Or the Peter Principle Revisited* (1984) provided additional examples of the phenomenon. *The Peter Pyramid: Or, Will We Ever Get the Point?* (1986) described businesses as inverted pyramids that start small but gradually grow upward and outward until they can no longer remain balanced.

The Peter Principle has become a standard term in the English language. According to this principle, every employee will eventually rise to the level of his or her incompetence. Peter describes his arrival at a teaching position only to discover that school personnel were more concerned about trivia than about education—that forms must be submitted on time and that "all window shades be on the same level." In this essay, Peter and Hull reach several conclusions, including the notion that "work is accomplished by those employees who have not yet reached their level of incompetence."

1 When I was a boy I was taught that the men upstairs knew what they were doing. I was told, "Peter, the more you know, the further you go." So I stayed in school until I graduated from college and then went forth into the world clutching firmly these ideas and my new teaching certificate. During the first year of teaching I was upset to find that a number of teachers, school principals, supervisors and superintendents appeared to be unaware of their professional responsibilities and incompetent in executing their duties. For example my principal's main concerns were that all window shades be at the same level, that classrooms should be quiet and that no one step on or near the rose beds. The superintendent's main concerns were that no minority group, no matter how fanatical, should ever be offended and that all official forms be submitted on time. The children's education appeared farthest from the administrator's mind.

2 At first I thought this was a special weakness of the school system in which I taught so I applied for certification in another province. I filled out the special forms, enclosed the required documents and complied willingly with all the red tape. Several weeks later, back came by application and all the documents!

3 No, there was nothing wrong with my credentials; the forms were correctly filled out; an official departmental stamp showed that they had been received in good order. But an accompanying letter said, "The new regulations require that such forms cannot be accepted by the Department of Education unless they have been registered at the Post Office to ensure safe delivery. Will you please remail the forms to the Department, making sure to register them this time?"

4 I began to suspect that the local school system did not have a monopoly on incompetence.

5 As I looked further afield, I saw that every organization contained a number of persons who could not do their jobs.

A Universal Phenomenon

6   Occupational incompetence is everywhere. Have you noticed it? Probably we have all noticed it.

7   We see indecisive politicians posing as resolute statesmen and the "authoritative source" who blames his misinformation on "situational imponderables." Limitless are the public servants who are indolent and insolent; military commanders whose behavioral timidity belies their dreadnought rhetoric, and governors whose innate servility prevents their actually governing. In our sophistication, we virtually shrug aside the immoral cleric, corrupt judge, incoherent attorney, author who cannot write and English teacher who cannot spell. At universities we see proclamations authored by administrators whose own office communications are hopelessly muddled, and droning lectures from inaudible or incomprehensible instructors.

8   Seeing incompetence at all levels of every hierarchy—political, legal, educational and industrial—I hypothesized that the cause was some inherent feature of the rules governing the placement of employees. Thus began my serious study of the ways in which employees move upward through a hierarchy, and of what happens to them after promotion.

9   For my scientific data hundreds of case histories were collected. Here are three typical examples.

10   **Municipal Government File, Case No. 17.** J. S. Minion[1] was a maintenance foreman in the public works department of Excelsior City. He was a favorite of the senior officials at City Hall. They all praised his unfailing affability.

11   "I like Minion," said the superintendent of works. "He has good judgment and is always pleasant and agreeable."

12   This behavior was appropriate for Minion's position: he was not supposed to make policy, so he had no need to disagree with his superiors.

13   The superintendent of works retired and Minion succeeded him. Minion continued to agree with everyone. He passed to his foreman

---

[1]Some names have been changed, in order to protect the guilty.

every suggestion that came from above. The resulting conflicts in policy, and the continual changing of plans, soon demoralized the department. Complaints poured in from the Mayor and other officials, from taxpayers and from the maintenance-workers' union.

14   Minion still says "Yes" to everyone, and carries messages briskly back and forth between his superiors and his subordinates. Nominally a superintendent, he actually does the work of a messenger. The maintenance department regularly exceeds its budget, yet fails to fulfill its program of work. In short, Minion, a competent foreman, became an incompetent superintendent.

15   **Service Industries File, Case No. 3.** E. Tinker was exceptionally zealous and intelligent as an apprentice at G. Reece Auto Repair Inc., and soon rose to journeyman mechanic. In this job he showed outstanding ability in diagnosing obscure faults, and endless patience in correcting them. He was promoted to foreman of the repair shop.

16   But here his love of things mechanical and his perfectionism became liabilities. He will undertake any job that he thinks looks interesting, no matter how busy the shop may be. "We'll work it in somehow," he says.

17   He will not let a job go until he is fully satisfied with it.

18   He meddles constantly. He is seldom to be found at his desk. He is usually up to his elbows in a dismantled motor and while the man who should be doing the work stands watching, other workmen sit around waiting to be assigned new tasks. As a result the shop is always overcrowded with work, always in a muddle, and delivery times are often missed.

19   Tinker cannot understand that the average customer cares little about perfection—he wants his car back on time! He cannot understand that most of his men are less interested in motors than in their pay checks. So Tinker cannot get on with his customers or with his subordinates. He was a competent mechanic, but is now an incompetent foreman.

20   **Military File, Case No. 8.** Consider the case of the late renowned General A. Goodwin. His hearty, informal manner, his racy style of speech, his scorn for petty regulations and his undoubted personal bravery made him the idol of his men. He led them to many well-deserved victories.

21   When Goodwin was promoted to field marshal he had to deal, not

with ordinary soldiers, but with politicians and allied generalissimos.

22 He would not conform to the necessary protocol. He could not turn his tongue to the conventional courtesies and flatteries. He quarreled with all the dignitaries and took to lying for days at a time, drunk and sulking, in his trailer. The conduct of the war slipped out of his hands into those of his subordinates. He had been promoted to a position that he was incompetent to fill.

An Important Clue!

23 In time I saw that all such cases had a common feature. The employee had been promoted from a position of competence to a position of incompetence. I saw that, sooner or later, this could happen to every employee in every hierarchy.

24 **Hypothetical Case File, Case No. 1.** Suppose you own a pill-rolling factory, Perfect Pill Incorporated. Your foreman pill roller dies of a perforated ulcer. You need a replacement. You naturally look among your rank-and-file pill rollers.

25 Miss Oval, Mrs. Cylinder, Mr. Ellipse and Mr. Cube all show various degrees of incompetence. They will naturally be ineligible for promotion. You will choose—other things being equal—your most competent pill roller, Mr. Sphere, and promote him to foreman.

26 Now suppose Mr. Sphere proves competent as foreman. Later, when your general foreman, Legree, moves up to Works Manager, Sphere will be eligible to take his place.

27 If, on the other hand, Sphere is an incompetent foreman, he will get no more promotion. He has reached what I call his "level of incompetence." He will stay there till the end of his career.

28 Some employees, like Ellipse and Cube, reach a level of incompetence in the lowest grade and are never promoted. Some, like Sphere (assuming he is not a satisfactory foreman), reach it after one promotion.

29 E. Tinker, the automobile repair-shop foreman, reached his level of incompetence on the third stage of the hierarchy. General Goodwin reached his level of incompetence at the very top of the hierarchy.

30 So my analysis of hundreds of cases of occupational incompetence led me on to formulate *The Peter Principle:*

In a Hierarchy Every Employee Tends
to Rise to His Level of Incompetence

A New Science!

31   Having formulated the Principle, I discovered that I had inadvertently founded a new science, hierarchiology, the study of hierarchies.

32   The term "hierarchy" was originally used to describe the system of church government by priests graded into ranks. The contemporary meaning includes any organization whose members or employees are arranged in order of rank, grade or class.

33   Hierarchiology, although a relatively recent discipline, appears to have great applicability to the fields of public and private administration.

This Means You!

34   My Principle is the key to an understanding of all hierarchal systems, and therefore to an understanding of the whole structure of civilization. A few eccentrics try to avoid getting involved with hierarchies, but everyone in business, industry, trade-unionism, politics, government, the armed forces, religion and education is so involved. All of them are controlled by the Peter Principle.

35   Many of them, to be sure, may win a promotion or two, moving from one level of competence to a higher level of competence. But competence in that new position qualifies them for still another promotion. For each individual, for *you*, for *me*, the final promotion is from a level of competence to a level of incompetence.[2]

36   So, given enough time—and assuming the existence of enough ranks in the hierarchy—each employee rises to, and remains at, his level of incompetence. Peter's Corollary states:

---

[2]The phenomena of "percussive sublimation" (commonly referred to as "being kicked upstairs") and of "the lateral arabesque" are not, as the casual observer might think, exceptions to the Principle. They are only pseudo-promotions. . . .

> In time, every post tends to be occupied by an
> employee who is incompetent to carry out its duties.

Who Turns the Wheels?

37   You will rarely find, of course, a system in which *every* employee
has reached his level of incompetence. In most instances, something is
being done to further the ostensible purposes for which the hierarchy
exists.

> Work is accomplished by those employees who have
> not yet reached their level of incompetence.

Why Women Are Paid Less Than Men

LESTER C. THUROW

Lester C. Thurow was born in 1938 in Livingston, Montana. He earned a B.A. at Williams College, an M.A. at Balliol College, Oxford, and another M.A. and a Ph.D. at Harvard University. After graduation, he served as instructor of economics at Harvard, became a research associate of the Kennedy School of Government, and eventually became professor of economics at the Massachusetts Institute of Technology. He served as dean of the Sloan School of Management at MIT from 1987 to 1993.

As a liberal economist, Thurow has written extensively about the nation's financial condition, and he paints a grim picture of a country crippled by debt and the loss of productivity. Some call him a pessimist, and while he admits to being an "intellectual pessimist," he maintains he is also an "emotional optimist." His 1980 work, *The Zero-Sum Society*, argued that special interest groups were causing the stagnation and paralysis of the economy. In 1992, he published *Head to Head: The Coming Economic Battle among Japan, Europe, and America*. In this book, he urged Americans to save more, endorsed higher taxes, and insisted that the government must play an even larger role in managing the economic stability of the nation. All of this came at a time when most Americans were insisting that government was the big problem. Nevertheless, Robert Z. Lawrence of *Fortune* says Thurow's final chapter, "An American Game Plan," should be "required reading for those occupying high office in this nation."

"Why Women Are Paid Less Than Men" first appeared in the *New York Times* in 1981. Here Thurow provides his analysis of the discrepancy in pay for men and women—a discrepancy that has baffled experts, raises plaintive cries of injustice from women, and remains to be remedied. Thurow focuses on the crucial decade in every person's career when major advancement must occur—the years from age twenty-five to age thirty-five, which is the very time that many professional and career-oriented women drop out of the workforce to have children. His solutions to the problem would require major changes in lifestyles and in the promotion system for business and industry.

1   In the forty years from 1939 to 1979 white women who work full time have with monotonous regularity made slightly less than 60 percent as much as white men. Why?

2   Over the same time period, minorities have made substantial progress in catching up with whites, with minority women making even more progress than minority men.

3   Black men now earn 72 percent as much as white men (up 16 percentage points since the mid–1950's) but black women earn 92 percent as much as white women. Hispanic men make 71 percent of what their white counterparts do, but Hispanic women make 82 percent as much as white women. As a result of their faster progress, fully employed black women make 75 percent as much as fully employed black men while Hispanic women earn 68 percent as much as Hispanic men.

4   This faster progress may, however, end when minority women finally catch up with white women. In the bible of the New Right, George Gilder's "Wealth and Poverty," the 60 percent is just one of Mother Nature's constants like the speed of light or the force of gravity.

5   Men are programmed to provide for their families economically

while women are programmed to take care of their families emotionally and physically. As a result men put more effort into their jobs than women. The net result is a difference in work intensity that leads to that 40 percent gap in earnings. But there is no discrimination against women—only the biological facts of life.

6   The problem with this assertion is just that. It is an assertion with no evidence for it other than the fact that white women have made 60 percent as much as men for a long period of time.

7   "Discrimination against women" is an easy answer but it also has its problems as an adequate explanation. Why is discrimination against women not declining under the same social forces that are leading to a lessening of discrimination against minorities? In recent years women have made more use of the enforcement provisions of the Equal Employment Opportunities Commission and the courts than minorities. Why do the laws that prohibit discrimination against women and minorities work for minorities but not for women?

8   When men discriminate against women, they run into a problem. To discriminate against women is to discriminate against your own wife and to lower your own family income. To prevent women from working is to force men to work more.

9   When whites discriminate against blacks, they can at least think that they are raising their own incomes. When men discriminate against women they have to know that they are lowering their own family income and increasing their own work effort.

10   While discrimination undoubtedly explains part of the male-female earnings differential, one has to believe that men are monumentally stupid or irrational to explain all of the earnings gap in terms of discrimination. There must be something else going on.

11   Back in 1939 it was possible to attribute the earnings gap to large differences in educational attainments. But the educational gap between men and women has been eliminated since World War II. It is no longer possible to use education as an explanation for the lower earnings of women.

12   Some observers have argued that women earn less money since they are less reliable workers who are more apt to leave the labor force. But it is difficult to maintain this position since women are less apt to quit one job to take another and as a result they tend to work as long, or longer, for any one employer. From any employer's perspective they are more reliable, not less reliable than men.

13   Part of the answer is visible if you look at the lifetime earnings profile of men. Suppose that you were asked to predict which men in a group of twenty-five-year-olds would become economically successful. At age twenty-five it is difficult to tell who will be economically successful and your predictions are apt to be highly inaccurate.

14   But suppose that you were asked to predict which men in a group of thirty-five-year-olds would become economically successful. If you are successful at age thirty-five, you are very likely to remain successful for the rest of your life. If you have not become economically successful by age thirty-five, you are very unlikely to do so later.

15   The decade between twenty-five and thirty-five is when men either succeed or fail. It is the decade when lawyers become partners in the good firms, when business managers make it onto the "fast track," when academics get tenure at good universities, and when blue-collar workers find the job opportunities that will lead to training opportunities and the skills that will generate high earnings.

16   If there is any one decade when it pays to work hard and to be consistently in the labor force, it is the decade between twenty-five and thirty-five. For those who succeed, earnings will rise rapidly. For those who fail, earnings will remain flat for the rest of their lives.

17   But the decade between twenty-five and thirty-five is precisely the decade when women are most apt to leave the labor force or become part-time workers to have children. When they do, the current system of promotion and skill acquisition will extract an enormous lifetime price.

18   This leaves essentially two avenues for equalizing male and female earnings.

19   Families where women who wish to have successful careers, compete with men, and achieve the same earnings should alter their family plans and have their children either before twenty-five or after thirty-five. Or society can attempt to alter the existing promotion and skill acquisition system so that there is a longer time period in which both men and women can attempt to successfully enter the labor force.

20   Without some combination of these two factors, a substantial fraction of the male-female earnings differentials are apt to persist for the next forty years, even if discrimination against women is eliminated.

The Efficient Society

JEREMY RIFKIN

Jeremy Rifkin was born in Denver, Colorado, in 1945. He earned a B.A. from the University of Pennsylvania and an M.A. from Fletcher School of Law and Diplomacy at Tufts University. As a social activist and head of the Foundation on Economic Trends, Rifkin has been involved with a number of different issues, including the Vietnam War, business and industry ethics, and genetic engineering. He has initiated lawsuits, organized demonstrations, established boycotts, and in general served as a public crusader on many significant issues. Among his writings are *How to Commit Revolution American Style: Bicentennial Declaration* (1973), *Common Sense II: The Case Against Corporate Tyranny* (1975), and *Own Your Own Job: Economic Democracy for Working Americans* (1977).

"The Efficient Society" is an excerpt from *Time Wars: The Primary Conflict in Human History* (1987). With satiric intensity, Rifkin explains how capitalists have promoted *efficiency* in order to gain greater production from the workforce. He examines in detail the innovation of the division of labor that made possible mass production and paved the way for scientific management that "calibrated worker performance to fractions of a second." The result was a system that stripped workers "of any capacity to make decisions regarding the conception and execution" of their tasks. Finally, Rifkin reminds us that the computer has increased efficiency and, again, diminished the worker's own creative motivations.

1   Clocks and schedules, and computers and programs, have transformed the sociology of human existence. The modern time world is fast-paced, future-directed, and rigorously planned. The new time technologies have changed our way of life and, in the process, have effected a fundamental change in the value orientation of Western culture. The artificial time worlds we have constructed have been accompanied by a radical new temporal value: efficiency. With its introduction, the modern temporal orientation is complete. Efficiency is both a value and a method. As a value, efficiency becomes the social norm for how all human time should be used. As a method, efficiency becomes the best way to use time to advance the goal of material progress.

2   To be efficient is to minimize the time in which a task is completed or a product produced and to maximize the yield, expending the minimum amount of energy, labor, or capital in the process. In less than two hundred years, efficiency has risen from obscurity to become the overriding value of society and the primary method for organizing the activities of the human family. Efficiency is the hallmark and trademark of contemporary culture. It binds the various temporal features of the modern world into a single unifying focus. Today efficiency pervades every facet of life: it is the primary way we organize our time and has burrowed its way into our economic life, our social and cultural life, and even our personal and religious life.

3   We have institutionalized efficiency through the schedule and now the program. Every activity is scheduled or programmed in advance so that we may use time in the most efficient manner possible. Optimizing schedules and programs means optimizing efficiency.

4   Efficiency was introduced into the popular culture through the workplace. If the first task of industrial capitalism was to make the workers punctual and to discipline them to accept clock time, the next major task was to make them efficient.

5   Efficiency is a product of three major economic innovations, each of which radically transformed people's relationships to their tools

and to their fellow beings: division of labor, mass production, and the principles of scientific management. These represent the cornerstones of the industrial pyramid, and each has played a key role in making efficiency the overriding temporal conception of the industrial way of life.

6   Efficiency's ascent to power began with the introduction of division of labor. Economic historian Harry Braverman contends that "in one form or another, the division of labor has remained the fundamental principle of industrial organization."[1] The first philosopher to articulate the importance of division of labor in industrial production was Adam Smith. Writing in *The Wealth of Nations*, Smith contended that the new principle of division of labor provided a means of "saving time" in the production process:

> This great increase in the quantity of work, which, in consequence of the division of labor, the same number of people are capable of performing, is owing to three different circumstances; first, to the increase of dexterity in every particular workman; secondly, to the saving of time which is commonly lost in passing from one species of work to another; and lastly, to the invention of a great number of machines which facilitate and abridge labor, and enable one man to do the work of many.[2]

7   Adam Smith came to this realization by observing the great strides taking place in watch manufacturing. It was there that modern industry first began to apply the principles of division of labor to increase production. As far back as 1703, master clock- and watchmaker Thomas Tompion was mass-producing timepieces. His biographer, Symonds, says that Tompion's success lay in organizing his workshop "in a way hitherto unknown in the English handicrafts."[3] Sir William Petty, one of the distinguished political economists of the period,

---

[1]Harry Braverman, *Labor and Monopoly Capital* (New York: Monthly Review Press, 1974), p. 70.
[2]Adam Smith, *The Wealth of Nations* (New York: New Modern Library, 1937), p. 7.
[3]Samuel L. Macey, *Clocks and the Cosmos: Time in Western Life and Thought* (Hamden, Conn.: Archon Books, 1980), p. 35.

wrote the following description of the new method Tompion and
others were applying to production:

> In the making of a watch, if one man shall make
> the Wheels, another the Spring, another shall
> engrave the Dial-Plate, and another shall make the
> Cases, then the watch will be better and cheaper,
> than if the whole work be put upon any one Man.[4]

Division of labor meant that more goods could be produced in "less
time" at a cheaper cost per unit.

8   The division-of-labor concept was followed in close order by the
second major economic innovation, the introduction of mass production principles. Eli Whitney introduced the idea of mass production in
1799. Frustrated over the long time delays that resulted from having
to teach workers the necessary skills to make the various component
parts that went into the assembly of a finished product, Whitney developed the idea of mass-producing standardized interchangeable parts
that could be easily assembled by unskilled laborers. He applied the
new principles of mass production to the making of muskets.

> To eliminate guesswork by eye, he invented jigs, or
> guides for tools, so that the outline of the product
> would not be marred by the fallibility of a shaky
> hand or imperfect vision. He made automatic stops
> that would disconnect the tool at the precise depth
> of diameter of a cut. He made clamps to hold the
> metal while the guided chisels or milling wheels cut
> it. By dividing his factory into departments—one for
> barrels, one for stocks, one for each lock piece—the
> parts could be brought into an assembly room and
> put together in one continuous uninterrupted pro-
> cess.[5]

9   Whitney's new mass production process became known as the
"American Method." Its principles soon spread to the watch industry, where they were further refined and eventually served as a model

---

[4]Quoted in ibid.
[5]Daniel Bell, "The Clock Watchers: Americans at Work," *Time* 8 September
1975, p. 55.

for the rest of American industry. The man responsible for applying Whitney's idea to watch production was Aaron L. Dennison. He joined forces with Whitney to set up a company which later became known as the Waltham Watch Company, the first mass production watch company in the United States.[6]

10   The principles of division of labor and mass production were both intended to save time. To be effective, they required the setting up of detailed work schedules so that every operation would be subjected to rigorous time standards. To ensure that every moment of the production process would be used to maximize output, a third and final innovation was introduced into the industrial process. It was called scientific management and its author was Frederick W. Taylor.

11   Taylor made efficiency the *modus operandi* of American industry and the cardinal virtue of American culture. His work principles have been transported to every sector of the globe and have been responsible for converting much of the world's population to the modern time frame. He has probably had a greater effect on the private and public lives of the men and women of the twentieth century than any other single individual. Economic historian Daniel Bell says of Taylor:

> If any social upheaval can ever be attributed to one man, the logic of efficiency as a mode of life is due to Taylor. . . . With scientific management, as formulated by Taylor in 1895, we pass far beyond the old, rough computations of the division of labor and move into the division of time itself.[7]

12   Taylor's principles of scientific management were designed with one goal in mind: to make each worker more efficient. His primary tool was the stopwatch. Taylor divided each worker's task into the smallest, visibly identifiable operational components, then timed each to ascertain the best time attainable under optimal performance conditions. His time studies calibrated worker performance to fractions of a second. By studying the mean times and best times achieved in each component of the worker's job, Taylor could make recommendations on how to change the most minute aspects of worker performance in

[6]Macey, *Clocks and the Cosmos,* p. 36.
[7]Bell, "The Clock Watchers," p. 55.

order to save precious seconds, and even milliseconds, of time. Scientific management, says Harry Braverman, "is the organized study of work, the analysis of work into its simplest elements and the systematic improvement of the worker's performance of each of these elements."[8]

13   Taylor considered his work principles to be scientific to the extent that he was able to eliminate all nonquantifiable elements of worker behavior. His time studies reduced every aspect of work to the dictates of time. Worker performance could now be reduced to numbers and statistical averages that could be computed and analyzed to better predict future performance and to gain greater control over the work process itself.

14   Taylor relied on a new approach to management. The stopwatch and statistics ruled the factory floor. "Management," by the way, seemed an altogether appropriate term to affix to the new scientism. Braverman reminds us that "manage" comes from the Latin *manus*, which meant "to train a horse in his paces, to cause him to do exercises of the manege."[9]

15   Taylor believed that the best way to optimize the efficiency of each worker was to assert complete control over all six temporal dimensions: sequence, duration, schedule, rhythm, synchronization, and time perspective. No aspect of the worker's time was to be left to chance or to worker discretion; from now on, the worker's time would fall under the absolute control of management. The most efficient state, said Taylor, was the most autocratic. Taylor's principles of scientific management represented the ultimate politicization of the new industrial time. Braverman argues that Taylor's work "may well be the most powerful as well as the most lasting contribution America has made to Western thought since the Federalist Papers."[10]

16   Taylor's first principle of scientific management was for management to seize control over the knowledge of the work process that had previously been in the hands of the workers. From now on, Taylor stated:

> The managers assume . . . the burden of gathering
> together all of the traditional knowledge which in
> the past has been possessed by the workmen and

---

[8]Braverman, *Labor and Monopoly Capital*, p. 88.
[9]Ibid., p. 67.
[10]Ibid., p. 88.

thereof classifying, tabulating, and reducing this knowledge to rules, laws, and formulae.[11]

Taylor's intention was to sever the labor process from the skills of the workers. Those skills were to reside only in the hands of management.

17 Taylor's second principle flowed directly from the first. Having gained a monopoly over the knowledge required to do the work, management must then assume the authority to plan and direct the work on the shop floor. Denied first-hand knowledge of how their work was to be done, the workers would become totally dependent on management in the execution of their tasks.

18 Taylor believed that as long as the workers maintained both knowledge and control over how their work was to be done, it would be impossible to elicit maximum efficiency. Left on their own, workers would let other "human" considerations enter into the work process. Feelings and emotions would come to the fore, tempering and even undermining the prospect of attaining maximum efficiency. For example, workers might consciously choose to moderate their work pace to accommodate the needs of slower employees. They may even relax their concentration by occasional socializing. Taylor argued that "if the workers' execution is guided by their own conception, it is not possible . . . to enforce upon them either the methodological efficiency or the working pace desired by capital."[12]

19 In order to secure maximum efficiency in the execution of the work process, a third and final principle of scientific management was called for: the implementation of the "work schedule." It was here that management cemented its control over the total work time of each of its employees.

> The work of every workman is fully planned out by the management at least one day in advance, and each man receives in most cases complete written instructions, describing in detail the task which he is to accomplish, as well as the means to be used in doing the work. . . . This task specifies not only

[11]Frederick Taylor, *The Principles of Scientific Management* (New York: W. W. Norton, 1947), pp. 37–38.
[12]Ibid., pp. 235–236.

> what is to be done, but how it is to be done and
> the exact time allowed for doing it. . . . Scientific
> management consists very largely in preparing for
> and carrying out these tasks.[13]

20 Taylor believed that the key to making a worker more efficient
was to strip him of any capacity to make decisions regarding the
conception and execution of his task. In the new scientifically managed factory, the worker's mind was severed from his body and
handed over to the management. The worker became an automaton,
no different from the machines he interacted with, his humanity left
outside the factory gate. On the factory floor, he was an instrument
in the production process, a tool whose performance could be timed
and improved on with the same cool detachment and scientific rigor
as might be applied to the machinery itself.

21 In the years following Taylor's pioneering efforts, the principles
he first enunciated were further refined. New scientific tools allowed
more exacting controls to be exercised over the work process. The
most interesting advance in the principles of scientific management
occurred with the introduction of motion-and-time studies. This
development was the brainchild of Frank B. Gilbreth, one of Taylor's
early disciples.

22 Gilbreth filmed the movements of each worker in order to establish
standard times for each body motion. Virtually every movement on the
factory floor and in the clerical offices was analyzed and assigned an
optimum time, usually calibrated down to a fraction of a second. The
various movements, in turn, were assigned standardized names, using
machine terminology. For example, "contact grasp" referred to picking
an object up with fingertips. "Punch grasp" meant thumbs opposing
finger. "Wrap grasp" meant wrapping one's hand around the object.

23 If the task required picking up a pencil, it would be described in
the following manner: transport empty, punch grasp, and transport
loaded. Each movement was assigned a standardized time. The sum
total of the individual times associated with each movement would
be the standard time for completing the task. The time calibration
in the Gilbreth motion-and-time study was perfected down to the
ten-thousandths of a minute.[14]

[13]Ibid., pp. 39, 63.
[14]Braverman, *Labor and Monopoly Capital,* pp. 173–174.

24   Today the science of motion-and-time studies is far more sophisticated than anything Gilbreth could have imagined. Sound waves are used to detect minute changes in body movement and are calibrated to an accuracy of .000066 minutes.[15] Even the worker's visual movements can now be timed and standardized. Through a process called electro-oculography, it is possible to time every single shift in eye movement as the worker scans the various monitors and controls with which he or she is working. Standardized times for each shift in eye movement are calibrated providing a norm for measuring the optimum efficiency of all eye movements.[16]

25   Motion-and-time studies have been used successfully in establishing time efficiencies in every work environment. In the clerical field, standardized times have been assigned to the smallest tasks, as evidenced by the following motion-and-time chart compiled by the Systems and Procedures Association of America.[17]

Open and close	*Minutes*
File drawer, open and close, no selection	.04
Folder, open or close flaps	.04
Desk drawer, open side of standard desk	.014
Open center drawer	.026
Close side	.015
Close center	.027

Chair Activity	
Get up from chair	.033
Sit down in chair	.033
Turn in swivel chair	.009
Move in chair to adjoining desk or file (4 ft. maximum)	.050

26   Taylor and his disciples turned efficiency into a science. They

[15]Ibid., p. 177.
[16]Ibid., p. 178.
[17]Ibid., p. 321. Note that the Systems and Procedures Association of America is now called The Association for Systems Management.

inaugurated a new ethos. Efficiency was officially christened the dominant value of the contemporary age. From now on, no other consideration would be allowed to compete with or undermine this ultimate value. It would not be long before Taylor's principles would find their way into the rest of the culture, changing the way we lived and interacted with each other in the modern world. The new man and woman were to be objectified, quantified, and redefined in clockwork and mechanistic language. They were to be turned into a factor and then a cog in the production process. Their labor was to be divided, standardized, and regulated to a fraction of a second, then regimented to the task of achieving maximum material output. Above all, their life and their time would be made to conform to the regimen of the clock, the prerequisites of the schedule, and the dictates of efficiency. . . .

27 Now with the clock and the schedule joined by an even more powerful time technology, the computer and the program, efficiency has assumed an unchallenged position in the social scheme of things, becoming the premier value of our age.

28 All around the world, businesses are making the transition to computer-run operations. As they do, the flow of work-related activity accelerates dramatically, and efficiency becomes reduced to a nanosecond time frame. Work that often took considerable time to "organize" and "produce" is now expected to be "programmed" and "processed" in a fraction of the time. Where a secretary used to average about 30,000 keystrokes per hour, the average VDT operator is expected to perform 80,000 keystrokes in the same amount of time. In brokerage firms, personnel responsible for customer accounts are now expected to handle one call every minute and a half, providing the shareholders with complete stock market information accessed from the computer console at their work station. An architect using advanced computer-aided design (CAD) can now "make nineteen times more decisions per hour than does a pencil-wielding colleague."[18] Mike Cooley, past president of the Designers Union of Great Britain, and an expert on computer-aided design, says that there are systems currently in use "where the decision-making rate of the designer can be forced up by 1800 percent." The frantic tempo established by these systems puts enormous pres-

[18]Craig Brod, *Technostress* (Reading, Mass.: Addison-Wesley, 1984), pp. 39–40.

sure on the designer, often crippling his or her creative contribution. According to Cooley, "the rate at which the computer demands decisions reduces his creativity by 30 percent in the first hour, 80 percent in the second hour, and thereafter he's just shattered."[19]

29   To insure "optimum interface" between the machine and the operator, computer experts are beginning to map the "peak performance age" for people working with computers in various fields of knowledge. People of different ages are scored on their ability to respond quickly to various problems on the visual display unit. The speed of their response is then used to calculate peak performance age. The peak performance age of a mathematician is twenty-three. A theoretical physicist peaks at twenty-seven and a structural engineer at thirty-four.[20]

30   The computer represents the ultimate technological expression of our culture's obsession with efficiency. It was introduced into our life as a means of helping us make the most efficient use of time. In the computer realm, time is information and information is utility. Time used in ways that cannot be broken down, quantified, and measured in terms of efficient inputs and outputs is of little or no value. Craig Brod's account of one of his patients, a supermarket cashier, is indicative of the way the new computer world transforms time into speedy, useful information while eliminating temporal activity without immediate instrumental value. When Alice's employer installed electronic cash registers, built into the computer-run machine was a counter that "transmits to a central terminal a running account of how many items each cashier has rung up that day."[21] Alice finds that she no longer "takes the time" to talk with customers as it slows down the number of items she can scan across the electronic grid and might jeopardize her job.[22]

31   In Kansas a repair service company keeps a complete computer tally of the number of phone calls its workers handle and the amount of information collected with each call. Says one disgruntled employee, "If you get a call from a friendly person who wants to

---

[19]Christopher Rawlence, ed., *About Time* (London: Jonathan Cape, 1985), p. 39.
[20]Ibid., p. 39.
[21]Brod, *Technostress*, p. 45.
[22]Ibid.

chat, you have to hurry the caller off because it would count against you. It makes my job very unpleasant."[23]

32   In an effort to speed up the processing of information, some visual display units are now being programmed so that if the operator does not respond to the data on the screen within seventeen seconds, it disappears. Medical researchers report that operators exhibit increasing stress as the time approaches for the image to disappear on the screen: "From the eleventh second they begin to perspire, then the heart rate goes up. Consequently they experience enormous fatigue."[24]

33   The computer is even being used to speed up normal conversation. Companies like Sony and Panasonic are now marketing variable-speech-control cassette tape recorders equipped with a specially designed, solid-state speech compression chip. The variable-speech-control chip speeds up the tape-playback motor while clipping off tiny audio fragments—lapping about 10 milliseconds off each sound. The remaining sounds are electronically stretched, producing a fast-paced, intelligible narrative.[25]

34   With the compression chip, it is possible to listen to any voice cassette in half the time without being subjected to the high-pitched sounds that result in fast-winding the traditional tape recorder. With variable speech control, a sixty-minute cassette can be listened to in half an hour. According to industry sources, about a million people now "speed listen," and millions more will in the years to come as the compression chip makes its way into schoolrooms, offices, and homes across the country.

35   The far-reaching implications of this accelerated time frame are difficult to assess. Like the clocks and schedules that preceded them, computers and programs cut deep into humanity's relationship with nature, severing many of the remaining temporal bonds between our species and the larger environment. Computer time bears no relationship to the rhythms of nature. It is an arbitrary temporal marker willed into existence by human ingenuity. The computer reduces time to numbers and turns duration into uniform segments

[23]Ibid.
[24]Rawlence, *About Time,* p. 39.
[25]Vic Sussman, "Going Nowhere Fast," *Washington Post Magazine,* 7 September 1986, p. 77.

that can be added, subtracted, accumulated, and exchanged. While the computer turns time into a purely manipulable commodity, programs turn human beings into instruments to serve the new efficiency time frame. With the computer and program, each person's immediate future can be predetermined down to the tiniest artificial time segments of milliseconds and nanoseconds. Computers and programs represent a new form of social control, more powerful than any previous means used to marshal and regiment human energy.

Acknowledgments

Agee, James, "Comedy's Greatest Era" from AGEE ON FILM by James Agee. Reprinted by permission of The James Agee Trust.

Bentley, Eric, "To Impersonate, to Watch, and to be Watched," from THE LIFE OF THE DRAMA. Reprinted by permission of Applause Books.

Carson, Rachel L., "The Moving Tides," from THE SEA AROUND US, Revised Edition, by Rachel L. Carson. Copyright © 1950, 1951, 1961 by Rachel L. Carson; renewed 1979, 1989 by Roger Christie. Reprinted by permission of Oxford University Press, Inc.

Catton, Bruce, "Grant and Lee: A Study in Contrasts" from Earl Scheneck Miers, Ed., THE AMERICAN STORY. Copyright U.S. Capitol Historical Society, all rights reserved. Reprinted by permission.

Cousins, Norman, "Pain Is Not the Ultimate Enemy." Reprinted from ANATOMY OF AN ILLNESS by Norman Cousins, with the permission of W. W. Norton & Company, Inc. Copyright © 1979 by W. W. Norton & Company, Inc.

Einstein, Albert, "What Is the Theory of Relativity?" From IDEAS AND OPINIONS by Albert Einstein. Copyright © 1954 and renewed 1982 by Crown Publishers, Inc. Reprinted by permission of Crown Publishers, Inc., a subsidiary of Random House, Inc.

Eiseley, Loren, "The Bird and the Machine." From THE IMMENSE JOURNEY by Loren Eiseley. Copyright © 1955 by Loren Eiseley. Reprinted by permission of Random House, Inc.

Jung, C. G., "The Shadow" from THE COLLECTED WORKS OF C. G. JUNG, ed. by Gerhard Adler, Michael Fordham, William McGuire, and Herbert Read, translated by R. F. C. Hull, Bollingen Series XX Vo. 9, ii, AION: RESEARCHES INTO THE PHENOMENOLOGY OF THE SELF. Reprinted by permission of Princeton University Press.

Marx, Karl, "Alienated Labor," from MAN ALONE: ALIENATION IN MODERN SOCIETY edited and translated by Eric and Mary Josephson. New York: Dell Publishing Co., Inc., 1962.

Mead, Margaret, "A Day in Samoa" from COMING OF AGE IN SAMOA by Margaret Mead. Copyright © 1928, 1955, 1961 by Margaret Mead. Reprinted by permission of William Morrow & Company, Inc.

Miller, Arthur, "Tragedy and the Common Man." Reprinted by permission of International Creative Management, Inc. Copyright © 1949 by Arthur Miller.

Peter, Laurence J. and Raymond Hull. Text of chapter 1, "The Peter Principle" from THE PETER PRINCIPLE by Laurence J. Peter and Raymond Hull. Copyright © 1969 by William Morrow & Company, Inc. Reprinted by permission of William Morrow & Company, Inc.

Rettie, James C., "But a Watch in the Night," from FOREVER THE LAND by Russell and Kate Lord. Copyright 1950 by Harper & Brothers. Copyright renewed 1978 by Russell and Kate Lord. Reprinted by permission of HarperCollins Publishers, Inc.

Rifkin, Jeremy, from TIME WARS: The Primary Conflict in Human History by Jeremy Rifkin. Copyright © 1987 by Jeremy Rifkin. Reprinted by permission of Henry Holt & Co., Inc.

Ross, Lillian, "The Yellow Bus" from REPORTING (Simon & Schuster), © 1960, 1988 Lillian Ross. Originally in THE NEW YORKER. Reprinted by permission.

Russell, Bertrand, "Touch and Sight: The Earth and the Heavens" from THE ABC OF RELATIVITY by Bertrand Russell. Reprinted by permission of Routledge.

Selzer, Richard, "Why a Surgeon Would Write" from MORTAL LESSONS: NOTES ON THE ART OF SURGERY by Richard Selzer. Copyright © 1974, 1975, 1976, 1987 by Richard Selzer. Reprinted by permission of Simon & Schuster, Inc.

Stafford, William, "A Way of Writing" first appeared in FIELD MAGAZINE and is © by Oberlin College Press. Reprinted by permission.

Thomas, Lewis, "The Long Habit," copyright © 1972 by The Massachusetts Medical Society, from THE LIVES OF A CELL by Lewis Thomas. Used by permission of Viking Penguin, a division of Penguin Books USA Inc.

Thurow, Lester C., "Why Women Are Paid Less Than Men," from THE NEW YORK TIMES, March 8, 1981. Copyright © 1981 by The New York Times Company. Reprinted by permission.

Woolf, Virginia, "The Patron and the Crocus" from THE COMMON READER by Virginia Woolf, copyright 1925 by Harcourt Brace & Company and renewed 1953 by Leonard Woolf, reprinted by permission of the publisher.

Index of Authors
and Titles